SPLIT ENDS

By

Beth Rubin

This book is a work of fiction. Places, events, and situations in this story are purely fictional. Any resemblance to actual persons, living or dead, is coincidental.

© 2002 by Beth Rubin. All rights reserved.

No part of this book may be reproduced, stored in a retrieval system, or transmitted by any means, electronic, mechanical, photocopying, recording, or otherwise, without written permission from the author.

ISBN: 1-4033-1211-7 (e-book)
ISBN: 1-40331-212-5 (Paperback)

This book is printed on acid free paper.

1st Books - rev. 07/23/02

"YOU'RE JUST IN LOVE" by Irving Berlin
© Copyright 1950 by Irving Berlin
Copyright Renewed
International Copyright Secured
All Rights Reserved
Reprinted by Permission
Warner Bros. Publications U.S. Inc., Miami, FL 33014

"SWEET LITTLE SIXTEEN" by Chuck Berry
© 1958 Isalee Music Co.
All rights Reserved by Permission
Isalee Music Co.

"COME FLY WITH ME" by Sammy Cahn and James Van Heusen
© 1958 Maraville Music Corp.
© Renewed, Assigned to Maraville Music Corp. and Cahn Music Co.
All Rights o/b/o Cahn Music Co. administered by WB Music Corp.
All Rights Reserved
Used by Permission
Warner Bros. Publications U.S. Inc, Miami, FL 33014

"SEND IN THE CLOWNS," music and lyrics by Stephen Sondheim
© 1973 Rilting Music, Inc. (ASCAP)
All Rights administered by WB Music Corp.
All Rights Reserved
Used by Permission
Warner Bros. Publications U.S. Inc., Miami, FL 33014

Dedication

To my mother and father

Acknowledgments

Many people helped me to conceive and birth this book. Some shared their own stories or read early drafts and offered suggestions. Others plied me with coffee, hugs and encouragement. Several pushed me to get dressed and leave the house once in a while, thank God. You know who you are. Hugs all around. Thank you from the bottom of my heart.

I'm especially grateful to:

My parents, children and brother for their love and faith that I could pull this off.

My grandchildren, for the joy they bring to my life.

Peter and Trish Benesh of AuthorAssist, editors and friends *par excellence,* for their insight, professionalism and pep talks every time I wanted to burn the manuscript. I bless the day I found them.

The Maryland Writers' Association and Carl Lau at 1st Books Library for the opportunity to make it happen.

My friends at the Maryland Writers' Association for their ongoing support.

Judi Scioli, for her friendship, faith in the project, editing skills and wisdom – professional and otherwise.

My wonderful girlfriends – Joyce Dumin, Bonnie Gibson, Ellen Goodman, Rosemary Mild, Judy O'Keefe, Barbara Rasin Price, Nancy Rosenshine, Billie Sandler and Mary Ann Treger – for their good humor, kindness, loyalty and putting up with my nuttiness; The Jersey Tomatoes – Chris Hildebrand, Sue MacKinnon, Bobbi Conway Fox and Suzanne Lyman Clark. I treasure our time together. May we never grow up.

Jaymie Meyer and Wendy Solomon – cousins by chance, friends by choice – who are always there for me.

My friends at the Maryland Youth Ballet, whom I miss every Monday, and my Sea Sisters at Women Aboard, Annapolis Chapter, who welcome me even though I'm boatless.

Brenda Castle-Young, LCSW, for her assistance with the therapy scenes and shrink speak.

The Center for Disease Control and Anne Arundel County Health Department for HIV/AIDS information.

Donna Vogel and Jane Hill for the crash course in Catholicism.

Jeffrey Fisch, Esq., for his help with the legalese.

Kathy Poerstel for her sailing expertise.

Penne Romar for the cover concept.

Hillary Frank for taming my split ends.

Eleanor Becker for keeping my back in line and nurturing my spiritual side.

My 4th grade teacher, Claire Auger, who said I had a flair for writing.

PROLOGUE

The wedding dress whipped at the flagpole like a hurricane warning to mariners. The sleeves had shredded and their ragged edges clawed at the wind, as if the tempest had ripped a tormented soul from their embrace.

Ashen sky mixed with charcoal sea and air turned to water. The horizon disappeared.

The undertow sucked Ellen down. She thrashed. Her feet hit bottom and she pushed up, up. Lungs imploding, she broke the surface, gulped in air and struggled toward the colored dots on the beach—dots she knew were Ron and the children.

She tried calling, "hus-band, hus-band." The word came out, "has-been, has-been."

Ron just sat in his canvas chair, ignoring her screams. Ellen harnessed her rage to subdue her panic. Rage at Ron that he would let her drown, panic that she would never again embrace her Michael and Lisa. The current seized her. She drove every ounce of will into her muscles.

Soft music, something by Sinatra, floated toward her from the ocean liner 50 yards away. Old Blue Eyes' voice lifted her like a life jacket. Friends cheered from the ship's rail.

The orchestra sat on the bandstand. Violin bows hung at half-mast from the string musicians' flies. A cigarette glued to her lip, Ellen's mother finished her eulogy and handed the microphone to a shapely woman Ellen did not recognize.

The woman rose from a director's chair with SHRINK on the back and curtsied to the screeching gulls.

She pulled a top hat from her cleavage, sprinkled M&Ms into it and lifted out a life-size marionette—a clone of Ellen.

With a slash of her jewel-encrusted knife, the shaman severed the umbilical cord and the puppet pirouetted around the stage. The melody bounced off the water and Ellen recognized "All the Way" rising to a climax. At the refreshment stand, the doll whirled like a dervish in the tattered wedding dress.

Ellen gave up the struggle and floated on her back, spreading her legs and praying for a savior. Ropes slung from giant pulleys in the sky lowered a man onto her. She felt his weight and heat but could not see his face, now pressed tightly to her own. Yet he seemed familiar.

As her arms were about to lock around him, he disappeared, leaving her bereft. She rolled onto her stomach and willed herself toward the beach. Some power answered her prayer. She body-surfed to safety.

As she lay gasping in the trough between the breakers and shore, the waves drove sand up her crack. She heard Ron challenge the Ellen doll to a game of badminton, using a pigeon for a shuttlecock. The game ended in a rout. The doll won.

Nearby, pelicans the size of linebackers hawked snacks to the sun worshippers. Ellen saw Ron buy two hot dogs and hand one to the pretty bitch next to him. A few feet away, the children had a tug of war with a two-headed fish. One end was Ron, the other herself.

With no conductor on the podium, the musicians began to play the Wedding March. The melody grated. As the music grew louder and more discordant, Ellen welcomed the sloshing in her ears.

A procession of hand-holding couples traipsed from the bathhouse, a neon Divorce Court sign blinking on its roof. On their march to the sea they trampled Ron and his hussy. Ellen eyed the burial mound where something poked through the sand—a coin, perhaps.

It was Ron's bald patch. Small change.

The doll clambered onto the lifeguard stand, satin shreds slapping at its goose bumps. As the wind began to lift it, the children raced over and hugged the legs, grounding it like a zeppelin.

The betrothed—extras from "The Ten Commandments"—squeezed together at the shoreline. Rabbi Charlton H. Prinski's dirigible face appeared in the sky, bulbous nose penetrating the marine layer. His voice boomed above the multitude.

"For better or worse, do you promise to take each other?"

"Sure, rebbe," they shouted in unison. "To the cleaners."

After exchanging smoke rings, the mob did a Red-Sea parting. The men dashed north; the women scrambled south in a tangle of arms and legs. Lying in the surf, Ellen sensed the stranger's presence again, his heat searing her loins. She struggled to see him but he was invisible. He tore away again.

Fear gripped her anew. A cramp paralyzed her leg. In agony, she fought for her life. She beat the water to keep her head up as the tidal wave's curling wall of foam blocked out the sun.

Penny swam up, a brown life preserver around her neck. Ellen mined her last reserve of strength and flailed toward the faithful retriever. As she reached for the chocolate doughnut it dissolved and the tsunami crashed down on them.

CHAPTER 1

I'm not ready to die.

Ellen swiped at the seaweed on her cheek. Her hand found Penny's tongue instead. The yellow lab stood next to the bed, tail thumping the mattress. The pounding of the surf and the tail merged into the rhythm of Ron's snoring. With each exhalation, he sounded like a train screeching to an emergency stop.

In her semiconscious state, Ellen struggled. Should she retreat into the maw of the nightmare or fight back by waking up?

In the limbo between dream and reality, she chose to open her eyes. The sun burst through her haze and she blinked. A boat roared up the river, jarring her alert. She covered her eyes with her hands and felt her forehead. Clammy.

God, what a pisser that was.

Nightmare number four that week. A few days earlier she had awakened drenched after careening down a mountain road in a driverless car. Too shaken to go back to sleep, she had padded to the kitchen and baked muffins before dawn.

Until recently her dreams had been more like cartoons, non-threatening and entertaining. Sometimes the plots had been so bizarre that she had jotted them down. Maybe a writing career lay ahead.

This morning, she would have killed for another hour of sleep. She had not gone to bed until 1 A.M. She had hung up her apron, left the stemware and platters unwashed and absolved herself for the sloth.

She hated the sight of dirty dishes the morning after a party, but exhaustion had overwhelmed her perfectionism. Ron had gone to bed at midnight after not helping. As usual. He had said, "Good dinner. See you in the morning."

Poor guy, he's had a rough week, she had told herself. As usual.

"Not so fast, lover," she had replied, and slipped her hand between his legs. He jumped.

"Jesus, Ellen. Don't do that."

"Did I hurt you?"

"No. I'm tired."

"Ah, c'mon."

But he'd backed away as she tried to rub against him.

"I thought you might like another piece of my pie. Me."

"G'night, Ellen."

She had lifted her skirt to her waist and slid her panties to the floor. "Pretty please?" He had turned away when she tried to kiss him. "C'mon, Ron. I'll make you feel good."

He had shot her a withering look. "Gimme a break."

* * * *

Ellen hunkered down in the kitchen after walking Penny. She stood under the skylight in her domain, communing with the pots of forget-me-not and bridal veil. She warbled with Sinatra.

Ron stormed in and yanked the plug.

"Hey, I was listening ..."

"I hate that skinny, no-talent, wop."

"I don't turn off your football games."

"That's different."

"Of course. How thoughtless of me." She watched Ron fumble at the counter, scattering crumbs everywhere as he butchered a bagel. He slammed it in the toaster and barricaded himself behind the paper.

Ellen sponged his crumbs into the sink. The toaster popped. Ron emerged to slather the bagel with cream cheese. She heard him chewing in back of *The Washington Post* sports pages.

"Ron, let's start over. Good morning."

He grunted.

"How'd you sleep?"

He turned the page with a cream-cheesey thumb. "'kay."

Ellen surveyed the unwashed dinnerware. *Oscars for last night's performance.*

The stemware was so delicate, a harsh look could shatter its stems. She loved to entertain, spending days planning and preparing. When she prepped for company she felt like an actress on opening night. Five minutes before guests arrived, she'd still be rehearsing her lines, plumping the sofa cushions and re-re-re-arranging the flowers.

She envied the Martha Stewart wannabes who luxuriated in aromatic baths an hour before the curtain rose. Only when the doorbell rang would Ellen drop her security-blanket sponge and step center stage.

She measured audience enjoyment by the noise level.

"It's beautiful, Ron. How 'bout a walk before the wind comes up?" she said to the top of his head. Sandy grass plugged his scalp. In the sunlight, it looked like a Chia pet.

"I have a lot to do before we sail."

"Oh. For instance?"

"Hose my boat, pick up beer."

"That'll eat up an hour, at best. I'd like to walk with you."

He groaned.

"A short stroll, Ron, not the Boston Marathon."

"I'm too tired."

Her jaw ached. She began emptying the dishwasher. "Why did you say *my* boat?

"Huh? I'm trying to read."

"You said, 'I have to hose *my* boat.'"

"You're putting words in my mouth."

"I don't think so."

He looked up for an instant. "Do you have to start an argument first thing?"

"I'm not arguing."

"Could've fooled me."

"I've always considered it *our* boat, even though…" At dinner the night before Ellen had bristled when she overheard Ron mention that he had taught her to sail. Her uncle had taught her, giving her the boat when he bought a larger one—before she met Ron.

The comment had rankled, but she let it go. Sailing was one of the few activities they enjoyed together. An able skipper under favorable conditions, Ron would freeze in an emergency and Ellen would take over.

Day sails on their 30-footer, *Golden Oldie*, to pick crabs at a waterside restaurant, were fun, but dropping the hook in a secluded cove overnight was sheer bliss. Stretched out in the cockpit at sunset, they would down

Split Ends

frosty beers, the bottle sweat cooling their sunburned foreheads.

"It doesn't get any better than this," she would tell Ron when they spent the night on the water. But that was then and this was nowhere. Ellen sighed.

"Do you think our guests had fun last night?" she asked.

"Probably." He surfaced for a moment as he turned the page, then submerged again.

Well, I didn't, you withholding bastard. Ellen wondered if naked cartwheels would get his attention.

Dis-tant hus-band, sis-boom-bah. Talk to me, you kiel-ba-sa!

"I forgot to tell Wilma and Steven whether we would meet them for dinner this week. It's their 25th anniversary. Ron?"

He put down the paper, glaring. Ellen expected flames to shoot from his nostrils.

"You know I don't go out during the week. I'm no good for work the next day."

"But they're our best friends. And a 25th is special. We can be home early."

"I have a heavy week coming up."

"Well, how 'bout the weekend after?"

"I'd rather wait until sailing season is over."

Ellen knelt down to put an arm around Penny. She lifted the dog's ear and whispered, "Let's run away together."

Penny licked her cheek.

Nearest thing to a kiss I'll get today.

Ron walked out, leaving his plate and newspaper on the table. Ellen knew there were worse habits, but it irked her. He was saying her job was to serve. All she asked was a little consideration. Was that too much?

She heard him peeing in the powder room. Why couldn't he close the door? He came back a few moments later, his hand behind his back. His nose twitched as though Penny had let one go.

"Why do you leave the dog's things lying around?"
"What?"

He shook the rawhide bone in her face. For a second she wished he was showing her the evidence of self-mutilation. Vincent van Gonads.

"This was in the guest john. You leave her crap all over the house."

"I meant to put it away. I guess I got sidetracked by the company."

"I don't think it's asking too much." Ron used his how-could-you tone. "Try to be a little considerate for a change."

Ellen's eyes burned. She turned to the sink, picked up and scrubbed a lipstick-stained goblet. The stem broke, slicing her finger. "Damn."

He rolled his eyes, pursed his lips. "I paid 60 bucks a piece for those in St. Thomas. You could be more careful."

The way he stormed out, she knew he was savoring his triumph.

Ellen sucked her soapy wound and wrapped a napkin around it. Wiping her good hand on her shirt, she dialed Wilma. She wondered if Wilma had noticed that Ron had been more subdued, moodier than usual last night.

Ellen envied Wilma's life with Steven. They laughed together. Even after 25 years. Especially after

Split Ends

25 years. She wondered how often they made love. A cloud grayed the scene outside, the way something had dimmed her romance with Ron.

Wilma's voice yanked her back. "I thought you might be sleeping in after last night."

"I was up early to walk the beast. I didn't see your kitchen light on so I kept going."

"Why doesn't Ron walk Penny?"

"He hates her." *Because he hates me.*

"Why, Ellen?"

"Damned if I know."

"By the way, dinner was great." Wilma's voice seemed to chirp as she changed the subject. "What are you doing today?"

"Well, Ron offered to bring me breakfast in bed."

"Hmmph." Ellen heard Wilma's disbelief. Or was it disdain?

"You're a lucky girl, Ellen. I'll bet he's doing laundry and darning socks too."

"How'd you know? Then he's making a soufflé."

"And I'm Bernadette of Lourdes. Any plans?"

"We're going on the boat with Michael. I can't believe my boychick is starting his last year of law school. I thought he'd never be potty-trained."

"Good thing we're not getting any older, girl."

"Seems like yesterday my little Michael was eating Play-Doh and singing, 'I Love Trash,' with Oscar the Grouch." Ellen felt woozy and sat down.

"Wilma, did you notice anything different about Ron last night?" she whispered.

"Different?"

Ellen sensed Wilma was stalling.

"No. Well, he looked heavier."

"I don't mean how he looked. I'm probably imagining things."

Ron came into the kitchen shaking his head and muttering. "Who's that?"

Ellen covered the mouthpiece. "Wilma."

"I can't believe you're on the phone to her. You saw each other last night. What can you possibly have to say?" He left as he had entered, still mumbling.

Schmuck.

"What's wrong, Ellen? You don't sound yourself."

You're right. I don't know who I am anymore. "Did Ron seem preoccupied to you, Wilma?"

"That's not news. You know what kind of party animal he's not."

"I know. He's the last one to wear a lampshade or moon the neighbors."

"Maybe he's stressed over work."

"Maybe." Ellen scolded the little girl inside her. *You're blowing things out of proportion.*

Split Ends

CHAPTER 2

A few days later, in her, "It Took Me 50 Years To Look This Good," T-shirt, Ellen pedaled next to Wilma at the Beautiful Body. Ellen struggled. Sweat soaked her T-shirt. Wilma exercised daily and weighed, at the most, 100 pounds after Thanksgiving dinner.

"How do you do this every day? Three mornings a week are punishment enough."

"C'mon, Ellen, it's not that bad."

"For you, maybe. I'd rather clean bathrooms, but gravity's been working overtime. My waist has wedded my hips and I want them to divorce."

"Hang in a little longer."

"I won't go gently so I rage against the cellulite. But only three times a week."

"What are you talking about? You have a lovely figure, Ellen."

"Puhleeze. There's enough cottage cheese in my thighs to feed the Naval Academy for a week." Ellen started to feel lightheaded. She let the bike slow.

"You're flushed. Are you all right?"

Ellen gasped. *Was this like drowning?* "My get-up-and-go got up and went."

They spread towels side-by-side for the floor exercises. As Donna Summer's "Last Dance" crackled, Ellen strained to flex her gluts and crunch her abs to the beat. More sweat ran down her face and dripped onto the towel.

She turned to Wilma. "I'll bet this carpet hasn't been cleaned since Millie peed on the White House lawn. In fact, it smells like Millie peed here."

"We'll be done soon."

Ellen liked talks with Wilma. But she thought their best conversations took place during their morning walks, while Penny sniffed every square inch of turf in Annapolis. Ellen admired Wilma's analytical mind and relied on her friend's sound judgment.

And, damn it, Wilma always looked good—even first thing in the morning. Ellen doubted she would ever possess Wilma's clarity of insight, but she thought that in her next life she might try makeup and big earrings at 7 A.M.

"You are getting thinner," Wilma said as they drove downtown.

"I guess I have lost some."

"Some? You're the incredible shrinking woman."

"Maybe Anorexics Anonymous will recruit me as their poster child."

"I'm worried about you."

"I'm pooped, Wilma. I don't know if my age is catching up or I have a bug." She polished her sunglasses with her shirt.

"You haven't been your usual zippy self. What's going on?"

"Not sure. I'm not firing on all cylinders. Been having weird dreams." Ellen gave a flip of her hand. "It's probably nothing."

"Maybe you should get a check-up. Just for your own peace of mind."

"I hate going to doctors. I'd rather give Mater Nature a chance. And I don't have the patience to sit in a room full of sickos where the latest *Newsweek* has Nixon on the cover."

Split Ends

Wilma wrinkled her nose under rose-tinted glasses. "I know what you mean. Why do doctors think their time is more valuable than ours?"

"I love it when the nurse locks you in a closet with a toilet-paper gown. Then the doctor pries you open with a cold speculum like you're a goddamn oyster."

"I went to my internist last month for something on my face and he ordered a chest X-ray."

"That's nothing, Wilma. I went to Dr. Applebaum with clogged sinuses. He asked me to lie down. I thought he wanted to listen for bronchitis or pneumonia. Next thing I knew, he had his finger up my ass. If I had hemorrhoids, he probably would have done a brain scan. All I wanted was an antibiotic."

Wilma eased the Lincoln onto Church Circle. A hot wind spun the leaves of the sycamore in front of St. Anne's church. They rolled up Main Street and pulled into a spot outside the Maryland Inn.

Ellen wondered if her symptoms might be psychosomatic. A few days before she had described to her mother the lethargy and sense that all was not right with the world. Her mother had said, "Sounds like you have the blahs. Are things all right at home?"

"Of course, Mom," Ellen had snapped. When she hung up she knew her mother saw through the lie.

Maybe I caught the blahs from Ron. He'd been absent for a long time. And he didn't have a note from home.

"Ellen? Ellen?"

"Sorry, Wilma. I was a million miles away."

They took a window table off by itself. Through the lace curtains they watched the day-trippers file by, tote bags in hand. A couple strolled into the restaurant in his-and-hers jogging suits. An electric-blue swordfish swam on the back of his jacket. Hers had gold trim. Hair the color of sweet butter crowned the woman's look of face-lifted surprise. Ellen shared a smirk with Wilma.

"New Yorkers," Ellen tsked.

"Philadelphia. He's had one too many cheese steaks."

"Do you mean his diet or his girlfriend?"

They laughed, then fell into silence as they sipped spritzers and ate crab cakes. Usually, they finished each other's sentences. But Ellen could tell that Wilma was avoiding eye contact. The way she fingered her short, wavy hair was a sign something was wrong.

Ellen fidgeted as Wilma thwarted her attempts at small talk with one-word responses.

Ellen couldn't stand it any longer. "Wilma, what's the matter? Have I done something? You haven't been like this in all the years I've known you."

"No, nothing."

Ellen searched Wilma's face. "I'm getting bad vibes. Are you sure I haven't done something to offend you?"

"You didn't do anything. Why do you always think you're at fault?" Wilma's face reddened and she snapped. "Did it ever occur to you that you might be the innocent party?" Her outburst attracted attention from the boaters a few tables away.

"What do you mean, 'innocent party?'"

"Nothing, Ellen. Nothing at all. Sorry I blurted like that."

"Don't tell me nothing. You reacted as if I'd stuck a hot poker in your eye. I want to know why."

Split Ends

"I've already said too much. Please, let's drop it."

"We can't drop it. You're my friend. It doesn't take a genius to see you're upset. And I can see it involves me."

Wilma let out a breath that could have triggered a tornado warning. She took Ellen's hand.

"I'm sorry. I had hoped it would fade away."

Ellen stared at Wilma, down at their locked hands. "Fade away? You're not making sense."

"Ellen, Ron's having an affair."

Ellen froze. She jerked her hand away. "What? What did you say?"

"Ron's having an affair. I don't know for how long, but Steven told me."

"Wait a sec. Ron's having an affair with Steven?" She felt dizzy. Her mouth went dry, her tongue thickened. She could barely get the question out.

"Remember last Tuesday night when it was raining?"

"No. Yes. Maybe. I dunno. So?"

"Well, Steven went to Samantha's for a drink after work. It was raining when he left Sam's. He went back to the office for his umbrella and walked in on them."

"Them? Who is them?"

"Ron and Casey."

"Ron and ... Casey? You mean his paralegal?"

"Yes."

"You're telling me that Ron and his ... were ... together ... after work? In Ron's office?"

"I'm afraid so."

"Oh God." Ron had called at about 4:00 on Tuesday to say he had to work late. Something about a brief for a hearing. "Don't wait dinner," he'd said.

13

Her stomach knotted. She lifted the water glass, put it down then chugged the spritzer.

"Maybe they were talking about a case. Or ..."

"I'm sorry, Ellen. I shouldn't have told you."

"It's okay. I'm glad you did. Right. I'm so glad, I could just … shit." She looked at her plate. What swill.

"I feel terrible, Ellen. But if it was Steven, I think I'd want to know."

"Yes, but it will never be the wonderful Steven. Oh my God, what did he say? About Ron, I mean."

"Are you sure you want to hear this?"

"I'm sure."

"Steven heard some noise as he got off the elevator. He followed it to Ron's office. The door was ajar and—I can't believe Ron didn't lock the door."

"And?"

"Ron's pants were down around his ankles and her knees were around his ears. He was doing her right on the desk."

"The desk? The George III pedestal desk with the leather top? That I found for him? It cost me seven grand, even with my discount." She wiped her eyes. "He never wanted to do me anywhere but in bed." She imagined Ron's ass flexing, as it might for his proctologist. The humor of it evaporated in an instant.

Ellen knew some of her friends overlooked their husband's affairs in trade for cruises and fancy jewelry. Gossip about these couplings had convinced her she'd rather live alone than fake a marriage.

"How could he do it? I've been faithful to him through our whole marriage. I'd never think of sleeping with anyone else."

Split Ends

"I thought Ron had more class," Wilma whispered. "Casey is cute, but she's not half as attractive as you are."

"Sure. But her boobs stand at attention and she doesn't have a line on her face."

"I'm not saying this to make you feel better. You're a beautiful woman. Everyone thinks so."

Ellen waved off the compliment. "Damn, Wilma, she's only a few years older than Lisa." She pictured Casey and suddenly felt like a bag lady. She wondered what Lisa would think of her moralizing father's extra-curricular divertissement.

"I know, Ellen. I couldn't believe it when Steven told me."

Ellen thought about how often she had talked with Casey when she called Ron at work. She wondered if she'd have an easier time accepting it if the woman were homely.

Edith Piaf gave way to "Ebb Tide" and Ellen's drowning nightmare flooded in. Ellen tried to focus on what Wilma was saying.

"You must be in shock. But I hope you won't do anything hasty. You and Ron have a lot of years together. And Ron is a decent guy. He's witty and he brings home the bacon."

"True. He doesn't beat me and he pays the bills. But he hid his salami in someone else's Kaiser roll."

Wilma winced. "How can you make jokes?"

"How not? It's my only defense, Wilma. Humor—the last refuge of the shafted. But I can't ignore this. Damn it, he betrayed me."

"You know how middle-aged men are. They drop their pants and lose their minds. A younger woman strokes their delicate egos."

"More than his ego got stroked. And I'd hardly call it 'delicate.'"

"It doesn't mean he doesn't love you."

"Yes it does. You don't cheat on someone you love. I can't pretend it didn't happen."

"I'd hate to see you give up on the marriage. When you've had time to think, maybe you'll decide you're overreacting."

"Overreacting? My husband fucked a co-worker on a desk I found for him and you think I'm overreacting? Shit." Across the room, she saw two blue-haired ladies flinch at every word they hung on.

"Perfect marriage is an oxymoron," Wilma whispered.

"Of course. But once the trust is broken …" The waiter arrived and asked if they'd like dessert.

They waved him away. "Maybe you should have a gyny exam."

"A gyny exam? There's nothing wrong with my equipment. It's a little rusty, but serviceable."

"Ellen, Ron might have had unprotected sex with Casey."

"So?"

"You need to find out."

"I'll ask him tonight. Right after, 'How was your day, Sweetie?' I'm sure he'll level with me. Then I'll kill him."

"I'm serious. You could have an STD."

"Isn't that a sorority?"

Split Ends

"I'm talking about a sexually transmitted disease. You might be infected."

"I might. But doesn't someone have to poke you first? We haven't done the deed in months. I thought it was my fault. But he already gave at the office."

"Let's leave this nastiness aside for a second. I've noticed that you've been uptight for a while. A check-up wouldn't hurt."

"A check-up?"

"I say this as your friend, I think you should see Dr. Applebaum."

Ellen pictured the kindly physician who performed internals like a prospector chasing the mother lode. She always wondered if he was digging a route to China. "I'll think about it, Wilma."

"That's all I'm asking."

"We'd better go. I have to start dinner," Ellen said. "For my loyal and loving husband." She thought of the hussy with the hot dog and stifled the urge to vomit.

Wilma paid. For the first time in her life Ellen left the chocolate mints on the table.

Ellen's shaking hands couldn't fasten her seatbelt. Wilma helped, then pulled into traffic. As they passed the courthouse, Ellen's eyes focused on the entrance. *That's where they issue marriage licenses and hand down divorce decrees.*

Wilma took the scenic route along the Bay, and Ellen gripped the door handle to resist the water's vortex.

CHAPTER 3

Wilma jabbered about harvest sales and Rosh Hashanah recipes. Ellen nodded like a doll with a broken neck.

Traffic stopped them on Bestgate Road. "Are you okay?"

"I'm numb."

"I feel so bad for you."

"I'll be all right."

"Of course you will. But I doubt even you can laugh this off. You may want to talk to someone."

"I'm talking to you."

"I mean a professional, Ellen."

"Nah." She tried to swallow the lump in her throat. "I'll be fine." *How can I face Ron? What will become of us? Of me?*

"You won't win a medal for martyrdom. Not that you don't deserve it."

Ellen could barely stay in her skin. "I could walk faster. If this traffic doesn't move soon, I'll have a major meltdown."

Wilma reached over and touched Ellen's bouncing knee. "Take it easy. We'll make the next light."

* * * *

Ellen's thoughts drifted to a conversation weeks earlier. She and Ron had been watching the Wednesday night races from the deck while a tuna steak sizzled on the grill.

Split Ends

"Ron, something's not right here," Ellen had said. "I know you work hard and put in long days, but for some time you've had nothing left for me."

His watery blue eyes had been vacant and he seemed to speak from a hypnotic state. "I have a lot on my mind."

"I'm sorry. I didn't know. Why don't you talk to me instead of withdrawing?"

"You wouldn't understand." He had emptied the beer.

"Wouldn't understand? Try me. I signed on for better or worse. Remember?"

Ellen's eyes had tracked his as watched the lead boat, its red-and-white spinnaker billowing on the downwind run.

"I feel neglected, abandoned in a way. We used to talk, among other things."

"I'm talked out at night."

"But you're shutting me out."

"I can't discuss anything with you. You're irrational." He had spat out the words on his way into the house.

Feeling that she'd left a homework assignment unfinished, Ellen had given it another try over dinner.

"We need to discuss this. I'm really blue. And losing weight."

"You must be happy about that." He speared a piece of fish.

"Happy?"

"You always said you'd like to lose some tonnage."

"Sure, a pound or two so I don't get a wedgy from my jeans. Not five pounds in a week."

His fingers drummed the table. "Is that all you have to worry about? I have more important concerns. Do you have any idea what we spend?" His voice rose an octave. "I lost a big client three months ago. There's less coming in."

"Lost a client? Three months ago? Why didn't you tell me?"

"I did."

"I'd remember something that important. How bad is it? Shall I get a full-time job?"

"No."

"Maybe we should sell the house. Move to something smaller. We don't need all this and, frankly, I'm tired of taking care of it."

"I don't want to move."

"We can cut back on extras then. Sell the boat."

"I don't want to sell the boat." Ron had pushed away from the table. He started pacing. "You know, I bust my ass so you can enjoy the good life. I don't think you appreciate that."

"Of course I do. But there's more to life than money and things."

"That's easy for you to say. You don't contribute anything."

Ellen had felt herself flush. "Not all contributions carry dollar signs, Ron. I'd rather live in a trailer and have a husband who's there for me. What good are the trappings if we can't enjoy them together? Or if we're barely speaking?"

Ron's eyebrows had flexed.

Ellen had tried to soften her voice. "Maybe I haven't made it clear. When I'm working, with family or friends, I'm upbeat. When I'm home, I'm empty and

Split Ends

sad. We used to be best friends. You're not here anymore."

Ron had banged his bottle on the counter and his eyes squeezed down to hyphens. "What the hell does that mean?"

His fury had sent a shiver through her and she had felt herself shrinking. "You're here in the physical sense. But you're absent in other ways. You're preoccupied, and you hardly acknowledge my presence."

"That's ridiculous. What do you want from me? I took you to Puerto Vallarta in February. I bought you a watch for your, I mean, our anniversary. I pay the bills and I'm nice to your mother when she visits. I'm good to your damn dog."

"But you don't talk to me! You used to let me know what you liked about me—loved about me. I get praise and attention from everyone but you."

"That's not true. I compliment you on your cooking."

"We're not speaking the same language."

She had swiped at a tear as she remembered when laughter filled the home. Sometimes Ron would sneak up and tickle her, making her squirm and squeal. She missed holding hands with him, lacing their fingers together. She couldn't recall when he'd last taken her hand.

He had grabbed his plate and dumped leftovers into the disposal. *He's feeding me table scraps.*

She had followed him into the family room, interrupting Dan Rather. "Ron, you're withdrawing. The more distant you become, the harder I try to please you. Maybe that's why I go to those damn fitness classes I hate. So I'll look good and you'll be proud of me. And why I cook a decent meal when our friends get take-out or eat in restaurants."

"You're way off-base. You should have your hormones checked."

"Hormones have nothing to do with this. We used to talk or watch a movie after dinner. Now you fall asleep before your head hits the pillow and I'm left wondering, is this all there is?"

He had clicked off the news and walked back to the deck. "You're never satisfied." He had slammed the door.

* * * *

Wilma turned into the development and pulled up to the house. "I'll come in with you."

"No. I *vant* to be alone. Talk to you later."

Ellen walked into what had been her dream house. Penny greeted her with a wet kiss and followed her into the bedroom. Ellen peeled off her clothes, leaving them in a heap on the carpet.

With luck—and divine intervention—Ron would trip over them and break his neck. She showered again, scrubbing her flesh, then threw on a tank top and shorts and dialed her mother.

"Is this the first time?" Mady asked.

"Who knows? I think so. Why did he do this?"

"Men are men, Ellie. They don't stray if they're taken care of, um, you know … sex. A man will overlook a lot, but not that."

"Thanks for the vote of confidence, Mom." *I tried that. No sale.* "What am I going to do?"

Split Ends

"Find a good lawyer."

"Isn't that premature?"

"You have to protect yourself. Ron could move out, run off with your assets. You know how important money is to him."

"I think I should talk to him first."

"I know you don't like me to tell you what to do, but I'm begging you, dear. The same thing happened to Jean Goldberg. Remember Peter? Always on the road? He took Jean to the cleaners. They were at the club for the Thursday buffet and he announced he was leaving. Had a chippy on the side for years. He'd been squirreling money away for ages. Jean was clueless. Don't be foolish. It may have been a one-time thing, but you never know."

"I'll think about it. Talk to you tomorrow."

The phone rang. "How are you?" Wilma asked.

"Okay," Ellen whispered.

"I feel terrible. If you hadn't pressed me, I wouldn't have told you."

"I would have found out one way or another." Ellen cradled the phone and cut up green pepper and onion for sweet and sour chicken.

"Do you want me to come over?"

"No, Wilma. Honest."

"Call me if you need me."

"I will."

Ellen covered the vegetables with plastic wrap. She mixed the sauce ingredients and set the bowl aside.

The heat pump rumbled, drowning out "The Blue Danube Waltz." Ellen shuffled to the family room to turn up the volume. Sometimes she danced to it, pretending she was Suzanne Farrell in Balanchine's

"Vienna Waltzes." But first she lowered the duette over the picture window. The last thing she wanted was an audience of jeering crabbers or gulls.

She stopped to look at their wedding album, lying next to the stereo. She sat on the floor and opened it. *How young we were. Ron looks like a kid in his rented tux. And all that hair. I look pretty good too—nice tits, no wrinkles, no gray.*

The bride wore a radiant smile and deep tan. *Was my waist ever that tiny?* Her throat ached at the sight of her father, dapper in formal attire. She recalled how he had ordered her a gin and tonic to settle her nerves. On their way to the ceremony he had pointed to the unopened gin miniature. For years they laughed that she got a buzz from tonic water.

She remembered every detail. For openers, her grandmothers delayed the ceremony an hour because they were primping in their rooms. At the time, Ellen couldn't imagine what the holdup was. The law of averages negated both women having heart attacks on the same evening. And the soaps didn't air on Sunday.

When the grannies finally showed up, oblivious to the ripple effect of their tardiness, perspiration had stained the ivory *peau d'soie* gown. Ron had to sweeten Rabbi Prinski's take because he was late for his next gig.

She wiped tears as she turned the pages. All her elderly relatives were dead. She wished she had told them how special they were.

The pastry chef had refused her request for an all-chocolate cake so butter cream had iced the dark layers. *How times have changed. Now couples play house before trading gold bands, and weddings take place in amusement parks, aboard yachts or on the beach.*

She turned to a shot of the newlyweds kissing and her eye began to twitch. *If we'd had the option of living together, I wonder if we would have married so young. Or if we would have married at all.* She would have been disinherited, probably dismembered, if she had announced to her parents that she and Ron wanted to practice first.

Carrying a basket of marguerite daisies, the toothless flower girl beamed in a lemon-yellow dress, scabby knees beneath the hem. Cousin Amy waved, in a pink taffeta number, from another page.

Ellen closed the album on the last photograph where she and Ron said good-bye before doing it as Mr. and Mrs. in Nassau. The social director had played Pied Piper to the honeymooners infesting the hotel.

Those were the days. Ron and I made love morning, noon and night, even when I had sun poisoning.

Ellen walked to the deck and dropped into a chaise. Her pulse slowed as she watched a crimson maple leaf floating onto some yellow gingkoes. *Golden Oldie* was docked at her L-shaped pier a few dozen yards away, ready to sail at a moment's notice. When not lashed to a TV remote or cell phone, Ron maintained her in grand style. Ellen had kidded him about the time he spent with his mistress. *Some joke.*

She thought back to the dinner party and how Ron had rebuffed her. It seemed that he was rarely in the mood—no matter what she tried to do to light his fire. Weeknights he was too tired for anything but channel surfing. And lately, on weekends too.

He had his routine honed to a science. She thought he would self-destruct if he deviated five minutes from his rigid schedule. Ellen often read in the family room, classical music soothing her, after Ron conked out. When the kids were little and life was a three-ring circus, they always found time to be together. Even on weeknights.

The noise from a motorboat drew her attention and startled a blue heron wading at the shoreline. The bird took off squawking as the bare-chested man cut his engine and dropped a line over the side. Ellen heard tapping on the stairs. It had to be Wilma. No one else in the neighborhood wore three-inch heels in the middle of the afternoon.

"I had to see for myself that you're all right."

"Help yourself to a cold drink. I can't move."

Wilma pulled a chair over. "How are you?"

"Fine. Hah! We'll see how fine when Mr. Big Shot Attorney gets home."

"You have the best view in Annapolis."

"Isn't it? I'd hate to have to leave."

"Leave? Why would you even think that?"

"I hope you're right." Ellen reached down to rub Penny's throat. The dog seldom left her side. She rolled onto her back, paws in the air. Ellen scratched her stomach. "She's my best buddy, Wilma. After you, of course."

"Don't get any ideas. I don't like my belly rubbed."

Ellen burst into tears.

"Poor thing. Want a tissue?" Wilma rummaged in her purse.

"I've been like this for weeks. Before you picked me up this morning, I bawled when Penny took a leak.

Split Ends

How sad is that? I've never been a crier. I'm turning into my grandmother. She cried at hockey games."

"Now you have good reason to cry. I turn on the waterworks every month."

"Well, I can't blame this on PMS. I had a hysterectomy, remember? The cutter gave me a bikini incision so I could parade down Ipanema in my thong." *A thong of love ith a thad thong.*

Ellen dragged herself from the chaise. "I have to feed the Hound of the Baskervilles."

"I'll be going. Book club meets at my house tonight." The women hugged. "Good luck. Call me if you need to. I'll see you tomorrow."

Ellen watered the impatiens, coral and white to harmonize with the interior. She went inside and paused to admire her handiwork, done in a palate of neutrals splashed with peach.

Mornings, the sun brush-stroked waves onto the ceiling and walls. Wicker and rattan added to the house's beachy feel, reminding her of summers at the Jersey Shore. Furnishing the house had been a labor of love and, for the most part, Ron had gone along with her. She used to flit from room to room savoring her skill. Oohs and ahs from visitors nourished her. Now, nothing did.

Ellen dumped food in the dog's dish. As she waited for Penny to eat, she wondered what Steven thought of his partner's desktop fornication. In the '70s, the two guys had opened a small office across from Ford's Theatre. A couple of years later they moved to a plush warren on Pennsylvania Avenue, hired three junior partners and began buying suits from a Greek on K Street.

As Ron glad-handed over prime rib and Macanudos downtown, Ellen ate with the kids and watched Mr. Rogers. Back then she couldn't wait for Ron to come home. On this evening she wished he would just vaporize.

She glanced at the kitchen clock. Her throat tightened. The man of the hour would be home soon—unless he had to work on Casey's briefs again.

Penny raced to the front door, nails tap-dancing on the oak floor. Ellen dreaded the mugginess of Maryland summers but, earlier, as she had cried over the wedding album, a thunderstorm had pushed the heat and humidity north.

The weeping willow formed a graceful *port de bras* in the yard. An osprey flew toward Cattail Creek over water that sparkled like a carpet of brilliants. The neighbors waved as she and Penny passed.

Ellen stopped so her neighbor's grandchildren could pet Penny. She couldn't wait to be a grandmother. But Lisa and Josh had been married only a year, so she kept her mouth shut. She felt lightheaded and wanted to move on.

Her neighbor whispered, "Are you sick? You're awfully thin."

"I'm fine."

Ellen and Penny both dragged as they neared the house. Ellen unleashed Penny. "Let's see if the bastard is home."

Split Ends

CHAPTER 4

Ellen walked into an empty house.
Stay of execution.
She ironed two linen napkins and set the table.
Why am I not angry?
She was heating water for rice when the rumbling garage door announced his majesty's arrival.
I wish I had a script. What do you say to your husband when you've found out he's shtupping a babe on the desk you bought for him?
Ellen cringed as he pecked her on the cheek.
"How was your day?" he asked, his voice cheery.
"Worked out with Wilma. Had lunch at Café Normandie." *He's smiling. Bet his one for the road was a blow job.*
"How's Wilma?"
"Good." Ellen picked up the rice package. Ron's face appeared on the box. She stirred grains of Ron into the boiling water.
"Did you pick up my shirts?"
"Yes." *I hope they choke you.*
"I'm working late tomorrow."
"Oh?" *On Casey's briefs?*
"Is that a problem?"
Ellen kept silent.
"Something smells good. What are you fixing?" He grabbed a beer from the fridge.
Why am I making dinner? How crazy is that? How crazy am I? "Sweet and sour chicken."
"My favorite. I'm starving."

Beth Rubin

Why was Ron so pleasant? 'Cause he'd be bonking the babe the next day? "We can eat in five minutes." *Please, somebody help me.*

* * * *

"Ron, dinner." She walked to the hall and heard water running. The powder room door stood ajar. The rustle of newspaper told her dinner had to be delayed. *Why does he tell me he's ready then disappear?*

* * * *

Ellen didn't try to make conversation. To her relief, Ron seemed to have run out of verbal steam too. Cutlery scraped stoneware. Penny snored in her corner.

Fifty feet from the kitchen, a cormorant dove into the water and disappeared. The bird resurfaced and spread its blue-black wings as Ron rested his fork on the plate. He pulled on his beer and eyed Ellen's untouched food.

"You're not eating. How come?"

"Big lunch. Heat zapped me."

"I have work to do. I want to get it out of the way before the O's game." He left the table and his dishes on it.

"Sure," Ellen said to his back. *Chicken shit. What are you waiting for?*

She cleaned up and poured some wine. In her head, Elvis sang, "It's Now or Never," as she walked to their bedroom.

She was in an unshored tunnel and wondered if she would survive the cave-in.

Split Ends

"Ron, we have to talk."

He looked up with an irritated expression. "Can't it wait?"

"No." Ellen paused, took a deep breath. "I understand you were caught in *flagrante delicto.*"

The color left his face. "What?"

Gotcha, you shit. "You were porking your paralegal. On your desk. The one I picked out. For you to work at. Not to fuck on."

Ron cheeks flushed, then fluttered as he let out a deep sigh. "I can explain." He used his Perry Mason voice.

"Save it. I don't want to hear it. I need time to think. Time alone. You better find another place. By Monday." *Kitchen and case closed.* Ellen couldn't believe the voice was hers.

"You can't be serious. This is my home. Why don't you go?"

"What?"

"It would be easier if you left." His cheeks had their normal color back. "Be practical for a second. I work full-time and you don't. You could visit your mother. She'd like that."

"I don't believe your chutzpah. It might be easier for *you* if I left. For your information, I am practical. And I work full-time too. At 97 jobs, for less than minimum wage. Four days, Mr. Lawyer. As you know, adultery is grounds for divorce in Maryland. You made your bed. Lie on her, I mean, it."

His jaw slackened, then tightened. He puffed himself up to his full five-feet-eight inches. "Listen, Ellen …" He approached the witness stand and his voice boomed.

"You're far from perfect. You're moody and extravagant as hell, always buying gifts for everyone. Do you want to live by yourself? Is that what you want? You can't possibly take care of yourself. Who do you think would have you at your age? You'll end up poor and alone."

His fangs showed as he spoke.

"Most women would love to be in your shoes. You've got a sweet deal. I feed, clothe, house and take care of you. Think about that before you jump off the deep end."

You take care of me all right, sonofabitch. Penny takes better care of me. The plaintiff faced the defendant. "What about you and Casey?"

His fist balled and she feared he would hit her. "If Steven hadn't come back for his effing umbrella, we wouldn't be having this conversation."

"Oh, so it's Steven's fault you were balling Casey."

"Don't be coarse."

Ellen began to giggle. Nerves. And empowerment. "You digress, counselor."

A pulse in his temple went off. "It happened. It's over. No big deal."

"It's a big deal to me." Before anxiety could crush her bravado, she snapped. "You have until Monday."

Ron went silent. His eyebrows headed for his receding hairline. Ellen knew that her assertiveness had surprised, even shocked him. Hell, it had shocked her.

"Where am I going to go?"

"Go to your brother's. Or the Salvation Army. Or Casey's. Or go to hell. I don't care."

"But …"

"No more buts. You can go back to Casey's b-u-t-t."

Ellen turned and walked to the front hall closet. She took Penny's leash. "C'mon, girl. We need a walk."

CHAPTER 5

Ellen looked at her uneaten sandwich, then at her children. Lisa fiddled with her hair and rocked. Michael stared at his plate. Ellen took a deep breath.

"Your father was supposed to be here." *Why am I always the one to deliver bad news? Is a vagina a prerequisite?*

"Kids, this is difficult ..."

Michael spoke. "Are you sick, Mom? You don't look so good."

"No, no. I'm not sick." *At least, not physically.*

"Then what is it?"

"Your father and I are separating. Maybe getting a divorce. Sorry to be so blunt. I don't know a pretty way to say it."

Michael bit his lip. He appeared on the verge of tears. Ellen looked away. She had never seen such pain on his face. Not even when he had fallen off his bike and broken his arm in two places.

"What happened, Mom?"

"We're not on the same page anymore. We've grown apart. We were very young when we married. It happens. Unfortunately." Her voice cracked. "We don't want the same things." *Like each other.*

Lisa pushed away from the table and ran, crying, to the powder room. Ellen followed her, held her and smoothed her hair. Lisa calmed down and they returned to the powwow.

Ellen cleared her throat.

"Your father and I love you both very much. That won't change. We'll always be your parents, always here for you. I'm sorry." She reached out to grasp their hands. "I wish things had turned out differently."

* * * *

Ellen tossed and turned in Michael's room, surrounded by his soccer trophies and baseball pennants. The next morning, as soon as she heard Ron leave, she walked Penny and dialed her internist. "Tell him it's an emergency. If he doesn't call back in the next five minutes I'm jumping off the Bay Bridge."

"Ellen, it's Dr. Applebaum. What's going on?"

"I'm falling apart. Going down the tubes." Her words exploded and she had trouble catching her breath. "I need a shrink. Yesterday."

"I can't refer you to someone over the phone. You know how your health plan works. Meet me at my office at 8:30 and I'll see you right away."

"Thank you." Ellen hoped she could make it in one piece. Her head swam and she trembled from head to foot.

"Ellen, don't do anything stupid. I'll see you in an hour."

* * * *

Straightjacket or Prozac? Ellen wondered as she waited for her first therapy session. The "Moonlight Sonata" played from an ancient radio on a parson's table. Ellen gazed at her mismatched socks—one white, one gray. She turned her attention back to the forms on the clipboard. The questions went on and on.

Beth Rubin

<u>Known allergies:</u> *Brussel sprouts and two-timing husbands.*

<u>History of heart disease:</u> *Heart broken. Need replacement ASAP.*

<u>Family history of mental illness:</u> *Descended from long line of neurotic Jews, starting with David.*

<u>Occupation</u>: *Cheated-on wife, loving mother, loyal friend, lapsed decorator.*

<u>How did you hear about our practice?</u> *Ad in Washington Post entertainment section.*

<u>Method of payment:</u> *Brownies and cookies.*

Ellen scoped out the waiting room, furnished in mauve and gray. It would have been elegant if the '80s hadn't been supersaturated with mauve and gray. She handed the questionnaire to the mauve and gray receptionist and sat down with *People* as a threesome entered the waiting room from the Other Side.

A young girl clung to a tall man and sobbed into his starched collar. Ellen assumed that the child, with wavy hair and coal eyes, was handicapped. "I don't want to leave you, Daddy. Please don't make me."

"You have to go with Mommy. I'll see you in a few days," he said, prying her hands from his neck. Mommy sat poker-faced while the girl's death grip tightened.

Thank God, Michael and Lisa are grown. I couldn't bear to put them through a scene like this.

Ellen crossed and uncrossed her legs as she counted down to her 10:30 appointment with Elizabeth Smythe-Tower, Ph.D. *Classy name. She's probably a polyester frump with chewed-up fingernails.* Ellen didn't know a thing about her healer-to-be except that

Split Ends

Dr. Applebaum had recommended her and she had an opening.

Where the hell is she? The clock read 10:40. Ellen struggled to fill her lungs and slapped the magazine, face down, on the table. One more picture of Cindy Crawford and she'd barf. Her staccato breathing played "The Pizzicato Polka" and her leg bounced to the beat.

Business was booming. *Everyone looks normal. I wonder why they're here.* She had the urge to roam the audience, a hyper talk-show hostess.

Let's have a show of hands. How many are here for dementia? Any anal retentives? You must have hired your own bus. Any pedophiles? Sir, please zip up your fly. A wagon is waiting at the stage door to take you to the funny farm. How many are in unhappy relationships? Whoa, knock me over with a feather! Tell you what I'm going to do for all you folks who are miserable with your partners: Dinner at Denny's and tickets to CATS! At the high school.

Ellen looked at her watch—10:45. *Where is she? I'm coming unglued.*

Ellen chewed the inside of her cheek and looked around the empty waiting room. *The cheese stands alone.* "How much longer for Dr. Smythe-Tower?" she asked the receptionist. "I have a noon appointment with my psychic."

"It should only be a few minutes. Her 9:30 was late."

Ellen felt dizzy. She had forced a bit of toast earlier, trashing the rest. She toyed with excess of her jeans, bunched and wrinkled around her legs. Two months ago she'd had to lie on a bed to get into them.

Beth Rubin

Ellen had been musing about her mystery therapist—probably 60-ish and rock solid in Easy Spirits and a bun—when the shapely woman in spike heels made a grand entrance from the hot zone. Ellen took her to be another walking wounded.

"Mrs. Gold?" The woman wore theatrical makeup and a bold print and spoke in a hush. She was dressed for a night on the town—L.A. or Vegas maybe. Annapolis? Never.

"That's me. That is I. She is me."

"Why don't you come on back? I'm sorry you had to wait." Ellen followed the fog of Shalimar—a lamb to the slaughter, or resurrection.

The therapist kicked off her pumps and rested her feet on an open drawer. *Painted toenails. Glitter yet. Probably a rose tattoo on her behind.* The wallpaper, a wavy pattern in shades of blue, reminded Ellen of the ocean. The ocean reminded her of the dream. The dream reminded her of reality. Photographs and an M&M dispenser sat on the blond desk next to a box of tissues. *Ah, yes, the requisite tissues.*

Ellen wondered if they'd flip a coin, but her shrink broke the ice.

"Would you like some M&Ms?"

"I'd love some." Ellen helped herself to a handful, setting them on the desk so they wouldn't melt in her sweaty hand.

"What are you looking for in a therapist?"

"Do you do windows? Contract murder? Sorry. I haven't thought about what I'm looking for besides relief. I've been too busy deciding what underpants to wear."

Split Ends

She licked a paper cut then held up the finger for inspection. "Hey, I didn't slash myself on purpose. What do I want? I want a therapist who will say something once in a while."

"Before we go any further, may I call you Ellen?"

"Sure."

"And you may call me Elizabeth if you wish."

"Good. Smythe-Tower is a mouthful."

"Ellen, do you have feelings of hopelessness?"

"Aye, aye, ma'am," Ellen saluted. "But no more than 24 hours a day."

"Do you wash your hands excessively?"

"No. But always after going to the bathroom. My mother taught me well. And always wipe front to back."

"Do you ever feel as if you're being followed?"

"Only when I am." Ellen felt silly. She tried to keep a straight face, but it was near impossible.

"Do you hear voices when no one is around?"

"Yes. Perry Como, 'I hear singing and there's no one there. I smell blossoms and the trees are bare ...'"

"Ellen, I need to ask you these questions to determine your course of treatment."

"Yes, ma'am."

Elizabeth took a steno pad from a worn attaché case. "Why don't you tell me what has been going on?"

Ellen's spine straightened. "Could we cut through the bullshit? My dimmer switch is on LOW. A hair more and I'll be OFF. I'm not eating or sleeping. I can't focus except on how lousy I feel. Last week I cried when my dog peed. I have warm, loving relationships with my family and friends." The words spewed like upchuck. "And I enjoy my work. Which leaves my marriage. It sucks. It's dragging me down. And he's cheating on me. With his paralegal, Casey. Casey at his bat. It's a soap opera. Except it's real." Ellen gulped. "I think I need to distance myself from my husband. Like move to Uranus. Speaking of which, I'd like to stick dynamite up his anus."

Elizabeth nodded as she wrote.

"If I do good in therapy, will I get a discount?"

"Why don't you tell me about your husband."

"Whattaya wanna know?"

"How you met, what attracted you. That kind of thing."

"I met Ron at a party in New York. He was pre-law at NYU. I was at Parsons studying design." Ellen shrugged. "We dated, fell in love, married. That's what you did back then. Anything else?"

"What drew you to him?"

"Besides the physical attraction?"

"The sex was good?"

"Past good. Hot. Then lukewarm. Lately, the big chill."

"What did you like about him?"

"He was smart, soft-spoken, grown-up. Someone I could count on. I thought."

"How old are your children?"

"Michael is 27. He's a law student at the University of Maryland. Lisa's 25. She's a social worker. And married."

"How is your relationship with your children?"

"Close. Loving. They're great kids."

"Do they know what's going on?"

"I told them Saturday."

Split Ends

"You told them? Where was your husband?"

"Good question. After I confronted him, I asked Michael and Lisa to come for lunch. My husband said Saturday was good for him. When I got up Saturday he was gone. He left a note. Said he was going to a boat dealer in Rock Hall. The kids arrived. I tried to act normal. Whatever normal is. They were hungry and Michael had to go to work. I gave them lunch. Turkey on rye. The bread was stale. I toasted it. Thawed cookies in the microwave. Cookies ... microwave ... Where was I? Oh yes, I tried my husband's cell phone. No answer. I had to say something. The kids kept looking at each other and at me. I'm not surprised. I used to be cute. I think. Time was, I wouldn't go out without lipstick. Now I look like an Auschwitz survivor. God forbid! I'm pathetic. What were we talking about?"

"What did you tell your children about your situation?"

"I told them we were having problems. That we were separating for a while. Maybe we'd divorce. But I hoped it would work out. Of course, I doubt it will. But they need time to adjust."

"So you bore the burden of telling them?"

Her voice rose. "I didn't want to do it alone. I had no choice."

"No need for you to be defensive. Where does that come from?"

"Habit probably. Been doing it all my life."

"It must have been difficult to tell them that you and your husband are parting after so many years."

"Mm-hm." Ellen tried to shake off the boa constrictor coiled around her neck.

"What was their reaction?"

"Lisa was upset. She thought we'd all sail off into the sunset together. I used to think so too. Then she got angry, said she'd heard enough. I told her I'd done my best. She said I should try harder. I heard that a lot growing up. 'Try harder.' Like what I did wasn't good enough." Ellen reached for a tissue.

"Did Lisa say anything else?"

"She said, 'You can make it work if you want to.' Most of her friends' parents are divorced. You know how it is. I guess she thought she'd dodged the bullet." Ellen wiped her eyes. "So did I."

"What was your son's reaction?"

"Michael seemed pained but less surprised. He's been around us more. He must have picked up on the distance between us."

"What about your husband's affair?"

Ellen raised her hand for a timeout. She took a breath, swallowed. "I didn't tell them."

"Why?"

"I don't want to turn them against their father. But they'd be furious if they knew."

"Let's get back to your husband." Elizabeth glanced at her notes. "I'm sorry. What is his name?"

"Schmuck."

"I could have guessed. Mind if I use his given name?"

"Knock yourself out. His name is Ron, but to me it's Schmuck."

"When did he come home?"

"Oh, he rolled in about 2:00, after the kids had left. I was so pissed off, I couldn't speak."

"I can guess."

Split Ends

"I asked where he'd been. Jeez, a new boat. That's what we need now. Something else to divvy up if we divorce. He'll get the head—you know, bathroom. I'll get the galley."

"What did you say to your husband about his missing the family meeting?"

"That he'd been expected at lunch. He said, 'No, you told me Sunday.' I reminded him that he had chosen Saturday. He blew. He gets angry at me when he screws up."

"How did that make you feel?"

"Frustrated. Ticked off." Ellen grabbed another tissue. "Wait a minute! I called the dealer when Ron didn't answer his cell phone. The salesman said Ron hadn't been in. Bastard. Bet he was doing flying jibes with his paramour—excuse me, paralegal."

"You sound angry."

"He's been out to lunch for years. He displays me like his high school tennis trophies. But he doesn't see me. Or hear me. Even when I repeat things six times, he forgets."

"What kind of things?"

"Phone messages. Requests. Social plans. Is it too much to expect a husband to keep track of his life outside the office?"

Elizabeth's concerned expression clashed with her dress. "Men, especially upwardly mobile men, often transfer the responsibility of preserving marital and familial harmony onto their wives."

Good one, Elizabeth. You hit a nerve.

"Is that the same as being self-absorbed and spoiled? He expected me to run the house, keep up with family obligations, volunteer for the right charities, entertain, look good, put up with his *mishigos,* and service him. And not much of that recently. He worked. Otherwise, he did *bupkes.* And he's a couch potato. The only thing he moves are his bowels."

"What about emotional support?"

"He gets plenty. When I need some, it's not in his lexicon. He accuses me of melodrama when I'm upset. What he doesn't perceive doesn't exist. My opinion counts for planning menus and picking ties, little else. Emotional support? I had a miscarriage, between Michael and Lisa. Needed a D & C. He couldn't leave work to be with me. My girlfriend took me to the hospital. He has this ... this attitude."

"What attitude?"

"He's like a guest in his own home. On second thought, he acts like a guest in his own life." Ellen's head throbbed. "Yes, Doctor Elizabeth, it'd be clinically accurate to say I'm angry."

"So what plans are you making for the separate time you need?"

"It's done. He left Sunday night. Found a place near his office. Month-to-month. He asked me to sign something."

"Sign something?"

"That his leaving for six months was a mutual decision."

"Oh?"

"So I can't hit him with desertion. He's a lawyer first."

"Why are you making a face?"

"He's running true to form—covering his ass, looking out for number one."

Split Ends

"Ellen, why six months? You need to live apart a year to divorce in Maryland."

"I know. Ron would agree to only six months. Maybe he thinks I'll come around. My lawyer, Marla Stein ... do you know Marla?"

"I've worked with her. She's tough."

"Good. I need tough. Marla said to take the six months. She thinks that once he's on his own, he'll agree to another six. I'm not so sure."

"But if he comes home, you're back to square one."

"I know. It's a risk. I just wanted him o-u-t."

"What about your financial situation?"

"He pays most of the bills. I'm a decorator. Work part-time. I took half our joint checking account. Opened an account in my name. I felt bad about it."

"Felt bad?"

"Sure. About not asking Ron. I'm used to asking first. For everything. Marla told me it was okay. And that I'll get a settlement—if, or when, we divorce."

"You sound unsure."

"I knew we had problems. What couple doesn't? Never thought we'd break up. This thing with Casey— I can't wrap my mind around it."

"Do you think you'll be all right financially?"

"I'm concerned over the short-term, and if ..."

"If what?"

"This isn't a community property state. I hope he doesn't pull a fast one. He's kept our finances under wraps. He always told me I had nothing to worry about."

Beth Rubin

"Keep in close contact with Marla, and write down your questions before you call. It'll save time and money."

"She charges an arm and a leg. But I wouldn't go to a country doctor for brain surgery. I figure I'm investing in my future."

"Where were you when he moved?"

"I walked around the mall. Went to a movie. For the life of me, I couldn't tell you what I saw."

"That was a good idea, to be away from the house when he left. How do you feel with him gone?"

"Unburdened. But also sad and anxious."

"You're in mourning. You can't walk away from a marriage, especially a long-term marriage, and feel nothing. Breaking away is like having a limb severed. It leaves phantom pain. To some people it can seem like a death."

Ellen shook her head and reached for the candy. "What a nightmare. I feel like I'm going under."

"How do you mean?"

"Drowning. I hope I don't sink to the bottom."

"You may be on the verge of a breakdown. However, I don't think you need a psychiatrist—that is, a medical doctor. I have a PhD in clinical psychology and more than 20 years' experience. I have helped many women in similar situations."

"Sounds like a plan. Can you wave your magic wand? Ship me to St. Bart's with *Self-Therapy for Dummies* and a bag of M&Ms?"

Elizabeth smiled. But without mirth in her eyes. "I wish it were that simple."

"What can you do for the anxiety? It's hell, especially at night."

"I can call Dr. Applebaum and suggest he prescribe something to help you sleep. I do not want to recommend an anti-depressant. At least, not now. Anti-depressants often mask symptoms, producing an inflated sense of well-being. The patient may feel better, but psychotropic drugs do not get to the heart of the problem. It is like putting a Band-Aid on an infection.

"I have nothing against Band-Aids." Ellen held up the paper cut.

"The first thing we have to do is cope with the crisis. The greatest progress will come later, once you're in a more comfortable place. Then we can create the kind of change you want for the future. Right now, you're in crisis."

"What was your first clue?"

"I'm trusting you to let me know if your depression gets worse. I can always recommend that Dr. Applebaum prescribe something. But I want to start with just therapy. We can begin by setting some goals and working through them together."

"What can I do for myself?"

"Nurture yourself. Do not worry about being on a schedule. I'll teach you relaxation techniques for the panic attacks. In the meantime, go to a quiet place and rest. Listen to soothing music. Take walks. Go out with friends. Draw on anything that brings you comfort and relief."

"Okay." Ellen made a mental list.

"Remember, you do not have to keep up the perfect person act anymore."

"That'll be tough."

"It is important, Ellen. It sounds as though you have been motivated by shoulds, instead of what you want."

"Shoulds are my specialty."

"I want to meet with you twice a week until things settle down. If you feel worse or if you have self-destructive thoughts, I am counting on you to let me know right away. And mark your message 'urgent.' Will you do that?"

Ellen rolled 'self-destructive' around her brain. "I've never felt worse, but suicide's not on my list. It'd be easier, faster, than climbing out of this pit. But, no, I won't self-destruct. Wouldn't burden my kids with that. Besides, I'm not ready to check out."

Elizabeth looked at her watch. "We have to stop now. I want you to make an appointment for Friday or Saturday."

Ellen dropped a wad of damp tissues into the wastebasket. "Thank you. I feel better than I did 50 minutes ago."

"That's because you have taken a big step in caring for yourself. I will see you in a couple of days. Be sure to make an appointment on your way out."

Ellen reached for Elizabeth's outstretched hand. *I like her. Elizabeth's voice is soothing. And she seems to care.*

Ellen hoped she could summon the strength for what lay ahead. As she walked to her car she made herself a promise: *I'm going to make it. Whatever it takes, I'm going to make it.*

CHAPTER 6

Ellen searched for words to describe the look and feel of the morning. She decided it wore the burnished mantle of late autumn. She passed a stand selling potted mums and cider and pulled into the lot behind the Hair House. Before heading north on a buying trip and to see old friends, she had to do something with her hair. It would be cheaper and less painful than a face-lift. She went into the salon.

A couple of years before, she had had her shoulder-length hair butchered to within an inch of her scalp. Ron had asked, "Did you fall into the lawn mower?" and turned back to "Wide World of Sports" before she could answer.

As the shampoo girl rinsed her, tears streamed down Ellen's cheeks. "It's PMS," Ellen croaked.

Turbaned in a pink towel, she waited as Jillian checked another customer's perm. The stylist's jaw dropped when she saw Ellen. Fists propped on her hips, she asked, "What truck ran over you? You look horrible."

"That good?"

Jillian fastened a cape around Ellen's neck and fluffed her hair with a fresh towel.

"What's goin' awn, hon?" she asked in Baltimorese. "You're skinnier than I am." At one time Ellen had envied Jillian's svelte body.

"No appetite. Sleep's messed up. Speaking of sleep, who are you bedding this week?"

The stylist snorted. "You're a piece of work. What are we doing today?"

"The usual. Take an inch off and make me 35 and beautiful."

Jillian untangled Ellen's hair with a wide-tooth comb. "You use conditioner?"

"No. Why?"

"You better do something. You have split ends."

In more ways than one. "I've been neglecting myself."

Jillian parted Ellen's hair into a checkerboard and clipped the sections. "I've missed seeing you. I like when you come in. You're always good for a laugh," Jillian said. Ellen had been going to Jillian for years. Sometimes, they met for coffee or caught a movie Ron had no interest in seeing.

"Give me a vicarious thrill, Jillian. How's your love life?"

"Pretty dull." Jillian trimmed Ellen's bangs. "I'm going out tonight with a guy who answered my ad in *The Washingtonian.*"

Jealousy gnawed at Ellen. *It would be fun to dress up and dine with someone new.* "What do you know about him?"

"He's single and lives in Chevy Chase. He's an attorney."

"Stay away from lawyers."

"Why?" Jillian drew two locks under Ellen's chin to make sure they were the same length. "Isn't your husband a lawyer?"

"Yes. Just kidding. Have a good time. In fact, knock yourself out."

Jillian set the shears on the counter and spoke to Ellen's reflection. "You know me well enough that I tell it like it is. I'm worried about you. You're always

Split Ends

upbeat and look good. I've never seen you like this. You're a mess." Jillian picked up the dryer, wielding it like a blowtorch.

Ellen raised her voice over the noise. "I'm in a funk. I'll snap out of it." *If I don't snap first.* Even without her glasses she could see the dark circles under her eyes.

After her haircut, Ellen walked next door to buy jeans. In the unflattering light she surveyed her beanpole body. A skinny little girl stared at her from the Fun House mirror. Ellen wondered what the child would look like when she finally grew up.

* * * *

"How's Cleveland, Mom? No, I'm not lonely. Penny's keeping me company." The dog napped on the Berber carpet in front of the fireplace. Home anywhere Ellen was.

"Therapy's going well. Two months down, 4,000 to go. Maybe I'll graduate sooner. Yep, I found the coffee pot." Ellen slouched on the gray flannel couch she had found for her mother.

She rested her feet on the cocktail table, watching the Five O'clock News. "Tell Amy I said hello." For years Ellen and her cousin had been closer than most sisters.

"No, the house isn't dirty. How dirty could it get in four days? Yesterday I found a Scalamandré silk and country French bombé dresser for a client. Then I met Trish at Serendipity."

Beth Rubin

Ellen used to have room for dessert after a footlong and frozen Mochaccino in a stemmed fishbowl. The day before she had trouble finishing a cup of soup.

Being with Trish had relieved her loneliness. She got a vicarious thrill from her younger cousin's escapades, her own life paling to winter white by comparison.

"Yes, Mom, the house is warm. I'm warm. Penny is warm. I scouted Soho for *tchotchkes* today. Yes, I wore a coat. No, I didn't go out with wet hair. I remember what you've told me for 50 years about that."

Ellen continued to field Mady's questions. Ellen was used to her mother's frustration with widowhood. Still, the interrogation rattled her. Ellen considered herself lucky that Mady hadn't smothered her before she entered kindergarten.

"Yes, I'm eating. Last night I ordered Chinese and watched 'Top Gun' for the 10th time." Ellen's body had ached during the love scenes. She doubted she would ever again know such passion. She'd mothballed that part of her life, storing it in the attic with out-of-season clothing. She felt she had lost the right to expect more.

After leaving in the '60s, she had seldom visited New Jersey except for weddings and funerals. With Ron bitching and moaning the length of the Turnpike, the four-hour drive seemed like 12.

So, early in the marriage Ellen had capitulated, letting old friendships fade. Since the separation she had begun to rekindle connections with childhood pals.

Ellen hesitated to tell Mady about her plans for the following evening. Then she thought, why not? *This is*

Split Ends

silly. I'm an adult. I have male friends. Nothing wrong with dinner with an old friend, just because he's a guy. Or because he moved me like no other.

She was having trouble thinking about anything else.

"Guess who I'm having dinner with tomorrow night."

"Who? One of your little friends from high school?"

Ellen laughed at how Mady still talked to her like she was a kid. He had been a high school friend all right. But he had never been little, in stature or significance.

"C'mon. Guess."

"I'm stumped. Who?"

"Drew Cushing."

"Oh, that's sweet, Ellie. Of course, you realize, by now he's probably fat and bald."

"M-o-o-o-o-m. What's the difference?" *Damn right, I wonder what he looks like.*

She hadn't seen a man, on- or off-screen, who measured up to the young Drew. *He's probably heavier. If he has any hair, I wonder if it's still chocolate brown.*

"How in the world did you find him?"

"I heard he lived on Long Beach Island. I always wondered what happened to him."

"You two were quite an item. Your father and I thought you might end up together."

I thought so too. "Remember when he gave me his letter sweater? Don't ask why, but I kept it all these centuries and through six moves. Before I left Annapolis—I mean I was already in the car—I felt compelled to find that sweater. I tore up the basement looking for it. It was weird, this little voice telling me, 'Don't leave home without it.' I found it with some scrapbooks in a mildewed carton."

"Then what? How did you find him?"

"Yesterday I woke up and thought, what the hell? No pain, no gain. I got the number from information and called. He sounded puzzled, probably didn't recognize 'Gold.' When I said 'Ellen Rosenberg,' he sounded happy to hear from me."

"That's nice, Ellie."

"I told him, 'I'm calling because I've had your sweater for 35 years and I thought I should return it. You may want to give it to someone else.' We talked so long, I missed the 10:15 train. He asked me to meet him for a drink. Then he upped the ante and invited me to dinner."

Ellen waited for her mother's inevitable cautionary advice—like the DANGER sign she had waved when they were high school sweethearts. Instead, Mady stopped clucking and asked, "Where are you going?"

"Who cares? I'd be happy with a hamburger and greasy fries at Butch's. He's picking me up at 6:30."

Whenever Ellen reconnected with old friends, she dredged up snapshots she carried in her head. She couldn't picture Drew any way but how he had looked the last time she saw him: blue shirt, Camels snug in the breast pocket, dungarees and loafers. That day so many years back—in her yellow shirtwaist and Keds, a ribbon tying her wispy ponytail—she had returned his ID bracelet and told him she couldn't be his girlfriend anymore.

Split Ends

"My gosh. Drew Cushing. He was a handsome devil. We liked him, your father and I. But there was something ... something ... about him. You were so gaga over each other, we went along. Until he got in trouble. Then we had to protect you."

From what? "I know." Ellen wanted to drop it. It had taken her years, and meeting Ron, to get over Drew.

"You know," Mady continued, "I was surprised you went along when we told you to break up with him. I think you two were really in love."

"Went along? You and Daddy left me no choice. Short of running away, what could I do? I was 16. Under your thumb." *Hmm, that has a familiar ring. Just like my marriage.*

"Calm down, Ellie. Why are you getting so worked up? It was years ago. You were a little girl."

And in some ways I still am, Mom. Listen to me confide all this stuff to you.

Her mother plunged into the pregnant pause. "Have a nice time tomorrow night. And say hello to Drew for me. I'll be dying to hear all about it."

"I'll videotape it. Let's talk day after tomorrow."

Ellen was watching the five-day weather forecast when the phone rang. *Must be my mother reminding me to lock the doors.* "Yes, Mom."

Her husband's voice triggered the tone she reserved for telemarketers. "I'm fine, Ron."

Steel butterfly wings began flapping inside her. *Why is he calling me here?*

"I'm busy. Going into the city. Seeing friends." *Gosh, he's cheerful. He must be missing my kugel.*

Beth Rubin

"Yes, I'm eating more. Why? Are you doing a study on anorexic women?"

She let him talk.

"So I'm short-tempered. Sue me. I'll be home Sunday night. Dinner next Saturday? Um, um ..." *Why does he think restaurants are closed Sunday through Friday? I better say yes. The piggy bank ruts on his side of the dresser.* "All right. I'll call you when I get back."

Ellen hung up and berated herself. "Penny, why am I still doing the shoulds?"

Penny awoke from her nap and stretched. "I can hear Elizabeth asking, 'Why did you accept if you don't want to go?' Because, Elizabeth, old habits—and husbands—die hard."

Ellen clicked off the sports and went to the kitchen. As she poured Penny's food, Drew's image displaced Ron's. The butterflies began to play a different tune, something light and upbeat from the '50s.

Ellen put on her jean jacket and clipped the leash to Penny's collar. She doubted her feet would touch the sidewalk. She couldn't wait to see Drew, even if he had gone fat and bald.

Split Ends

CHAPTER 7

She'd had a crush on Drew Cushing since ninth grade, since the day when she had been watching for her mother's car after checking out "Catcher in the Rye." Across from the library the bank had already swallowed the sun. A woman had stopped to let her beagle pee. Ellen had buttoned her camel-hair coat, flipping the collar up against the late afternoon chill.

When she had looked up, there he was. He loped down the avenue in a black and gold athletic jacket, broad shoulders drooping like spruce boughs after an ice storm. He moved like a panther and prowled the sidewalk. Maybe he thought it held the answers to the next day's English quiz. Ellen had stared. Her eyes tracked him as he padded past the drugstore, past the record store and the movie theater.

His acolytes trailed, leaving a flash flood of saliva in their wake. Not once did Drew acknowledge his fan club's presence. Maybe he had been soaking up the adulation so he could later squeeze it out and pore over it in the privacy of his room.

Ellen tried to picture his room. Were photos of Mickey Mantle or movie stars taped to the walls? Did he have his own phone?

Ellen's pulse had quintupled the pace of his footfalls. He'd swung round the corner and disappeared in a veil of smoke. She'd known that, for the rest of her life, she would think of Drew whenever she smelled burning autumn leaves. He was more perfect than Elvis, who was marching somewhere in Germany. And about as accessible.

Beth Rubin

Ellen knew where he lived—in a white house with green shutters and pachysandra necklacing the throat of a huge oak. She knew because she and her best friend, Meg, walked by it all the time, hoping for a glimpse of the Chosen One. Afterward, over cheeseburgers and fries at Butch's, they'd concocted outlandish plans for meeting him.

Although the girls were in the top 10 percent of their class and smart enough to know that the Drew Cushings of this world were trouble, they kept hatching plots. It beat the hell out of helping their mothers with chores.

Drew was almost always trailed by a swarm of pointy Maidenforms. And Ellen was seldom dateless on a Saturday night. But she thought she didn't have a prayer of penetrating his Maginot Line. Aching to know him, she had settled for admiring him from afar, like the postcard of Michelangelo's *David* on her bulletin board.

* * * *

Ellen hugged her books to her oxford shirt and wormed her way through the crowded halls. Her tight skirt made her mince. Gunmetal lockers lined the walls like troops at attention. Their doors slammed an erratic drill to the squeals and yells of friends reuniting.

Ellen always looked forward to the first day of school and counted September, rather than January, the start of a new year. The shiny, waxed floors and virginal textbooks, their spines uncracked, worked their magic again. At last, she was an upperclassman.

Split Ends

She threw back her shoulders and swept the dip from her forehead.

Ellen suffered withdrawal in June when her friends scattered like pollen. Some fled to the shore to hawk fudge on the boardwalk. Others traipsed through Europe, leashed to their parvenu parents. Some traded organdy curtains for torn shades to play God at New England camps. Ellen had toiled as a gofer for the *Maple Shade Gazette*, then spent a week at the beach with relatives.

She spotted her friend, Jane. Her pace quickened, restrained by her skirt. Overweight and brainy, Jane was a social outcast. Ellen liked Jane because she was funny as well as smart. She didn't give a rat's ass what her cool friends thought.

"Hey Ellie, you look great."

"Great? How? I just had gym. I don't know if my underwear is inside out. Or even on." Changing out of the bloomers that made her narrow hips look like the Hindenburg and reinflating her hair were major pains in the ass.

Amid "Hi's" and "How-are-you's?" the girls climbed the stairs. "Where ya' headed, Ellie?"

"Latin. Mrs. Strong."

"Me too."

They hustled. Even a few seconds late meant detention. No excuses—even if you gushed en route and had to wad the scratchy girls' room towels in your Spanky pants.

"What's with your hair, El?"

"Peroxide and ammonia. My mother threatened to cut it out. Thinks bleached hair is for whores. How bad is it?"

Beth Rubin

The bell blared, the question unanswered. The girls breezed into class under the dour glare of Isabelle Strong, square-shouldered in a print dress and orthopedic sandals. As Ellen searched for a seat, she spotted him. Her heart tingled as if zapped by a cattle prod.

The teacher greeted the class—"*Salvete discipuli*"—and the students responded with a sing-song, "*Salve magistra.*"

Ellen slid into the chair not two feet from him and dropped her notebook on the small patch of floor between them. In an abortive *pas de deux*, they leaned over to retrieve it and clunked heads. The collision and whiff of Canoe left her almost unconscious. *I want to get close to him, but not like this.*

She massaged the egg bulging on her scalp. Drew handed her the binder with a smile that turned her insides to marshmallow cream. *God, he has beautiful eyes, green like a cat's.*

Their fingers brushed and she thought she would *plotz.* "Thank you." *Was my whisper too faint? Is my deodorant working?* She folded her trembling hands in her lap. From the corner of her eye she could see him watching her. His gaze bore into her like the shoe-store X-ray scanner.

How can I conjugate, much less pass the course, with him so close? When she tried copying the homework assignment, her pencil squirmed like an eel.

She nearly went walleyed trying to watch him. His Hershey-colored hair was Brylcreemed into a D.A. With his ruler-straight nose and square jaw, he looked like the Roman soldier in her Latin book.

Split Ends

Slumped almost to horizontal, he wore a bored expression and red polo shirt. His right arm draped over the chair back as it might some girl's shoulder. Ellen quivered at the thought of that arm around her. He held a ballpoint as if it was a cigarette, tapping it on the desktop. Thrust into the aisle, his legs stuffed pegged pants like sausage in its casing. Ellen tried to appear nonchalant while his scuffed black loafers flirted with her polished burgundies. She pressed her knees together to stop their jitterbugging.

The teacher droned and Ellen considered names for their children. *Cathy Cushing? Chuck? No. Friends might call him Chuckles.* She had been scribbling, "Mrs. Andrew Cushing," in the margin of her notebook when the bell freed them from Brundisium.

She took a breath of chalky air that tickled her throat. Stalling to allow him time to leave, she rummaged in her purse for a stick of gum and regained her composure. When the coast was clear she gathered her books and flung her bag over her shoulder. A husky voice startled her.

"How's your head?"

"Fine. Woke me up for class." Ellen wondered if her smile was more sophisticated than she felt. She hoped that lettuce from her baloney sandwich wasn't clinging to her braces like seaweed to a crab pot.

He moved closer. He flashed two neat rows of whiter-than-white teeth. They reminded Ellen of the Chiclets her grandmother kept in the drawer of her mahogany drum table. His mouth was within kissing distance and Ellen feared she would melt down to her socks.

"I hear you're a whiz in Latin. I stink." He said it with an "aw, shucks" shrug. Ellen swallowed hard. She had one thing on her mind. Not irregular verbs. She wanted to drag him into the parking lot and lose her virginity before sixth period. Or her next period.

"I'm off the team if I bomb."

Ellen lived to cheer his quarterback butt on Saturdays. Hot dog in hand, she dreamed that someday he'd squeeze her like a pigskin.

"Can you help me?"

Name it. Write your exam? Wash your jockstrap? Bear your children?

"If you really think I can help."

"Cool." He winked, grabbed something from behind his ear and popped it in his mouth. "ABC gum. Already been chewed."

She stood rooted to the spot and watched him saunter off.

Head and heart pounding, she stumbled down the corridor, searching for Biology. She finally found the room, right across from Latin, after the bell.

Ellen barged in as the teacher summarized the unit on reproduction. *Reproduction. Drew. Hot dog. Pigskin. Foreskin. Amo, amas, amat. Maybe an extra-credit project?*

She had been picturing them making out in his '55 Bel Air when the teacher flushed the daydream. Dripping sarcasm, he hissed, "Nice of you to bless us with your presence."

Cheeks flaming, she embraced her books for protection. *Christ, I don't need his grief. Not now.* Her new shoes squeaked as she edged to the far side of the room and parked her firm behind next to Tiny. She

Split Ends

watched the 12-foot boa constrictor swallow a white rat. She thought about Drew and gulped.

* * * *

A week after they bumped heads, Drew asked for help with Latin.

Ellen called her mother first.

"Will Drew's mother be home?"

"Yes. So will Willie. That's his cocker spaniel."

"No need to get cute, Ellen."

She thought the day would never end. Sitting in class was a complete waste of time. He arrived at her locker with a smile that left her speechless.

"Thanks for rescuing me, Ellen."

She grinned, relieved not to be drooling.

They talked about the Top 10 and their least-favorite teachers and the team's chances of winning the state championship. By the time they reached his house, she felt as though she'd known him ever since she was a 32AA.

A statuette of the Virgin Mary stood near the hedge in his yard. Ellen had never given a thought to Drew's religion. He had not asked about hers.

The house was so dark Ellen thought she had entered a crypt. Heavy floral drapes blocked out the sun. Antimacassars protected the arms of the horsehair sofa, olive drab like the carpet. Ellen wanted to fling open the curtains and turn on all the lights. Her own living room was bright and cheery, with pale yellow walls and sheers. *It's a morgue. I'd go nuts here.*

A Sacred Heart of Jesus hung over the mantel. The boss's son pointed his right index finger at the crown of thorns around his heart. Ellen thought the caption should read, "It hurts only when I laugh."

Mrs. Cushing ghosted in from the kitchen. She had tight lips and permed hair the color of ginger. *Drew must get his height and good looks from his father. Either that or he's a mutant.* Over her apron hung a gold cross as big as an albatross. *How come she doesn't tip over from the weight?* Many of Ellen's friends wore crosses, but she had never seen one that large.

"Nice to meet you," his mother murmured without a hint of interest.

She's a better ventriloquist than Paul Winchell.

"What parish do you belong to?" she asked. Ellen could tell Mrs. Cushing was staring at her nose.

"Beg your pardon?"

"What parish? St. Stephen's or St. Paul's?"

"Neither. I'm Jewish."

Her nostrils flared. "Jesus, Mary and Joseph." She fingered her rosary and looked as if she needed smelling salts.

"I'll be saying novena and watching my programs. Drew, there are oatmeal cookies in the breadbox. Help yourself."

What about me? Is it a sin for Jews to eat oatmeal cookies? "Drew, I don't think your mother's thrilled with my being Jewish," Ellen whispered.

"She doesn't know the meaning of thrilled. Don't let her get to you."

They sat at the kitchen table, elbows on the Kelly-green oilcloth, and translated Cicero among the cookie crumbs and Yoo-Hoo bottles. Ellen wondered what Mrs. Cushing would do if she found out a Jew had

Split Ends

eaten her cookies. Maybe she'd call in a priest for an exorcism. But more strange was Drew—he knew his Latin.

He doesn't need help from me or anyone else. What gives?

His mother was upstairs watching soap operas. Ellen recognized the theme whenever the saga broke for a Fab commercial.

* * * *

The next time Ellen tutored Drew, his mother was away. *I should probably call home. But how's my mom going to know we're alone?* The Latin book sat unopened. They were laughing about their teacher, Mrs. Strong.

"She's plug ugly. Her husband must be blind," Drew said.

"But she's a sharp dresser." Ellen thought of the teacher's huge bosom. It was only a matter of time before the buttons exploded, like corn popping.

"Let's take a break," he said. "Want to go for a walk?"

They headed toward the village, the autumn leaves crackling beneath their feet. Over vanilla Cokes at Butch's, they discovered they both liked Sinatra and the shore.

Drew slid off the stool and reached in his pocket. "Any requests?"

"Surprise me."

He headed to the jukebox. She heard a coin drop and recognized the strings introduction of "All the Way."

They locked smiles. Ellen thought she was hallucinating every time she glanced in the soda fountain's mirror.

"I'm full, Drew. The fries are yours." *So am I.*

On the way back he took her hand. It felt as natural as brushing her teeth. He checked to see that his mother was out. Then he turned on the radio and sat on the sofa with her.

The horsehair scratched her bare legs and she wished she had worn knee socks. Drew moved closer and rested his arm on her shoulder. She shivered.

"Are you cold? I'll turn up the heat."

If I was any warmer, I'd be hot cocoa. "It's just a spasm, from carrying books."

"Love Me Tender" came on. Drew tried to sing with Elvis. Ellen nearly lost it and bit her lip. *He can't carry a tune worth a damn, but otherwise he's perfect.*

They turned to each other and next thing she knew they were kissing. Ellen felt as if she was on "Queen for a Day." She couldn't believe how soft and warm his lips were. He smiled then buried his face in her hair.

"Do you want to see the rest of the house?" His voice was low. She followed him up the worn staircase to his parents' room.

It looked like it hadn't been slept in for 20 years. Rosary beads hung from a post of the twin maple beds. *Green spreads. Of course.* On the dresser, a tiny Virgin Mary prayed on a lace doily. Crystal rosary beads spilled from an open jewelry box. *Probably blessed by the Pope.* Another rosary lay on a blue novena book. *This room gives me the creeps. All that's missing are stigmata on the headboards.*

Split Ends

Ellen heard scampering overhead. "What's that noise, Drew? It sounds like squirrels."

"Oh, that's my Black Irish grandfather." She wondered if the old man was really black and whether he came down for meals. She was too embarrassed to ask and Drew didn't offer to introduce them.

"Where's your room?"

"Over here." He took her hand.

Ellen held her breath. *Don't let it be green.*

The walls and spread were the color of sesame seeds. *Thank God.* Over the roll-top desk a bulletin board held autographed pictures of sports figures. Ellen had never seen such a neat room. Not even a pencil out of place. Her own room was a dump. She often piled clothes on her chair until it fell over. And she had back issues of *Seventeen* and *Photoplay* strewn everywhere.

* * * *

One afternoon they had been making out on his bed when she heard crunching gravel. They slipped into their loafers and raced downstairs as Mrs. Cushing walked in the door. Ellen looked down and noticed the beige fuzzies clinging to her navy skirt.

"Where ya' been Mom?" Drew asked, stuffing his shirt into his chinos.

"At church, ironing altar linens for Sunday Mass." She hung her green coat in the front hall closet and headed toward the back of the house without acknowledging Ellen.

"I'll be in the kitchen having tea and starting dinner."

Beth Rubin

"What are we having, Mom?"

"Haddock and macaroni and cheese."

Ellen felt grateful that they hadn't asked her to stay. Mady had promised brisket and potato pancakes.

* * * *

"Those socks make your legs look like stove pipes, Ellen."

"Thanks, Mom." *Love you too, bitch.*

"Remember your curfew. And keep your legs crossed." It was the 11th commandment at the Rosenbergs. She pictured her headstone: "Here lies Ellen—with her legs crossed."

* * * *

They had caught the first 15 minutes of the movie before the steamed windows blocked the view. Ellen envied Sandra Dee's perfect blond flip and cute *shiksa* nose.

"She's so pretty."

"I prefer brunettes." He squeezed her shoulder, nibbled her ear. She felt dizzy. And damp.

I want him. But I don't want a rep. The guys were always mouthing off about their conquests, real and imagined, after they burst their lunch bags.

What if we did it and my parents found out? I'd die of embarrassment. If they didn't kill me first.

"My nose is too fat. Think I should have it done?"

"Don't you dare. I like that nose." He tweaked it and pulled her to him.

"Ouch!"

Split Ends

"What?"

"Banged my knee."

"Let me kiss it and make it better."

"You need a bigger car, Drew."

He nodded over his shoulder. "More room there."

"Last one in the back buys popcorn." She kicked off her shoes and shimmied over the seat.

* * * *

After the movie, they stopped for sundaes at a place known for its fountain treats. On a clear night you could see the twinkling lights of Manhattan—Oz on the horizon—from the naugahyde booths. The hangout filled with teenagers. It was better than homework or watching Justine and Bob do the Stroll on "American Bandstand."

* * * *

Ellen checked her watch. "I should have called home. My mother goes ape if I'm five minutes late."

He mussed her hair. "You worry too much."

They sat hip to hip in his Chevy. A St. Christopher medal dangled from the mirror, swaying with every bump and corner. The windshield wipers squeaked as Chuck Berry sang "Sweet Little Sixteen." Ellen boosted the volume. "Just got to have tight dresses and lipstick ..."

She hit a clinker and he laughed. "Maybe we'll cut a 45."

"Think Elvis would lend us Col. Parker?"

Beth Rubin

Ellen checked her watch again. "Damn, I'm going to catch it. It's 10 of 12."

"Betcha your parents are asleep."

"My father maybe. My mother never. She's gotta make sure her precious teen angel didn't die in a flaming wreck."

They pulled up to the house. It was too late to ask Drew to stay. *Just as well. I'm spent from all the heavy petting.*

Drew followed her up the walk. *Please, don't creak.* She turned the key in the rain-swollen door. He followed her into the living room where Mady stood in a flannel robe and curlers, a cigarette dangling from her lip.

"Hi, Mrs. Rosenberg," Drew said.

Ellen knew that look on Mady's face—disapproving and put-upon. "Do you have any idea what time it is?"

"Yes, Mom."

"Haven't we always told you to call if you're going to be late?"

Ellen's reply caught like stale bagel. "I thought you'd be sleeping."

Ellen saw Mady eyeing the misaligned buttons on Drew's shirt.

"Sorry we're late, Mrs. Rosenberg. The traffic was heavy."

On a Saturday night? Jeez, Drew, couldn't you have come up with a better excuse?

"I'll talk to you tomorrow, Ellen. Good night, Mrs. Rosenberg."

Mady ignored him. Ellen heard his car rumble off and knew what to expect.

"Where were you?"

"We went to the movies and stopped for ice cream."

"What movie?" Ellen was no better off than Meg. Her parents nailed a list of verboten flicks next to the kitchen Crucifix. Mady carried a similar list in her head.

"We saw 'Imitation of Life.' You'd like it. Lana Turner is in it." *Thank goodness I have my coat on. Lawrence Welk could play "The Beer Barrel Polka" on the wrinkles of my blouse.*

"Where did you see it?"

"In Morristown."

"The Morristown Theater?"

Ellen stared at an old stain in the carpet. *She's got me. I'm a lousy liar.* "No, the drive-in."

"In the rain?" Her mother's eyebrows met her pink curlers.

"It was only drizzling."

"You know how your father and I feel. No drive-ins. I thought we made it clear." Ellen heard her father snoring upstairs.

Why does she have to be such a witch? It's not like I'm giving blow jobs like some of the girls. She couldn't imagine doing anything so disgusting. Not even to Drew. Or her husband—*if* she ever married.

Ellen turned to go. "Good night, Ma."

"Don't walk away from me, young lady."

"I'm tired. I'm going to bed."

"We're not done. We'll talk more tomorrow."

Ellen sighed.

"By the way, you're going to Amy's over your spring break."

"I'm what?"

"You leave for Cleveland on Good Friday."

"Drew is taking me to see 'My Fair Lady' Easter week. He ordered tickets ages ago."

"He'll find someone else."

"But I want to go. I've been looking forward to it. Why didn't you ask me first?"

"We thought you'd be pleased. Is this the thanks we get?"

If I stay here a second longer, I'll kill her. "I'm not a baby. Stop running my life." Ellen stomped upstairs.

She changed into pajamas and peered into her dresser mirror. Lipstick tattooed her cheek. Her hair looked as if it had been styled on the bow of the Staten Island ferry.

She drew back the blanket and crawled into bed. She would have called Drew, but her parents had disconnected her phone for a month over two C's on her last report card.

Why couldn't her parents just leave her alone? Her anger faded as she fantasized about Drew. *What a dreamboat.*

* * * *

The fragrance of cucumber magnolia wafted through the open window. Ellen had been listening to Cousin Brucie and painting her nails with Cherries in the Snow, a dry run for the Junior Prom in two weeks, when the phone rang.

"Why weren't you in school?"

"That's why I'm calling."

Split Ends

Ellen didn't like the sound of his voice. "Are you sick?"

"No ... I wanted you to hear this from me first." Ellen shivered. *Oh God, something awful's going to happen.*

"What is it? Don't keep me in suspense."

"I was caught shoplifting a 45."

"Oh, Drew. You didn't. Tell me you didn't." She knew that most of her friends had palmed a record. It was like a game to see if they could get away with it. "Why did you have to be the one to get caught? When?"

"Yesterday. It was stupid. I don't even like Roy Orbison. I'm lucky Mr. Conway didn't call the cops. But he came by the house. My mother was hysterical. Of course, that's nothing new. You'd have thought I shot an Eagle Scout. My father'll have a stroke when he finds out. I wish we could run away."

Ellen felt sorry for Drew. She thought Mrs. Cushing was *meshugana.* And his father worked long hours in the city. Her stomach churned. "What did Mr. Conway say?"

"He said he wouldn't report it, but I better keep my nose clean. He plays golf with my father at the country club."

"That's a lucky break."

It's not like he set fire to the school. But my parents will flip if they find out. They've been bugging me for weeks.

"Why do you have to go steady?" they had asked after he gave her his ID bracelet and letter sweater. "Why don't you go out with other boys?" her mother had said. "My friend So-and-So's son is dying to take you out—and he comes from a good family."

"He has zits the size of Montana and bad breath, Ma. Do me a favor and don't find me dates."

"It's not healthy to see so much of just one person."

By 'not healthy,' Ellen knew they feared she'd lose her virginity. They probably worried over that more than whether she'd get into a decent college. *Why don't they just stuff me in a convent?* She was surprised that they hadn't given her a chastity belt for her 13th birthday.

"You're too young to be this serious over a boy," her father said one night.

"Weren't you 19 when you married Mom? And didn't I come along a year later? I guess I'll be starting a family soon."

Ellen had found herself grounded for impertinence. She had hated missing Meg's slumber party that weekend. It would have been a chance to see Drew. The guys always stopped by for potato chips and to make out in dimly lit basements before the girls rolled their hair to gossip all night.

Ellen began to meet Drew on the sly. She put away his sweater and wore his bracelet only at school. Meg covered for her most of the time.

The following Monday her mother wore "that look." *What did I do now?* Dinner was a silent event. Ellen could usually count on her father for chitchat, but he didn't speak.

As Ellen carried in the dessert, her father said, "We have to talk to you." *It better not have anything to do with Drew.*

Split Ends

"We heard that Drew stole a record."

"Who told you?"

"That doesn't matter. This person knows you two go together. He told us out of concern."

Ellen put down her fork. Mady's chocolate cake turned to sawdust in her mouth.

"Ellen, we like Drew. He's always been polite and respectful around us. But this can't go on. He's a bad influence. You've changed. Your grades have slipped. You've been short-tempered. You won't consider dating anyone else. In fact, you hardly spend time with your girlfriends. And we know you're sneaking out to see him."

Ellen froze.

"We know. It doesn't matter how."

"He told me about the record, Daddy. He did a dumb thing and he feels terrible."

"Your mother and I have given this a lot of thought. You can't see him anymore. You're going to have to cut it out. Like a cancer."

"A cancer? Drew's not a tumor, Daddy."

Her mother reached over to pat her shoulder. Ellen threw off the gesture and ran to her room, slamming the door behind her.

Sobbing, she dialed Drew.

"Take it easy. Maybe if we cool it for a while and you bring up your grades, they'll come around."

"Do you think so?" Her finger had turned white from twisting her hair.

"I hope so. I can't imagine not having you in my life."

"Me neither. They've been looking for a reason to keep us apart."

Beth Rubin

"I'm catching it too. My mother is on my case worse than ever. She's threatening to send me away."

"Oh no, Drew, anything but that!"

"Don't worry. I'll never leave you."

"I wish I could see you this weekend, but we better not."

"I love you, El."

"I love you too, Drew."

"Meet me in front of school first thing Monday."

"All right."

"It'll work out." Drew didn't sound convinced. "You take care of you."

The weekend dragged. She went to school early Monday.

They continued to meet at Drew's locker but otherwise kept their distance. She was losing hope that her parents would soften. Evenings she turned up the radio to call him. She couldn't hold a thought in her head and studying was futile.

Every night her parents harped on it. "Have you done it yet?"

"No," she would whisper.

Her father had lowered the boom on a Wednesday.

"You have to tell him by the end of the week or we'll do it for you."

Ellen felt like she'd been thrown from a plane. No parachute.

Her hand flew to her heart. "Don't make me do this."

She pushed away from the table, knocking over her chair, and ran to her room, tears streaming down her face.

Split Ends

She sat on her bed, clutching her stomach and rocking.

Her spirit broken, Ellen picked Thursday to die. Friday the Rosenbergs were going to the shore for Memorial Day weekend.

At midnight, her parents knocked.

"Go away. Just leave me alone."

"Do you want anything?"

"I want Drew."

* * * *

The alarm rang at 6:00. Her pillow was soaked.

There was a soft knocking. "Ellen, are you all right?" her father asked.

"Yes. No. What do you care?"

"Why don't you stay home and take it easy. I'll call school."

* * * *

That afternoon Ellen walked to Drew's, a mourner at her own funeral. She passed yards of lilacs, certain that if she breathed on the lavender flowers they would blacken and wither.

The door was ajar. She found him sitting on the floor behind a smokescreen. His mother was out. *Probably at confession saying a thousand Hail Mary's.*

An empty Rheingold bottle sat on the mantel—at the feet of the Suffering Jesus. Drew's eyes were as red as hers. Ellen mumbled something and handed him his ID bracelet. He hurled it across the room.

Beth Rubin

They wept and clung to each other for a long time. There was so much she had wanted to say, but the words got trapped between her heart and mouth.

"I'll drop off your sweater sometime." She looked away, wiped her tears with the back of her hand.

"No. I want you to have it." He reached for her and held her. "Please don't leave me. You're all I have."

A car door slammed and Ellen broke free. She ran out the back door and kept running—past the library and the movie theater and Butch's—until she could run no longer. She would have thrown herself into Madison Creek, but the water wasn't deep enough.

She stayed locked in her bedroom with the flowered wallpaper and a box of tissues until the next afternoon.

* * * *

Over the weekend her parents left her alone to cry and read on the beach. Tuesday she looked for Drew. He wasn't at his locker. Or in Latin. No Drew. Had he overslept or caught a cold? She phoned at lunch. The line was busy. She tried after school and his mother answered.

"May I speak to Drew, please?"
"No. He's not here."
"When will he be back?"
"I don't know."
"Don't know? I don't understand. Where is he?"
"At my sister's."
"Your sister's? Where?"
"In California."
"California? How long is he staying?"

Split Ends

"I'm not sure."

"Where in California?"

"San Diego."

"Could I have the address and phone number, please?" Dizzy, she leaned against the wall.

"No."

"Mrs. Cushing, please. I have to talk to him."

"Don't call here again." The phone went dead. Ellen slumped to the floor.

CHAPTER 8

Awakening early, she walked Penny. She filled a trashcan with sketches for a client, plucked her eyebrows until they looked like Jean Harlow's. A dozen times she went to the refrigerator trying to decide on lunch.

Too nervous to eat, she picked up a book. She read the same sentence three times and gave up. With Penny in the backseat, she drove to the store for cheese and wine, passing the ochre stucco library where she had first seen him.

By 3:00, Ellen had laid out her clothes. Hairstyling equipment and makeup blanketed the bathroom vanity. Most of the time she slapped on blusher and lipstick, disdaining the heavy artillery except for special occasions.

Well, this is special.

She hauled out her big guns. On the third round the eyeliner hit within target range, landing closer to her lashes than her brow.

Ellen checked her watch every five minutes. Was it running? She didn't know what to do with herself until Drew picked her up.

Skinnier than she'd been since adolescence, she bunched the black, knit dress over her favorite silver and turquoise belt and planted the earrings she had picked up from an Indian in the Santa Fe Plaza. She checked her watch again. She had spent less time dressing for her wedding.

At 5:30 she had nearly chewed a hole in her cheek. At 6:00 she needed another shower. She slid "Come Fly With Me" into the CD player and set the hors

Split Ends

d'oeuvres and cocktail napkins in the den. The only thing missing was the leading man. With half-an-hour to curtain time, she paced, her black pumps clicking on the hall tile.

She sang along with Frank. "If you can use some exotic booze, there's a bar in far Bombay."

I hope Drew likes wine or vodka. If he asks for a frozen drink with a paper umbrella I'm S.O.L.

"I'll be holding you so near, you might hear a whole gang of cheers just because we're together."

What if we're not together? What if he doesn't show up?

"Weatherwise, it's such a cuckoo day ..."

It's cuckoo all right. I'm not depressed; I'm manic.

"Come fly with me, let's fly, let's fly ..."

I am flying. Elizabeth should see me now. I'm in interstellar orbit.

"Pack up, let's fly away. And don't tell your Mama," Ellen crooned.

Of course, I'll tell my Mama.

At 6:35 she was sure he was stuck in a meeting until midnight. Or banging a co-worker à la Ron. At 6:40 she poured a glass of wine.

Shit, maybe it's payback time for breaking up with him in high school. Wonder where I can order a pizza.

At 6:45 the phone rang. She tripped answering it. "Hi, it's me. I'm on your street. What's the number?"

"Nineteen."

She peeked out the window as a car pulled up, then gulped some Chardonnay and popped an Altoid.

He knocked. Drawing a breath, Ellen smoothed her hair in the foyer mirror.

She could feel her heart beating, lub-dub, lub-dub, lub-dub, as she wrestled open the massive door. She stared. He stared. A freeze frame.

"Hi!" they said with one voice.

"You look just like you, El."

He flashed that smile, his Chiclets as bright as ever.

"It's good to see you," she said in lieu of a hug. *How could I be so insipid?* She knew she was grinning from ear to ear. "You look well." *That's the understatement of the century. He looks fucking gorgeous.*

Her hand shook pouring his wine. When she gave it to him without spilling a drop, her inner voice whispered, 'There is a God.' They sat catty-corner in the den. She imagined themselves as a couple of wind-up toys. Yakketa yakketa yakketa.

Drew pulled a pack of cigarettes from his breast pocket. "Okay if I smoke?"

"Sure. Can I have one?"

"It's bad for you."

"And you?"

"I gain 20 pounds every time I quit."

"I started a couple of months ago. It's a temporary crutch."

When he lit her cigarette, she whiffed his aftershave. Opium. *It could become addictive. So could he.*

Penny took to Drew's navy pinstripe like a bitch in heat. In seconds her hair covered his pants. The efficient housewife jumped up. "Can I get you a damp towel or lint roller?" she asked. "Masking tape? Electric broom?"

"Don't worry about it. I'll get the suit cleaned."

Split Ends

I'd like to clean it with my bare hands and you in it.

"How long have you had her?" he asked, stroking Penny.

"Almost 12 years." *If I sit at your feet, will you stroke me too?* Ellen imagined his fingers caressing her own neck.

"I'd love a pet, but I'm not home enough. She's a great dog."

A great dog? Ellen heard Ron shouting expletives at Penny anytime they were in the same room.

Ellen's eyes stuck to Drew. His words blurred like Monet's *Water Lilies*. He laughed at her quips and asked all the right questions. He was heavier. Not fat, but chunky. His hair was still brown, with only a hint of gray. *Maybe he colors it?*

AJC imprinted his shirt cuff and a Patek Philippe, with black alligator band, adorned his right wrist. He smoked like a chimney and Ellen wondered how he kept his teeth so white.

"How long have you been a stockbroker, Drew?"

"Since the '70s. I'm hoping to retire in a few years. I'd like to travel before everything falls apart."

"You mean the market or your body?"

"Both."

"I know what you mean. I want it all now." *Oy, why did I say that?*

He asked, "How long have you been married?"

"Long enough. Twenty-eight years."

His eyes widened. "I wasn't married half that long. I can't imagine ..."

Ellen felt the draft of melancholy. *Don't even try. It hasn't been a day at the beach.*

She told him about her kids, her work, and how she loved sailing. "Listen to me. I haven't talked this much in years. I'm a Chatty Cathy."

"I want to know everything."

"To be continued ..." She excused herself. In a minute she came back wearing his letter sweater, spotted and riddled with holes.

"I know you've been missing this," she said, twirling. He laughed until tears ran down his cheeks.

"You still have your sense of humor."

Thank God, or I'd be up shit creek without a paddle.

"Maybe you'll wear the sweater to work for Show and Tell."

"Won't fit anymore. I've gained a lot since high school. But you haven't changed. You're as slim and pretty as ever."

"I'm not usually this thin. I'm going through a tough time."

"Oh?"

"Nothing that can't be fixed." *Enough. Subject closed.*

Drew set his glass down. "Considering how thin you say you are, we should probably think about dinner."

Dinner? Who cares?

"Do you like Italian? There's a place nearby. It's nothing fancy but the fish and veal are fine."

"I love Italian." Ellen doubted she would swallow a morsel, even though she hadn't eaten since breakfast. The wine had kicked in. She wondered if she was acting sloppy. Despite her growling stomach, she had

Split Ends

shied away from the Brie. It could coat her teeth or sour her breath.

She slid onto the leather seat of his Mercedes SL 500. "Drew, the clock must be broken. It can't be that late."

He checked his watch. "It's right—9:15. Buckle up. I don't want anything to happen to you."

With one hand on the wheel, the other on the seatback, he kept glancing at her.

* * * *

Ellen struggled to read the menu. The flicker of the candle in the Chianti bottle may have been romantic, but she had difficulty seeing in broad daylight. The waiter opened a bottle of Pinot Grigio and described the specials.

"I'm not very hungry. I'll have an appetizer."

"Order something you like. You don't have to finish."

"What about all the starving orphans?"

Drew laughed. "Did your parents hand you that line too?"

"Natch. I picked at my food just to irritate them."

"You can doggy-bag it for Penny."

She confessed that she'd been a little depressed and had almost no appetite. Then she cleaned her plate. The salmon was perfect. She devoured the angel hair with tomatoes and fresh basil and vacuumed Drew's Fra Diavolo.

"Pretty good for someone who doesn't eat much."

Ellen blushed.

"Don't be embarrassed. I like a woman with a big appetite."

You don't know the half of it.

The waiter returned to market dessert.

"What would you like, Ellen?"

You, silly boy.

"I'm stuffed, but my sweet tooth craves a fix."

"Go for it."

"What appeals to you?"

"Mixed berries."

"Berries?" Ellen's nose twitched, as if he'd said cow pie. "With tiramisu and cannoli, you want berries?"

"Call me crazy. What would you like?"

"I love mousse. But I'm kind of full. Want to share it?"

"Sounds good to me."

"It comes with raspberries. You can have my half."

If I had my cherry, I'd give you that too.

He laughed again.

Am I that funny? Maybe I should audition for Saturday Night Live.

She started to ask questions. His work, his hobbies and favorite vacation spots.

God, he's easy to be with. He smiles a lot and he's so laid-back. And he pays attention to me. Ron would have gone into anaphylactic shock sitting in a restaurant that late. When they ate out he got *shpilkes,* often settling the check before Ellen had finished eating.

She felt like Cinderella. It was plain as the pantyhose eating into her crotch that he didn't want the evening to end either. She couldn't afford to wait another 35 years for an encore.

They sat in the car, listening to k.d. lang. Ellen needed to throw her arms around him and kiss him until he screamed, 'Uncle.'

"It's getting late," she said.

They walked up the flagstone path. He had said he was an early riser. But he hadn't yawned once, at least not in her face, and it was nearly 1:00. "Would you like a cup of coffee?"

Penny greeted them as if they'd been gone for three weeks. Coats on, they leaned on the granite countertop, still babbling. She thought of inviting him into the den. But what if he said yes? What if he said no?

"I have to walk Penny," she said, thinking he would leave.

"I'll walk with you." They strolled side by side through the sleeping neighborhood. "I can't remember when I've had this much fun, or laughed so hard, El."

"Me too."

A plane approaching Newark Airport drowned their conversation with its roar. Ellen hoped her mother's nosy neighbor, Mrs. Feldman, wasn't up late. They passed a street lamp and she admired Drew's features. She felt herself caught between dreaminess and lust. Vulnerable as a bug in a spider web.

Penny sniffed every bush as if she were buying fish.

Drew followed Penny and Ellen back into the house.

He licked the corner of his mouth. "How long will you be staying here?"

"Until Sunday."

He loosened his tie, blue with green doodads that matched his eyes. "What are you doing this weekend?"

She clasped her hands to stop their fluttering. *Masturbating.* "Hanging loose."

"I'm taking Friday off. Why don't you come to the shore for the weekend?"

Whoa! Hold the phone! Her pulse began to race. "I don't think ..."

"It has three bedrooms. One for you."

"It's tempting. I love the ocean. You wouldn't have to entertain me. I'm reading a good book and ..." She struggled for rationality, but that part of her brain had shut down. "It'd be nice to relax."

"It's settled then." He smiled and his lips parted like the gates of paradise. Ellen wanted to stick her tongue in his mouth clear to his tonsils.

"I'll ... I'll think about it."

Drew began to scribble on Mady's message pad. "Here, I'll draw you a map."

"What about Penny?"

"Penny's invited too. But she won't get her own bedroom."

Ellen walked him to the door. "I had a wonderful evening, Drew."

"Me too. I'll call you."

Ellen Windexed the cocktail table.

"Jesus H. Christ, Penny. What's happening here?" The letter sweater sat on the sofa. Penny's head lay on it.

CHAPTER 9

Ellen couldn't make up her mind. Knowing Drew was working at home, she stopped at his office and left his sweater with a co-worker, in case she decided against going to his place. Then she drove to the mall.

She wanted to give her shlumpy uniform a rest—as if jeans were inappropriate for the beach with a blast from the past. She skipped down the marble promenade, 50 going on 15.

I may be nuts. But I'm alive. And happy.

Ellen felt like cornering the haggard mothers pushing strollers and blurting, "I'm shopping for a dirty weekend and I'm having a ball!"

She combed the stores, settling on a cream tunic and dark tights. *Might as well accentuate the positive.* In high school Drew always told her she had good legs.

My mother is right as usual. T-shirts and flannel are not feminine sleepwear.

The Victoria's Secret clerk showed her a rack of satin seducements. She had always hated nightgowns. They rode up, strangling her during the night like a sweaty noose. As a newlywed, she had tried to look sexy. Ron hadn't seemed to notice if she was wearing charmeuse or cellophane. He was into goods, not packaging.

She had donated her peignoir sets to Goodwill and reverted to T-shirts. *If it's coming off anyway, I might as well be comfortable.*

The clerk had left her alone to browse. A short time later she walked out with a purple, silk teddy, matching robe and a receipt for $80.

Beth Rubin

I should have myself committed. If I go, I'll never wear them again.

In Bloomie's she found a terra-cotta dish and had it gift-wrapped for Drew. Ellen loaded the bags into her car. *So much for my austerity program. I've blown $200 for a walk on the beach.*

* * * *

That night Ellen ate Italian again. This time at Vacarro's. Because the pasta near her home tasted canned, Ellen loaded up whenever she traveled north. She was excited to see Sandy, a former neighbor and friend who had moved to New Jersey 10 years ago.

Ellen noticed several satin bomber jackets invading the field of mink. Probably from the bowling alley across the street. Her leg jiggled and she kept touching her face to make sure it was still there. *Wonder if they have a belted high chair in my size. Or a straightjacket.* The friends made small talk as Ellen shredded the cocktail napkin.

In a corner of the bar area, a pockmarked Al Pacino tickled the ivories. His repertoire was limited, but Ellen applauded live music even when it was secondrate. She'd chosen a seat against the wall where she could keep an eye on the door. In case someone had a score to settle with old man Vacarro, or Ron had trailed her, she wanted the chance to duck. She had enough *tsuris* without having her brains splattered on the mirror.

"While I think of it," Sandy said, "I'm going to my condo in Florida for Thanksgiving. Why don't you come down?"

Split Ends

"I'd been wondering what I'd do. The kids will be with Ron and my mother's gone to Cleveland."

"Try to get a flight."

"I will. Thanks." Ellen fiddled with the salt and pepper shakers.

"Are you all right?"

"Right as acid rain."

"You're shaking like someone with the DT's. Want to talk about it?"

A sensible eater since her mastectomy, Sandy ordered broiled rockfish. Thinking something spicy would whet her appetite, Ellen sprang for Linguine Puttanesca. The parchment menu footnoted it as "whore style."

How fitting. Forgive me, Rabbi Prinski, for what I'm thinking.

"Like I said, I'm a wreck."

"I hope you're not sick."

"In a manner of speaking, I am." Ellen dipped Tuscan bread in the herbed olive oil.

"Let it out, Ellen. That's what you've always told me. You'll feel better."

"I think I'll feel better if I throw up." She forced a small bite of Caesar salad and heard her mother chanting, "Here comes the choo-choo."

"We've always been able to talk. What's going on?"

"I've got a dilemma."

"You mean you've got a man."

"Not just a man." Ellen put down the quivering fork before it could inflict harm. "A very attractive man. He lives at the shore and he invited me to spend the weekend. No strings—you know, I'd *never* jump into bed—but I'm petrified."

Suddenly nauseated, Ellen fled to the ladies' room. The pink-flocked wallpaper and plastic flowers didn't help. She splashed water on her face, blotted it and waited for the sick feeling to pass.

She returned to the table, passing gold-chained men and women with decaled nails. "Sorry, Sandy. At least it's not morning sickness. Where were we?"

"A man you're attracted to invited you for the weekend. Is that it? What's the problem?"

Ellen pushed the pasta around the plate.

"The problem ..." She leaned closer and whispered, in case the feds or Ron's lawyer had bugged the bread basket. "The problem is I'm still legally married."

"But you're living apart." Sandy's fork was a baton. "You can do what you want as long as you're discreet."

"That's what my lawyer says. As long as I don't get caught in a sleazy motel with a tattooed biker."

"That I'd like to see."

"Sandy, I still feel tied to Ron. And I don't know how this hunk views me. But there's chemistry."

"You'll do the right thing. Follow your heart."

"If I had followed my heart the other night, I wouldn't have let him leave. Here I am all worked up and he probably thinks of me as a sister."

"Then you have nothing to worry about."

"Why am I so nervous? I'm nuttier than Natalie Wood in 'Splendor in the Grass.' Yesterday I washed my hair with cough syrup."

"Sounds as if he's more than a brother to you."

Split Ends

"I really like him," Ellen said to her plate. "I've never felt this way. Like Jimmy Carter, I have lust in my heart. I never screwed around, Sandy. My conscience is big enough for the entire free world."

"Ellen, you're fighting to break out of an unhappy marriage. It's your turn. Do what *you* want. Breast cancer was my wake-up call. I decided then that it would be me first."

"I hear you. But I want to do the right thing. And I'm afraid of getting hurt. I'm still licking my wounds over the marriage."

"Of course you are. Look, I can't tell you what to do. Don't let analysis paralysis prevent you from going after what you want. Hold your nose and jump in the deep end. What's the worst that could happen?"

"I could drown."

"Ellen, life is to be lived. All we have is the moment."

"True. This is the first time I've been on my own. The little girl in the starched pinafore and perfect pigtails went from being Daddy's girl to Ron's girl—from one controlling man to another. No wonder I lost myself in the shuffle."

"It's a generation thing. We grew up on those sitcoms. Hell, my mom thought she was starring in 'The Donna Reed Show.'"

"Really, Sandy? You ate that white bread?"

"It was the only bread around. Remember? It was pre-Cosby. There weren't any sitcoms with African Americans—Negroes, in the parlance of the day. I don't count 'Amos 'n' Andy.' My parents were the black June and Ward Cleaver of our neighborhood. I was raised on the same crap you were."

"It sure was crap. But we bought into it, didn't we? Hell, my mom's role model was Jane Wyatt and my dad was Robert Young in 'Father Knows Best.' And I was supposed to behave like Kitten. Just an obedient little bitch. Come to think of it, I deserve an Emmy for my performance."

Sandy rested her elbows on the wine-stained tablecloth.

"I have lots of newly single friends, Ellen. And I think inertia keeps most of the marrieds where they are. Where have all the couples gone?"

"Beats me. Natchez?"

"Now we're doing what we should have done in our 20s and 30s, instead of playing Florence Nightingale to everyone."

"Our fathers passed the staff of office to our husbands." Ellen poured more wine. She knew she'd get a headache but the hell with it. "Remember the ballet where four male dancers pass a woman around and she never touches ground? I used to feel like that ballerina. But I didn't have the guts to shout, 'I'm getting a nosebleed at this altitude. Put me down so I can dance with you.'"

"I remember. How are you doing on your own?"

"I'm free."

"I never thought Ron was right for you. You deserve more."

"Thanks, pal."

"Divorcing is the pits. Things will only get better."

"Not to change the subject, but what do you think I should do about the weekend?"

"What do you want?"

"Waaaaa, I don't know!"

Split Ends

Sandy turned heads with her laugh.

"How did you meet him?"

"Old boyfriend. Phoned him a few days ago. I always knew I'd bump into him again." *I'd like to bump into him for about 48 hours straight.*

"Well, go if you want to."

"Sounds simple enough, but logic has never been my strong suit. It's hardly ego-boosting to find out your husband screwed a nymphet while you were at home cooking his fucking beef stew."

"You're attractive, bright and a wonderful friend. Why are you agonizing?"

"I graduated *summa cum laude* in agonizing." Ellen tried a forkful of stone-cold linguine. A headache cruised her forehead searching for a berth.

Wonder where I rank on Drew's list of eligible weekend guests. Probably at the bottom, next to his parents and the homeless.

"What did you tell him?"

"I told him I was addressing the UN and, if I could find a stand-in, I'd join him."

"You're a stitch. Seriously, what did you decide?"

"I didn't. He's calling in the morning for the verdict. The jury is hung." *Bet he is too.* "I have 12 hours to hand down a decision."

"Be sure to let me know."

"I will."

"Did you make it to the Sotheby's auction?"

"Spent the morning swigging Kaopectate."

"You're a wreck, Ellen. Did you go out at all?"

"I went to the mall this afternoon. On the way, I stopped at his office to drop off his high school sweater. In case I don't go to the shore." *Who are you kidding? You're going. You know you're going.*

"He wasn't in. I handed the bag to a co-worker. The guy held it to his ear and asked, 'Is it ticking?'"

"I said, 'No, it's the strong, silent type.'"

"Sounds like your friend has a reputation, Ellen. Be careful."

"I think the guy was joking."

"Well, watch your flank." Sandy reached into her purse and took out her wallet. "I want to give you something. You're a single woman now. You need to be prepared."

"You carry mace in your wallet?" Sandy handed Ellen a foil-wrapped condom. "You're kidding, Sandy. It'll decompose before I ever use it."

"Always carry one, Ellen. Don't rely on a man to be prudent."

"Sandy, I just had dinner with him. You don't think … I would never …"

CHAPTER 10

Ellen woke with a start Friday morning. It was still dark. Penny licked her arm.

"I'll bet he's not going to call, Penny. I ought to have my head examined. I missed an important auction, spent a fortune and poured my heart out to Sandy. And for what? I'm a fool. If he calls, I'm in doody up to my eyeballs because I want to go. And who knows where it will lead?"

Penny licked again.

"And if he doesn't call, I wasted a day and I'll have to return everything I bought. But if that's the case…" She stopped to fondle Penny's ear. "… better to see his true colors before I get in any deeper."

She was baking chocolate chip cookies when Drew called at 8:00 sharp. Ellen phoned her mother.

"Mom, I'm going to Sandy's for the weekend. She's down in the dumps. Maybe I can cheer her up." Ellen coughed up Sandy's phone number. It was easier than arguing. Besides, there was a 50-50 chance Mady would call to see if she had warm pajamas.

Ellen ran from room to room, collecting her belongings, changing her mind, arranging piles of clothing and rearranging them.

You made your decision, lighten up.

Penny trailed as if to say, "Don't forget me." When Ellen backed out of the driveway, she couldn't see out the Celica's rear window. Penny huddled on the front passenger seat.

Whenever Ellen strayed into the next lane, her guardian angels—a mug of French Roast and Vivaldi—took over, guiding her safely. Leaving the parkway, she pulled into a gas station for a fill-up and to comb her hair.

She picked at a hangnail, glancing every few minutes at the directions she'd taped to the dash. The sky had begun to darken and the wind had picked up. She hoped to get to Drew's before the rain did. She crossed Manahawkin Bay and dried her palms on the new tights, then hung a left onto Long Beach Boulevard.

Anticipation nearly levitated her off the seat. She ran a finger over her teeth and winked in the mirror. "I'm ready for my close-up, Mr. De Mille." *I think.*

* * * *

Ellen felt Drew's presence before she turned the corner. She didn't have to hunt for his house. He was waiting for her in the middle of the street. His eyes drew her like the green light on Daisy Buchanan's dock. He looked dreamy in grungy jeans, sweatshirt the color of surf spray and tired boat shoes.

He grinned. "How were the directions?"

"Perfect. I didn't get lost once." Ellen could barely recognize her own voice, as if cotton plugged her ears. Could Drew hear her heart banging? It was loud enough to march to. He took Penny's leash, grabbed the suitcase and some bags from the backseat.

"I feel like 'The Man Who Came to Dinner.' Don't worry, I won't stay a month."

"Stay as long as you like."

Besides the suitcase, dress bag and attaché case, there were two shopping bags from the mall, a sack of leftovers and a bottle of wine. Penny had her own

Split Ends

canvas satchel on which Ellen had penned, "Have Bones Will Travel."

"My bird cage and steamer trunk will be delivered later."

The A-frame sat on a bluff overlooking the ocean. Ellen thought she'd died and gone to heaven.

Drew led the way up the stairs and through the porch where a rocker creaked in the breeze. The hairs on the back of her neck snapped to attention when she crossed the threshold, as if she had been there before.

A stone fireplace dominated the living room, furnished with dark wicker and mismatched accent pillows. A plaid stadium blanket hugged the sofa back and a tower of books stood in a corner. *It's cozy, but it needs a woman's touch. I'd love to get in here with a bucket of shell white and bolt of chintz.*

The house was immaculate, the clutter neatly arranged. Ellen smiled to herself. *Just like his house in Maple Shade.*

He dropped her things in the guestroom. "Anything else in the car?"

"You never know, there may be an armoire in the trunk."

"I'll check."

Ellen tapped the wall separating the bedrooms. Thin wallboard. *Christ, he'll be within pissing distance.*

Penny sniffed the oak dresser and looked to her mistress. Ellen patted the dog's rump. "It's okay, girl. I wonder if he has a bungee cord. So I can strap myself in tonight."

She didn't hear Drew come in. "What's this about a strap?"

99

"I was talking to Penny."

She joined him in the living room.

"Here's your wallet. I left the candy bars. I have a one-car garage. I'll park your car and be back in a flash."

Ellen squeezed the leftovers into the refrigerator, stuffed with gourmet items and wine. "He must be expecting an army, Penny." Her lips stuck to her teeth and she opened a cabinet to fetch a glass.

How the hell did I know which cabinet?

He came in and handed her the car keys. "C'mon, El. I'll give you the nickel tour."

She flashed back to his house in Maple Shade as he showed her around. His room faced the ocean. A king-size bed and dresser ate up the space. A blue and white quilt lay folded at the foot of the bed. *At least it's not green, thank God.*

The sheets had little sailboats on them. *How boyish. I wonder if he has a rubber ducky.* She had envisioned a tailored check in taupe and white or quiet print by Ralph Lauren.

Through the window she saw a keep-off-the-dunes sign and, beyond it, the beach and ocean. Books were stacked on the dresser and floor.

"That's quite a collection. Anything to recommend?"

"'In the Lake of the Woods.' It's a page-turner about a guy with a dark secret. Terrific read."

"Sounds interesting."

"I'll give it to you when I'm done. I think you'll like it."

Seascapes and photographs covered the living room walls. She moved closer to inspect a picture of

Split Ends

Drew. Ski goggles on his forehead, he stood next to a blond man about 40, straight out of *GQ*. A snow-mantled mountain loomed behind them.

She didn't know why but she felt uneasy. "Who's that?"

"A friend. He has a condo in Aspen where I ski. Do you?"

"Only on water over 80 degrees. I hate the cold."

Ellen sat down on the sofa and kicked off her shoes. "It's nice, Drew. Very cozy." *Wonder if you'd like a roommate. I'll do your windows. I'll do you.*

He shrugged. "It's just an old bachelor's beach pad."

"How long have you lived here?"

"Three years. Had my fill of suburbia. I made the third bedroom into an office."

"What about your old clients?"

"Not a problem. Most of my work is over the phone. I go to the old office once a week."

Penny begged for attention as Drew opened Ellen's gift.

"I love presents." He reminded Ellen of a child on Christmas morning.

"I'm glad you like it."

He set the dish on the trunk, next to some *Ski* magazines.

Penny paced at the door. Ellen put on her shoes and got up. It had begun to drizzle. Drew handed her a jacket big enough for the two of them. Thrilled to be wrapped in something of his, she rolled up the sleeves and they headed out.

The wind whipped sand in their faces, twisted Ellen's hair into corkscrews and savaged the beach.

Beth Rubin

The breakers jockeyed for position, spewing foam into a pewter sky.

Ellen pushed her bangs from her eyes. "I wouldn't want to body surf today, but it's a beautiful sight. Maybe the most beautiful sight I've ever seen."

Drew smiled and reached down to pick up a piece of blue sea glass. Placing it in Ellen's palm, he closed her fingers around it with his own. She shivered at his touch.

"Thank you." *Does this mean we're going steady again? Grow up, Ellen. He's just a friend.*

They turned to each other and their eyes met. What was it about his eyes? She felt under his spell. *Isolde to his Tristan?*

Penny nosed between them.

"She's jealous, Drew."

He let go of Ellen's hand to pat the dog's head. "It's okay, Penny, you're still numero uno. I'm getting hungry. How about you, El?"

"Me too."

They went back to the cottage, left Penny with a Milk Bone and a, "Good girl, we'll be back soon," then drove to Beach Haven.

He offered her a cigarette.

"No thanks."

"We're going to a place that reminds me of Butch's."

"Hamburgers, onion rings and vanilla Cokes?"

"All of the above."

"My kind of gourmet cuisine."

"Remember how we used to share French fries?"

"It's a wonder my arteries flow at all."

"And how we planned to run away to Paris?"

Split Ends

"Sure. On $49."

"But back then those dollars were worth something."

* * * *

The hostess at the '50's-style luncheonette greeted Drew by name and sat them in a booth under screen star glossies.

Drew was talking about the subs when the Chairman of the Board began serenading them. Ellen wondered if Drew noticed. Did he recall how they had listened to Old Blue Eyes while their friends were hooked on doo-wop and Conway Twitty?

This is too weird. Nobody would believe it.

Drew tried to sing "I've Got You Under My Skin" with Frank.

God help him, his voice hasn't improved with age.

"That has a familiar ring," Ellen said and sipped her water.

"Do you listen to him anymore?"

"I built an addition for my collection. How 'bout you?"

"Nope. No addition. But he's still the greatest, El. I don't guess …"

"What?"

He blushed. "Do you have any of the albums I gave you?"

"Every one. They're my dowry. Don't say you want them back."

He laughed. "You're too cute."

He likes me. I think he really likes me.

Beth Rubin

The food arrived to "At Long Last Love." Ellen bit into her BLT, tonguing the bacon so it wouldn't catch in her teeth. Drew grinned at her between mouthfuls of a meatball sub as though he'd won the lottery. She felt unworthy of his attention. Too thin.

He put down his sub and wiped tomato sauce from his hand. *Oh, let me lick that off for you.*

"I'd like to cook for you tonight," he said. "I hate restaurants on weekends. Too crowded and noisy. Okay with you if we stay in?"

"That's great." *Jesus, he cooks too?*

"My Way" was playing when they left.

A steady rain fell as they walked past storefronts boarded-up for the winter. The occasional car and pickup whooshed by. They had to press against the buildings to avoid a drenching. Their hips bumped and she went weak in the knees. *I'd like to do him 'my way.' His way. Any old way.*

They stopped in a shop selling bric-a-brac and Drew bought her a bud vase held by a painted tin Cupid.

"I've always liked the beach off-season," Ellen said. "My Dad and I used to walk the boardwalk in winter. We'd eat caramel corn and candy apples."

"What about your mother?"

"She stayed home to dust."

"You're joking, right?"

"No. They'll bury my mother clutching a dust rag."

"You're funny. You always made me laugh."

"This is wonderful, Drew. I feel at peace."

"I know. That's why I moved here."

"What do you do when you're not working?"

Split Ends

"Read, golf, fish. But mostly I veg." *He probably veges with a succotash of women. I sure would like to be his favorite lima bean.*

She stepped in a puddle, shook the water from her foot and laughed at her own clumsiness. "Thank you."

"For what?"

"For inviting me."

"I'm happy you're here."

She thought she saw sincerity in his expression. And something else. Lust?

They drove to a supermarket on the mainland and pushed a cart together, as if it were a weekly ritual.

It's a food store, for God's sake. But I feel like it's prom night. Get real. He puts his pants on one leg at a time.

Drew grabbed groceries left and right, slam-dunking the non-breakables into the cart. Ellen wondered who would eat them all. She paused to admire his chiseled profile against a backdrop of cookie boxes. *It's the simple things that give pleasure. I almost forgot the cliché during my marriage.*

In the produce section Drew sized up the pink grapefruits. "Don't forget the berries," Ellen ribbed.

"I won't, Smarty." He began to fill a bag with oranges.

"What are those for?"

"Juice tomorrow morning."

"That's a lot of trouble. You can buy fresh-squeezed you know."

"Uh-uh. I like to squeeze them myself. It tastes better."

Ellen tried to picture Ron squeezing oranges, but outside interference scrambled the image.

They drove back in a downpour. Just another bad hair day, Ellen thought as she finger-combed the sopping tangle. In the living room the wind indicator bounced around 35 mph. Drew handed her a towel and asked if she liked champagne.

"I love it but I can handle only a glass, two at the most. It gives me a headache."

He went to the kitchen and returned with two aspirins and a glass of water. "Here, take these first. It works for me. No headache."

He filled two hollow-stemmed flutes, put out smoked bluefish and crackers, then built a fire.

"More food, Drew?"

"In case you're not hungry."

Cold and figuring she had made an adequate fashion statement, Ellen changed into sweats.

Drew puttered in the kitchen, refusing her offer of help. She settled on the braided rug in front of the hearth, the fire rouging her cheeks. The chill had finally left her bones when she remembered Penny. *Damn, I don't want to go out again.* She fed the dog and was zipping Drew's jacket when he interceded.

"I'll walk Penny. You stay in and keep warm."

He is too good to be true. So kind and thoughtful. Wonder if he's on something. Ellen felt guilty but relieved.

Wet sand caked Penny's fur when they returned. Ellen jumped up. "I'll dry her on the porch."

"Don't be silly. It's only sand. I'll vacuum it later."

Ellen recalled how Ron had gone ballistic whenever Penny tracked in dirt or leaves. *Why did I put up with him for so long?*

"You sure you don't want me to clean her?"

Split Ends

"Nah. I'll do it. You relax."

"I'm relaxed. I'm a baby step away from catatonia. Thank you for walking her."

They settled at opposite ends of the sofa, feet flirting on the coffee table as they had in Latin class, and sipped champagne. Outside of weddings and bar mitzvahs, Ellen couldn't remember ever drinking bubbly in the middle of the afternoon.

They listened to vocalists they had enjoyed in their youth—Bobby Darin and Judy Garland and Broadway musicals—and played "What Ever Happened To ... ?"

The champagne working its magic, Ellen spilled some of her unhappiness and frustration over the marriage.

Drew listened, his forehead creased. He appeared tearful and she thought he might be revisiting his own painful memories.

"Do you think there's a chance you'll get back with Ron?"

"I doubt it. Too much sewage under the bridge."

"Have you considered counseling?"

"Too late. A huge weight has lifted. I can't ignore the feeling."

"How do you like living alone?"

"I love it. It's the first time I can do what I want, when I want and how I want. Without censure."

"What do you mean?"

"My husband liked to keep me in my place."

"But you're such a free spirit."

"So I'm rediscovering. I buried that part of me for a long time."

"Welcome back to the living."

"It's good to be back. I like sunshine. I used to think cloudy was normal."

"I'm sorry for your pain. I know you'll be fine."

"I am fine."

"I envy your sharing so many years with one person. I've never been lucky in love. I'm reconciled to living alone. Too set in my ways." He flicked the stub into the fire. "I don't make a good couple."

I think you'd make a wonderful couple. Maybe you've been burned once too often. Maybe we'll be different. Nothing like a good challenge.

He went to the kitchen and came back with more champagne.

"You're a dynamite woman." He refilled their glasses. "You won't have trouble attracting men."

He might as well say I won't have trouble running for Congress. "I can't imagine dating. Do you think I'm marketable?" *Would you make a bid?*

He laughed so hard he nearly snapped the flute. "Marketable? What do you want? A Filipino cabana boy? Wall Street banker? Trust me. You'll be one busy lady."

But I want you. Maybe I can break your losing streak.

Ellen imagined a party on the beach. The barefoot bride wore a Mexican wedding dress, no underwear and a gardenia in her upswept hair. The groom, also barefoot, was in jeans and a guayabera shirt as white as his teeth.

After the ceremony on the jetty, presided over by Rabbi Prinski and Fr. Dimmesdale from Our Virgin by the Sea, the newlyweds hosted a clambake on the sand. Tables cloaked in white circled a fire pit where the

Split Ends

lobsters cooked. As the guests sipped champagne and ate all-chocolate wedding cake, Frank Sinatra—also barefoot—stepped up to the mike to sing "All The Way." Maybe for another 50 grand he'd do "Second Time Around."

"Ellen? Earth to Ellen."

They laughed and made small talk. An hour or so passed. Maybe it was a year. She couldn't be sure. It was dark out.

"How long were you married, Drew?"

"Twelve years."

"What happened?"

"She came home one night and said she was leaving. Met someone."

"I'm sorry. Are you in touch?"

"No. No reason to be. She remarried and moved to Ohio. It's history."

"How come you didn't have kids?"

"She couldn't. I wanted to adopt. She didn't. I love kids."

Ellen sliced some fish and put it on a cracker.

"You've been on your own a long time."

"About 15 years."

I'm surprised someone hasn't grabbed him up.

"Are you getting hungry, El?"

"A little."

He slipped into his shoes and got up. "I'll start the fire."

"You already have," she said under her breath.

"Pardon?"

"You're not going to cook outside, are you? It's blowing a gale. We can broil the steaks in the kitchen."

Beth Rubin

He hesitated a second. "No, I'm going to grill them. They'll taste better."

What's he trying to prove? She grinned. "I think you're crazy, but it's your house. How 'bout I do the garlic bread and salad?"

"Deal." He gave her a high-five and went outside.

Ellen gathered stainless from a warped drawer. She rummaged around and went to the back door. "Drew, where are the paper napkins?"

Rain slid down the hood of his yellow jacket. He resembled a mad monk in a sci-fi thriller. "I don't do paper. You'll find cloth napkins next to the blender."

She chose navy and set votive candles around a spray of daisies she'd bought at the market.

Champagne chilled in a brass bucket.

Ellen was dressing the salad when Drew dripped into the kitchen with the steaks. She took the platter from him and, without thinking, wiped a raindrop from his cheek. As the aroma of the meat filled the room, Penny's tongue unrolled to the linoleum.

Ellen couldn't believe it. At home she needed a list to prepare dinner: Meat in 6:30. Start vegetables 6:50. Remove meat 7:00. Ellen hadn't consulted her watch once. Hell, she didn't even know where it was. Their timing was impeccable, perfect synchronicity.

As she lit the candles, he said, "You look beautiful." They unfolded their napkins.

I feel like a washerwoman—faded makeup, tired eyes, unkempt hair. "I think you've had enough to drink." She snatched his champagne. He feigned wrestling her for it.

Split Ends

The steak was exactly as she liked it: charred on the outside, pink on the inside. Drew complimented her on the salad and garlic bread.

"No big deal." She hoped she would soon have the chance to cook for him. He had already made a dent in the chocolate chip cookies she had baked at her mother's.

They talked until the *au jus* had turned to gelatin. Hunched over the table, their flushed faces mere inches apart, Ellen felt naked under his penetrating stare.

She watched him lick his lips and went all soft inside.

"I can think of a thousand things I'd like to do with you," he whispered.

She replied with a smile. *I can think of two thousand. Give me a minute and I'll make it three.* "I hope I find the strength to do what I have to … with the divorce."

"You will. You're tough."

She frowned. "How do you mean, tough?"

"I mean you're strong. You'll do what it takes."

How can he be so sure? One thing's certain. No one has ever paid such close attention to me. And nobody ever grilled steak for me in a nor'easter.

He loaded the dishwasher. She washed the serving pieces. They chatted and laughed, creating a fête out of doing dishes. *Look at us, Ma and Pa Kettle at the beach.* Ellen recalled how she and Ron used to get in each other's way in the kitchen. With Drew it was different. Everything was different.

Drew brewed cappuccino, which they carried with the cookies into the living room. He threw a log on the fire and Ellen drank in the view of his backside.

Still dig those buns, even though they've spread a bit since football practice.

"Do you like Bruch?" he asked.

"Yes. Especially his violin concerto."

He shuffled through his CDs.

Ellen settled against her end of the sofa, careful to avoid crossing the 50-yard line. Drew rested on an elbow and faced the fire. His long legs dangled over the arm.

"I don't know if you were aware, but I was crazy about you in high school," he said over his shoulder.

"The feeling was mutual."

"You were hot."

"Hot?" She never would have described herself that way.

"Yes, hot. Very attractive. You must have known."

"Not really. I was always worrying about my slip showing or a chin zit."

"You were—are—very pretty."

Champagne talking. Don't let it go to your head. "Thank you."

"Remember when we went to New York?"

"Sure. You knew so much about art, especially for a *pischer*."

"Pischer?"

"Kid. Wet behind the ears. It's Yiddish."

"I thought it was Latin."

"You nearly put me to sleep at the Museum of Modern Art."

"How?"

"On and on about *Guernica*."

"I've always liked Picasso."

Split Ends

"Remember how I choked on the hot dog? In front of St. Patrick's? And how we laughed?"

"That was funny, sauerkraut hanging from your mouth, you trying to push it back. I thought I'd bust a gut."

"I almost died and you laughed. Fine friend you were. You know, your mother would have had a fit if she'd known we ate kosher franks on holy ground."

He shook his head and made a funny face. "She's nuts."

They began to giggle. Their laughter seemed to fuel each other's. Ellen had to hug her stomach. She wiped her eyes. The room grew quiet, except for the crackling flames and Bruch's beseeching violins.

"I'm glad you're back in my life," he said. "I know we'll always be friends."

"I hope so." *Maybe I should grab the friendship and run. How can two people living 200 miles apart maintain anything more than a friendship? Some people thrive on a commuter relationship. Being with a lover only on weekends might keep things smoldering, instead of drowning in familiarity. It just might work.*

At her last haircut, she had read an article about couples who had broken up and reunited. The longer the separation, the more likely they were to stay together. When these couples reunite they feel their bond is more spiritual—that they've found their soul mates. Ellen wondered if she and Drew would inflate the statistics.

He stoked the fire. "I wanted to call you after my mother shipped me to my aunt's in California. I wish I had. But I didn't want to cause you more trouble with your parents."

Beth Rubin

Ellen sighed. "I was a mess. It didn't occur to me that you might be hurting too."

"I was hurting big time. Strange place ... new school ... my best friend 3,000 miles away."

"I thought of tracking you down."

"Why didn't you?"

"How? Your mother wouldn't speak to me. I didn't even know your aunt's last name. I figured you didn't care. That it would be a waste of time."

"I missed you something awful."

"How long were you in California?

"I finished high school there. When I came back, you had left for college. I joined the Air Force. Moved around a lot, then settled back in Jersey."

"I always wondered about you, where you were, how you were. Even my parents have asked about you. Damn, they were strict. I felt powerless. I wonder what would've happened if ..."

"I liked your parents. I could talk to them."

"I remember. They liked you, Drew, but they freaked over the record thing. Compared to what goes on today, it was nothing. They felt bad about making us break up, but ..." Ellen couldn't go on. She fought back the tears.

"I know. And I understand. They thought I was a bad influence."

"I told them you were kind, treated me well. They didn't want to hear it." Ellen let go a little laugh. "To tell you the truth, I think they were afraid I'd surrender my precious virginity, or we'd run off together."

"Or both."

Split Ends

He tossed another log on the fire. "They did what they felt was right. If I had a daughter, I'd do the same. Don't be angry with them."

"I'm not." Ellen shivered. "I'm angry with myself. I wish I had stood up to them. I didn't think I had a choice. I was only 16—and a good girl."

"You sure were. You would have made a good Catholic."

"They didn't let up. I couldn't take it." Ellen shook her head. The memories were vivid. "I wish I'd had the guts to say, 'I'm going to see him, whether you like it or not.' You know, I carried the same passive behavior into my marriage, repeating it *ad nauseam*. What an eye-opener."

Breaking up with Drew, she realized, had been harder than separating from Ron. For the simple reason that she hadn't wanted to. She was beginning to understand that she had been burying Ron for a while. Or maybe he had been burying himself.

She had always wished her relationship with Drew had run its course, dissolving over time as most teenage romances do. Like all unfinished business, it had shadowed Ellen for years. Even now, perhaps, it still did.

Drew rearranged himself so he was resting against Ellen's legs. She froze. *A forklift couldn't budge me. Now what . . . ?*

"Too bad we didn't meet again 20 years ago."

"Timing is everything. I was busy PTA-ing and driving carpools."

"You're right. It wouldn't have worked then. But we've always had chemistry." He reached back and took her hand. Ellen felt a surge from her split ends to the tips of her toes.

God, take me now. No, wait. Cancel previous message. I'm already a goner. She wondered if he would make another move. And when. At 50, she didn't know if she could maintain the good girl persona. *You can run but you can't hide. All that history and chemistry. Might as well try to stop the tide.*

The storm raged. The lights flickered and the wind howled, rattling the windows as if it wanted to break the two of them apart—a parental storm. Ellen listened to the rain hammering the roof and hoped Drew had flood insurance. She pictured the house washing out to sea, them in it, still talking.

He got up to cover her with a blanket and returned to using her legs as a backrest. She had lost feeling there, but gained it everywhere else.

Snug, and hypnotized by the embers, she felt herself slipping away. *I can't keep this up much longer. I'm exhausted.* As Drew toyed with her fingers, "Strangers in the Night" replaced Bruch.

"Am I losing you?"

Her body jerked.

"I didn't mean to scare you."

She yawned. "I must have dozed off. I'm going to pack it in."

Drew moved aside.

"Okay if I take a quick shower?"

"Of course."

She paused on her way to the bathroom and turned to him. "Shall I say goodnight?"

"No, not yet. I'll stay up."

Split Ends

She shaved her legs for the second time in 24 hours and returned, perfumed and primed, the purple robe tied tightly around her.

It took a minute for her eyes to adjust. Except for the embers and his smoldering cigarette, the room was dark. Ellen wondered if the storm, or the host, had dimmed the lights. Neither uttered a sound. She intended to give him a hug or chaste kiss before retiring to her room, where she knew she would stare at the ceiling and wish she were sharing his bed.

The moment of truth is upon us. Whichever bed I land in, I'm not going to sleep.

She heard him get up. He moved toward her, a blur in the darkness. She held her breath. As if by rote they fell into each other's arms, clinging as if their lives depended on it. One image filled Ellen's heart and mind: sanctuary.

The tempest tore at the cottage, but she had never felt so safe.

"I've wanted to kiss you all day. May I?"

"You're very polite. Did you think I'd say no?"

They kissed. Gently.

Please don't ever stop.

His arms encircled her waist. They kissed again and he drew her closer.

"I always liked the way you kissed."

"Just hold me, hold me tight and don't let go," she whispered.

"I'd like to spend the night with you. It has to be your choice. I don't want you to do anything you'll regret."

For a moment Ellen hesitated. But she knew she could not retreat.

"I vote yes."

"Are you sure? I don't want to complicate your life."

"I can handle it." She took his hand and led the way.

CHAPTER 11

They kissed and hugged in the doorway. And hugged and kissed.

This is a nice doorway. Oh my God. I don't want to leave this doorway. What am I doing? Is that the bedroom I see before me? Or the abyss?

Her feet refused to move.

The foot bone's connected to the headbone. The headbone's connected to the pubic bone. Will my aging body gross him out? I've had two kids. First they stretched everything. Then my boobs shrank. Maybe I'll disgust him. What if he sees the gray hairs down there? Hell, he can't see them in the dark. Damn, this is show time. Where is Mel Brooks when I really need him? It was easier being a vestal virgin. She giggled. *Great timing, moron. Stifle it, girl.*

"What's so funny, El?"

"I don't … I can't … This is …" She crossed her arms over her chest. *What am I supposed to do next?*

"What is it? Tell me."

"I feel foolish. I don't know how to act. Jeez, I'm 50 years old, for God's sake. Aside from a doctor here and there, you're only the second man to see me in the buff."

"I haven't seen anything yet. It's dark. My night vision is terrible. And it won't get better. I took out my contacts. Whatever you think your flaws are, I'm blind to them. I'll be using braille."

"Let your fingers do the walking."

"I could put my contacts in if you want me to pander to your fears."

She slapped his chest. "That's not funny."

"Then why are you laughing?"

"Nerves. I feel shy ... modest. Maybe you won't like my body. Maybe you'll laugh at me. Kick me out into the storm."

He kissed her forehead. "You're being silly. If you were perfect then I'd have to be perfect. And then we wouldn't be able to be real with each other. We'd both be on pedestals, trying not to be the first to fall."

But you are perfect and I'm not. She began to giggle again. *Get a grip.*

He touched her lips. "What?"

"My boobs."

"What about them?"

"They're small."

"I like small. Means I can fill my hands without getting carpal tunnel."

His hands left her waist to unknot the belt of her robe.

Something came over her. She flashed him. But she wasn't fast enough. His hands went inside the robe.

"They were fuller and perkier before I lost weight. How about I give you a rain check, good for two handfuls?"

"They're beautiful." He slid his hands up her rib cage, bent and kissed her breasts.

She felt her nipples harden.

"You're beautiful. And wonderful. You should be proud of yourself. Stop worrying."

"I'll bet you tell that to all your guests." *Okay, time to act grown-up. At least, pretend.* She exhaled.

She stepped into the room and smacked her shin on the bed frame.

"Ouch! Another bruise to add to my collection."

Split Ends

"The bed does that to all my guests. Cripples them so they can't run away. Let me kiss it and make it better." He knelt in slow motion.

Damn, you're good, Drew.

His hands slid from her ribs to her hips and to the backs of her legs.

She stood with her robe open. *It's like he's praying to me. Preying on me?* He kissed her shin, then the inside of her knee. He pushed her back with a gentle but irresistible force.

His tongue flicked on her thigh. Her knees trembled. Everything trembled. *What's that furry thing behind my legs? Drew's on his knees in front of me. Who's behind me?* She fell backwards over Penny.

Penny yelped and slunk away.

Damn dog. Don't let me lose this moment, pleeeeeeease.

Drew was on her belly. His tongue began to search.

"Mmmm ... Drew ..."

"I want to make you feel good, El. Tell me what to do."

"You damn well know what to do." She dug her fingers into his hair and held him to her. His tongue found that perfect place. *Take that, Ron, you selfish bastard.*

* * * *

"Oh my God, Drew, no more." She squirmed away and tossed her purple robe aside. She saw it land on Penny, lying in the corner. *Thank God, Penny can't talk. If she went on Jerry Springer, I'd be dog food.* She scrambled under the quilt.

Beth Rubin

Drew stood up. Moonlight bathed his body. She had fantasized about him naked since dinner: *Stallion? Average Joe, er, Dick? Teeny weenie? The envelope, please. Will the real Drew please stand up?*

He had a good body for a guy of 50—broad shoulders, nearly flat stomach. *What the hell, he was a little meaty. So what?* He turned. The silver glow from the window held him in silhouette. *Oy, Jeez, look at that hardware. Am I really supposed to get that into me? Twenty-eight years with Mr. Asparagus and now this?*

He pulled her to him. She closed her eyes. He ran his finger across her forehead and down her cheek, under her chin and up the other side of her face.

She shivered.

His hand caressed her neck. He stroked her stomach. His touch was tender. Loving. She felt his heat. Then her own. Again.

He began to kiss her—softly—on her cheeks, forehead, eyelids. He moved to her mouth, brushing her lips. They teased each other with small kisses and murmurs. The pressure increased. Drew nibbled her lower lip, sucked it as if it were a ripe Jersey peach. Juices flowed.

You like Picasso. How do you like this abstraction? She painted swirls in his mouth.

His hand felt like a feather on her breast. Teasing. Exquisite. Her nipples grew harder than she could remember.

"I like your breasts, El." He squeezed them.

Can he see them without his contacts? How do they look? "Keep your eyes closed."

Split Ends

She cupped them and held them, in turn, to his lips. He worshipped them equally.

She moaned. Her modesty—what was left of it—evaporated. *Thank God.* She tried pulling him closer, but he resisted. He grazed on her ears. He nuzzled her neck. He moved to her shoulders, marking them with love bites that made ecstasy of pain.

You know how to make love—where to go, what to do when you get there, how long to stay and when to move on. Ron thought foreplay was turning off the TV.

Images flashed behind her eyes. They were teenagers again. Feverish. Out of control. A match.

His lips found hers and she heard "Kisses Sweeter Than Wine."

Her self-control dissolved. *I want to feel you. All of you.* Her arms locked around him. The urgency of his response sent a shock through her. He grabbed her rear and squeezed her against his hips. They fused. She gasped. He groaned.

She ran her fingernails over his chest and belly, slowly, until she discovered him. Her fingertips tingled.

Christ, he's circumcised. I can't believe his cross-hugging mum stood still for that. Maybe they did it to reduce the weight. She giggled.

"Found a new toy, Ellen?"

"The bigger the boy, the bigger the toy." A realization hit her. *Jeez, if I put that thing of his inside me it's going to come out my throat. I'll be a kabob on his skewer. I don't remember that from the acne years. Moby Dick. Mo Big Dick.*

She giggled again. He responded with a kiss.

His foot grazed hers. He froze.

123

"You make love in socks?"

Oh my God. How ridiculous must I look in anklets and nothing else?

"I have to." She wiggled her toes against him. "These are my icebergs. Watch out, or they'll sink your Titanic."

"Ice is nice, but sex is best. What should I do next?"

"I have a few ideas."

She rolled onto him and trailed her breasts across his chest. She played her nipples against his. To her surprise, his went as hard as hers.

He reached up and around her, fingers dancing on her back.

"You have a sexy back."

"Sculpted it just for you."

He pulled her downward. She wrapped her legs around his. *Glad I shaved my legs again. Twice in one day. Double your pleasure, double your fun, Drew. Two, two, two shaves in one.*

Their bodies braided like challah. *Challah and Irish soda bread.*

Ellen felt her thermostat skyrocket. His warmth and weight felt so good. Tears welled. She let them run down her cheeks. They kissed and caressed, exploring each other.

Do this. Don't do that. Careful. He might not like it. What's he thinking? What's he really thinking? What the hell am I thinking? Why can't I stop thinking?

"You have magic hands, Drew. From your quarterback days?"

"Just don't say it's from massaging the pigskin."

Split Ends

She slapped his chest again. "I'll make the jokes around here, buddy."

"And I'll laugh at every one. You're sexy and funny. You could drive a man crazy."

Is that what happened to Ron? Burned out by sexual insanity? "That's what I had in mind."

"You gonna talk, girl, or you gonna do?"

She licked his neck and shoulders. She proceeded to his nipples, citrusy and salty. *Better than a margarita.* She traveled south, taking the side roads, enjoying the scenery along the way.

Damn, I should have insisted that he use a condom before we got this far. Another image crashed in on her. She was having a heart-to-heart with the kids about safe sex. *Here I am, post-menopausal and reasonably intelligent and I haven't told him.*

"Drew, we need to use a condom. I have one in my purse." *Thank you, Sandy.*

"No need." He reached over and groped in the drawer of his bedside table.

"Do you want to do it, El?"

"My pleasure."

He handed her the packet. "It's chocolate."

"Really? Godiva?"

"I hope it's not Nestlé's Quick."

She tore open the foil, placed the condom on him. "Ah, that's cute, Drew. It's like a little crown."

"God save the King."

"And his Queen," Ellen said. She unrolled the condom with her mouth. It tasted like a diet drink. *Great gimmick, but it won't put Hershey out of business.* She thought of saying it out loud. *But mom told me not to talk with my mouth full.*

Beth Rubin

She tucked her hair behind her ears, teased him with her tongue, then took him deep in her mouth. Well, most of him. He groaned. *God, a gorilla in my midst. King Kock.*

He became both supplicant and predator. His pelvis began to heave. Seismic shocks coursed through his body. "Oh, God, Ellen. Don't stop. Please don't stop."

Stop? When I'm in control and you're the slave? Forget it, pal. You're mine. Lock, stock, Tom, Harry and Dick. Eat your heart out, Ron, wherever you aren't.

He clawed at the sheets and arched his back, then clutched her hair. She took in another inch.

Christ. He could do a root canal and a tonsillectomy while he's in there.

"Oh, yes, Ellen, yes," he gurgled from somewhere in the back of his throat. He squeezed her thighs. Her jaw started to ache. He saved her from calling a time-out. He reached and pulled her upward until their heads met on the pillow.

In an instant, he rolled her over as if she weighed nothing. He lifted her knees and knelt between them. She saw him in the moonlight. He looked like an Aztec priest and she was the ritual sacrifice. *Mistaken for a virgin to be sacrificed to the Moon god. Does the Moon god take old babes? I hope I survive this to be a grandmother.*

"I'm ready, I think." She took a deep breath.

"I've been ready for decades."

"Easy cowboy. It's been a while." *Wonder if he has a broom on that handle, to sweep out the cobwebs.*

Split Ends

His hands rippled down the inside of her legs. "I want you, Ellen. I've always wanted you." He slid into her with an easy motion that made her gasp.

"How did you do that?"

"What?"

"Go into me so easily?"

"Homing instinct. Like riding a bike. You never forget. I could never forget you, El."

"But we never …"

"Yes we did. In my fertile imagination. More times than you'll ever know."

She wrapped her legs around his waist. He went deeper. *Oh my God. First down my throat and now he's going to come up it. Thank God he doesn't have two of those things.*

She flung her arms around him and pulled him to her. He lowered his full weight on her.

"I can't breathe, lover boy."

"Good. Means you'll stop talking." But he propped himself on his elbows.

She squeezed his waist between her knees.

Keep this up and I'll need a hip replacement.

He began to move, not just in and out, but in a spiral. She rotated her hips with him.

So it was true. The Declaration of Independence lied. All men were not created equal. Or, as Sandy put it, "I don't need a man for his brain. I already have one of those. I just need eight inches of him. If he can take out the garbage, great, he can do two things."

Drew was good. He found and matched her tempo. Still, her mind continued to wander. She pictured her Tiffany-set solitaire nestled in its velvet pouch. On her lawyer's advice, she had put her jewelry in a safe deposit box. *I hope I don't have to sell it. I want the kids to have it. I wonder what it's worth.*

As Drew humped away, she went further out of sync. *Is he just getting off on consummating his teen romance—at last? Maybe he hasn't had any in a while. How can that be? He's such a stud muffin. And he's making me his sex crumpet. Strumpet.*

"You fill me up, Drew." *My cup runneth over. And under. Will goodness and mercy follow me all the days of my life? Will you dwell in me forever?*

"Being inside you is fantastic."

Ellen felt herself shudder. *Damn that shudder of distrust.* Something about his tone set off an alarm. *A hollow compliment? How many times has he said that? And to whom? Next he'll tell me my apple pie is better than his mother's and I'm the best piece of tail he's ever had.*

Throat parched and head pounding, she wanted an aspirin and glass of water. *Maybe I can help get this over with.*

She tried to match his cadence. She grabbed at the baby-soft skin of his rock-hard buns. She never imagined a man, so furry elsewhere, could have such a smooth derrière. *Maybe he shaves his butt? Laser treatment? Nair? East is East and West is West and Nair the twain shall meet?*

She started liking him again. Kneading his ass warmed her as bread-making did on winter afternoons.

"Come with me, Ellen. Come with me."

Come, go, in, out, stop, start. "I'm trying." *Christ, does he think I'm playing Scrabble here? How about a seven-letter combination of two words, beginning and ending in F. Please, Drew, do it before you herniate*

Split Ends

six of my disks. You're a pile driver on steroids. You could pound me all the way back to Maryland.

Without breaking his rhythm, he lifted his chest and locked her in his sight. He looked like a Top Gun pilot marking a target. "I want to help you come."

"I'm a little rusty. Don't worry about me. Knock yourself out." *Please.*

She wrapped her legs around his waist again, lifted her hips off the bed. Her teeth clenched. "Harder, Drew, harder." She clawed his back.

Perspiration dripped from his chest to hers.

"Do me, do me, Drew." *Dooby dooby do. I could love this man. But if he doesn't finish soon, I'll be crippled.* She pictured herself in leg braces.

An image raced past her mind's eye, like a downhill racer. It could have been a downhill racer. It was Drew and the young man in a skiing ad. *Where did that come from? What am I worried about? At least he doesn't leave pictures of his ex-wife lying around.*

He gasped. He moaned and mumbled her name.

I don't care what you say about me as long as you get my name right. Maybe he's back in high school, boffing Sweet Little Sixteen. Am I a good lover? Or is he noisy for effect? Is all this just special effects? The moonlight? The dog snoring in the corner, my aching back?

But his vocalizing turned her on. Ron had made more noise eating mashed potatoes than making love. He always seemed to be going through the motions while reviewing the Dow or his wardrobe *du jour.*

She wanted Drew, needed him. She loved the kissing and fondling, their slippery bodies in a horizontal dirty dance.

She could no longer hear. She could only feel. She touched his flesh, tasted his sweat, fingered his hair, kissed his mouth, felt his weight. She wanted only to stroke him and suck him and fuck him and love him. On top of her underneath her inside her upside down and alongside her. She wanted to swallow him up and feel forever the way he melted her.

Drew is doing all the right things. I haven't been this wet in years. If ever. Why am I stuck in second gear? Where the hell is my loose wire? I need time. We need time. With a little practice maybe we'll be gangbusters in the sack. I might even scream. Better than hyperventilating.

The red diodes of the bedside clock glowed 4:18. *How did that happen? I haven't been up this late since college. It's almost time for Weekend Edition on NPR.*

Her back chafed against the sailboat sheet. *Hi, sailor. Push your tiller hard a'me.* She cracked a smile over his choice of the kiddie bedding. *You can take the man out of the boy, but ...* The thought floated off in the sweaty air.

She imagined the sailboats would tattoo her, leaving imprints like Hester Prynne's scarlet A. The bright badges of infidelity would be tough to hide in a bathing suit. *That should be my biggest problem. C'mon, Slugger, swing that bat of yours and belt one out of the park. I don't mind if I get left on base. If you wait for me to steal home, we'll be here until the World Series.*

Ellen swept a strand from her mouth along with the notion that it couldn't possibly work out between them. *I'm going to look like shit in daylight.* She touched her puffy eyes. *Did I pack concealer?*

Split Ends

His cry shattered the night and 200 pounds of beefcake collapsed onto her. She unlocked her legs, numb from hips to toes.

"Thank God." *Oops, too loud, girl.*

"What?"

"Oh God."

"Are you okay?"

"Yes, I'm fine." *How long till I can stop faking it? I faked it with Ron and I'm faking it now.* "All hail, Adonis. Could his Greek godliness roll over, please?" Taking a deep breath, she murmured, "Was it as good for you as it was for me?"

No answer.

"Drew?"

He snored.

Thank God. She reached down for the quilt. Lulled by his breathing and the rhythm of the sea, she settled against the headboard and pulled the cover up to her chin. She stared out into the moonlight. *Can I get to the john without waking him?* She kissed his half-smile, traced his face with adoring eyes. *Please, let me adore him.*

Silver spray danced in the night and sparkled beyond the glass. *So what if I never walk again? I made the right decision. I'm done coloring inside the lines. It feels good to be scribbling on a blank page.*

CHAPTER 12

"Sleeping Beauty."

Something tickled her face. "Huh?" She didn't know where she was. "Go away, Penny."

She felt a kiss on her forehead. She opened her eyes and fumbled for her glasses. If she was dreaming, she never wanted to wake up. Drew sat on the edge of the bed.

"Woof," he said.

Where'd he get that robe? Salvation Army? She stretched.

"Do I look like a dog?"

"More like a kitten. I brought you juice and coffee. Are you going to stay in bed all day?"

"Meow." She wiped the sleep from her eyes. "What time is it?"

"Ten after 9:00." He caressed her cheek. "How are you?"

"I'll know when I try to walk."

He laughed. "You were incredible. You wore me out last night."

"I wore you out? I'm ready for physical therapy. How long have you been up?" *So to speak.*

"About an hour. I was watching you sleep. You looked so angelic."

"Did the angel snore?"

"She didn't."

"There is a God." She sipped the juice. Fresh-squeezed, as advertised. "Oh shoot. Penny." Ellen's feet hit the floor. "She has to go out first thing."

"I walked her and fed her. She's in the living room behaving herself."

Split Ends

"She won't want to leave." *Neither will I.*

"I'm glad you slept well. It means you're comfortable here. What do you want to do today?"

Ellen winked at him.

"Besides that." He mussed her hair. "Why don't we drive to New York?"

"New York?"

"You've heard of it? Bright lights. Tall buildings. Drunks and junkies. Maybe see a show."

"Sounds like fun. Can you get tickets?"

"I can squeeze orange juice and I can get tickets."

"What about Penny?"

"Leave her to me."

Drew called the widow next door and asked if she would keep an eye on Penny.

"She said to have fun, El. And not to hurry back."

He made more calls. She finished the juice, savored the pulp and drank the coffee—cream only. How had he remembered? Ron still thought she wanted sugar, when he thought about what she wanted at all.

She scanned the desolate beach. The storm had left flotsam, jetsam and standing water.

"Done deal. We have tickets for 'Show Boat' and a suite at the Four Seasons."

"I can't let you do all that. I'll pay for the tickets."

"No way. You're on my turf so it's my treat."

"You'll spoil me."

"You deserve to be spoiled."

"Would you hand me my robe, please?"

"Shall I close my eyes?"

"Only if you want to."

"I don't. I like what I see."

She took her time getting out of bed and putting on her robe. He wrapped his arms around her and kissed her hair.

"How about breakfast? I have the makings for a Western omelet."

"Good. I'm starving. And I want a garlic bagel. Maybe two. With lots of cream cheese. Got any bacon?"

"How do you stay so skinny?"

"Angst."

A few minutes later, Ellen minced onion, green pepper and ham at the sink. Drew whisked the eggs, carried the bowl to the stove and dropped a pat of butter in the skillet.

She felt his heat before he touched her. Pressing her from behind, he fondled her breasts and began rubbing against her. Her knees buckled when he kissed the back of her neck. He untied her robe to slip a hand inside. She moved the cutting board out of harm's way and gripped the sink.

"Mmm." Ellen watched the butter melting in the skillet and reached back to find his robe open. She ran her hand between their bodies and found him. She could barely close her fist around him.

"Bend over," he said.

"What?"

"Bend over the sink."

"I-I'm not into kinky."

"Don't worry."

She heard foil tearing. *What flavor condom for breakfast? Banana? Passion fruit?*

Then he was inside her. A raging bull. She braced herself, the cold stainless catching her belly.

Split Ends

"Am I hurting you?"

"Yeah. Hurt me some more."

He held the counter with one hand, stroked her with the other while thrusting deeper, deeper.

"Oh God Oh God Oh Go-o-o-o-o-d." Ecstasy overcame her and she hit her head on the faucet. *So much for my loose wire. Cancel the electrician. I've reconnected.*

He held her tight, resting his head on her shoulder, as the butter burned.

"You okay?"

"Beyond okay."

She turned to face him and they held each other. Ellen's stomach growled. "I hate to spoil the moment but I'm about to chew my arm."

"Uh-oh. Now I have to feed the woman to keep her happy."

They ate breakfast without more digressions.

Shortly after noon they came out of the Lincoln Tunnel, drove to the hotel and left their things with the bellman. Hand-in-hand they walked to the Museum of Modern Art, passing St. Patrick's.

"Shall we stop to light a candle?" Ellen asked, a tease in her tone.

"I wish I had my camera. You could re-enact the hot dog scene."

"Once was enough."

At the museum they went straight to the third floor where they had viewed *Guernica* as teenagers. It was gone. Picasso's *The Charnel House* hung in its place.

"What happened to it, Drew?"

"They sent *Guernica* back to Madrid when Franco died in 1981."

"You know so much stuff."

He shrugged. They visited the Pollocks for him and the Monets for her. After a snack in the café overlooking the sculpture garden, they went back to the hotel.

Later that afternoon as she rode him, she felt light-headed. She steadied herself by planting her hands on his chest. "I think I'm going to faint."

"You're hyperventilating."

"Thanks for the diagnosis, doc. Got a paper bag?" she asked before collapsing in laughter on his chest.

Drew had wangled fifth-row seats for "Show Boat." Ellen could see the sweat pouring off the actors' faces. When Magnolia and Ravenel sang, "You Are Love," he kissed her fingertips, one by one. In the crowded ladies' room after the show, she wondered if anyone noticed the flattened nap of her velvet pants where he had palmed her thigh.

Humming, they left the theater. He offered her a cigarette. She said no. He paused to light his. "What do you feel like eating?"

"You."

He touched his ear. "Did I hear you right?"

A woman in a full-length fur shot Ellen a look. *Jealous bitch.*

"Anything. I'm not very hungry."

"I've heard that line before. French? Italian?"

"You know what I'd really like?"

"Indian? Thai? Name it."

They picked up corned beef sandwiches, potato salad and cream sodas from the Carnegie. Drew ordered champagne from room service and they

Split Ends

picnicked in bed while watching "It Happened One Night."

"Great idea, El," Drew said as mustard dripped on the sheet. "I never would have thought of it. But I owe you a dinner. A real dinner."

"You don't owe me diddly. This weekend has been perfect."

"It has, hasn't it?" He leaned over to give her a mustard kiss. "I'm so glad you called and that you're back in my life."

"I hit the jackpot—my favorite city, great corned beef and you."

"Damn. Upstaged by corned beef."

"Don't go turning hypersensitive on me." She put the Kosher pickle down to give him a garlicky lick and tickled him until he begged for mercy. They snuggled and half-watched the rest of the movie locked in each others' arms.

"I was thinking, this beats Meg's slumber parties."

"I hope so." He spooned her.

The next morning they bathed in the oversized tub. She choked on the soapy water as the SS Drew, periscope raised, maneuvered into position and torpedoed her.

"I have to wash my hair," she said as the tub drained.

He turned the shower on. "Let me wash it for you."

Ever since she had seen "Out of Africa," Ellen thought it was the sexiest act a man could perform for his woman. As Drew massaged her scalp, she recalled how she and Ron had showered together occasionally. But he'd never shampooed her—not that it would have made a difference in the rinse water of their marriage.

Drew toweled her hair and, still damp, they made love again on the huge bed. *Wonder if housekeeping can get me a wheelchair.*

After breakfast they window-shopped on Fifth Avenue. Ellen stopped at a chocolate boutique.

"You're drooling, missy. What's your desire?"

"I love their champagne truffles."

"I'll be right back." He left her on the sidewalk to browse through designer knockoffs and returned with a two-pound box. "Here, try to save some for later."

She kissed him and hung the ribbon around his neck. "I'd rather have these than a trinket from Tiffany's."

"You're funny. And fun. I love to do things for you."

She kissed him. "You give great courtship." Ellen raised a cocoa-dusted truffle to him. "L'chaim."

They left the city about noon. Somewhere near Woodbridge he picked up Sundays With Sinatra on a Philadelphia station. After songs from the Dorsey years, "All the Way" began.

Drew winked at her. "I couldn't have made this up."

"Did you call in the request?"

"I'd like to take credit, but no." He reached over, slid his hand under her skirt and squeezed her thigh. His fingers crept higher. She wiggled out of her pantyhose and threw her coat across her lap, so the truck drivers wouldn't have something to talk about on their CBs. Then she leaned back and spread her legs.

"You are hot, woman."

"I'm a shameless slut."

"I'm hard as a rock."

Split Ends

"Please ... my virgin ears." He took her hand and placed it on his erection. "Another half inch, Drew, and it'll steer the car."

"I want to make love to you, Ellen."

"You'll have to wait. In the meantime, let me help you out of your distress." She unzipped his fly. "One good turn deserves another." When he started pumping the brakes Ellen prayed they wouldn't make *The Star Ledger's* obit page.

Melancholy overtook her as they neared his house. For the first time in 48 hours the conversation died. Her mood turned dour, as though they had already parted. She began to wonder when they would see each other again.

As if reading her mind, he said, "I have business in Baltimore I could take care of Tuesday. How far is that from Annapolis?"

"Only 40 minutes."

"Can you meet me for lunch?"

"Just tell me where and when."

"I'm leaving town Wednesday. We might not see each other for a while."

"I'll be away too. My kids are having Thanksgiving with Ron and I'm going to my girlfriend's in Florida."

"That's good. You shouldn't be alone." He kissed her hand and held it.

"Where are you going?"

"Aspen. Early skiing."

They picked up Penny and walked to the beach. Ellen squinted at the water, glittering in the afternoon sun. She wished she could bottle the scene. Then she could keep it with the sea glass and Cupid vase Drew had given her.

As Ellen packed, Drew built a fire and made coffee. She knew she had to leave but her feet were lead. He stuck his head in the room. "I'm not kicking you out. Why don't you stay over tonight?"

Just tonight? I want to stay forever. "I have an appointment with a client tomorrow morning. I need to get back." *To what? The empty house? More divorce negotiations? Where am I going? I'm already home.*

An hour later the Sunday *Times* littered the floor. Two empty mugs sat on an end table. Ellen put down the travel section and walked to the sofa. She climbed onto his lap and wrapped her arms around him. They remained that way for a long while, not saying a thing. When they separated their cheeks wore Rorschach tears.

They stood up and embraced. He began to grind his pelvis into her. She reciprocated. He reached down and shook hands with her crotch. *It's like he's doing a laying on of hands. Make it better, Drew. Make it all better.*

His hands moved to her ass. He lifted her. She curled her arms and legs around him. He carried her into the bedroom where they fell onto the bed and squirmed out of their pants.

He opened the drawer. "Damn. I'm all out."

"Shoot. We used my one and only."

She grabbed him, put his thing between her thighs and squeezed.

"C'mon, Drew. One for the road."

"I want to, El, but … "

"C'mon, just this once."

Split Ends

"Uh-uh. No tickee, no washee." He hugged her.

I want to feel him once without a raincoat. I've waited 35 years.

"Please, Drew."

"It's okay, El, we can cuddle."

"Cuddle, my ass."

She threw a leg over his belly and climbed aboard.

* * * *

Ellen had planned to leave by 3:00 to have daylight for part of the drive. He put her things in the car. They clung to each other before the sunset, struggling to say good-bye. At 5:00 she finally pushed off. The parting seemed almost as painful as their teenage separation had been.

The ache cut into her.

"Drive carefully." He mussed her hair. "Call me when you get home."

"I will. Thank you." Ellen drove at a snail's pace, stopped and lowered her window. Drew loped over, smiling, always smiling. They kissed once more.

"Drew, do you think this kind of thing really happens?"

"It just did. Take good care of yourself."

"I love you, Drew."

"I love you too."

She watched him in her rearview mirror until he was a fleck against a darkening field of fountain grass. Dusk, and Drew, slid into night.

CHAPTER 13

Tuesday they met at a place in Fells Point, a block from the water. He had been waiting at the bar. Who's the handsome guy, she mused. He must have seen her reflection. He got off the stool. The way he smiled made her feel like royalty.

They kissed. "You look wonderful, El. On the phone you said you were tired."

"I haven't slept much since the beach."

"Well, you look rested. And delicious, as always. I like your suit."

They had a glass of wine at the bar. It went to her head. They moved to a window table. She hardly touched her Crab Imperial. She kicked off her shoe and stroked his thigh. He squirmed and bit his lower lip, then mouthed something.

"What?" She leaned forward and tried to lip read. She thought of his mouth on her body and pressed her legs together.

"I want to fuck you," he whispered.

Ellen glanced at the lone man at the next table. "Drew, I think he knows this isn't a business lunch."

Drew leaned across the table, his yellow power tie in her coleslaw, and purred, "Maybe I'll just kidnap you."

The prospect intoxicated her. She would have followed him anywhere that day. Never had she felt so full of life, so desirable or desirous.

"I have something for you." He pulled a gift-wrapped box from a shopping bag. "But you have to promise to wait."

"You're a tease. I want to open it now."

"Not here, El. You'll understand why when you get home."

"If you insist."

He kissed her palm and held it to his cheek.

"I'll miss you. Take care of yourself."

"Ditto. I hope you'll visit me after your skiing trip."

"We'll make plans when I get back. Have a nice time with your friend in Florida."

"I will."

"Don't eat too much stuffing, El."

"I won't. I don't have much of an appetite." *For food.* "I wish we were going away together, Drew."

"Be patient. We have the rest of our lives. We might not see each other all the time, but I'll always be here for you. I'm in this for the long haul."

She gulped. *Is he saying what I think?* She tried to think of a reply, but couldn't.

The bar had filled. She looked at her watch. "How did it get to be five o'clock? Jeez, I have to feed and walk Penny."

"I have to go too, not that I want to. I have a long drive and I have to pack."

He handed her the gift. "Next week you can tell me how you like it. Think of me when you use it."

He paid the check and belted his trench coat. They stepped into the fog. He put his arm around her shoulder.

"Be careful driving, El."

"I will. You too." She spied his car, the tag with a lighthouse and "Shore to Please." She wanted to get in his car and be with him forever.

Beth Rubin

Tears burned. "Don't walk me to my car, Drew. I hate good-byes."

She kissed him and tore away.

* * * *

Ellen filled Penny's bowl. She looked at the gift box. *Wonder what it is. Too big for jewelry, too small for clothing.*

She ripped off the ribbon and shiny red paper. "The Tongue" was printed in bold letters above a grotesque picture. *What the hell is this?* She pulled the plastic gadget from the box and held it away from her. *Gross! It's a tongue, all right. I don't want it licking any part of me. What was he thinking? That I couldn't wait for the real thing?*

Penny sniffed it and barked.

"Yuck, Penny. I feel like barking too."

Ellen read the instructions. "Let's see, two power sources: 4 AA batteries and an electrical adaptor. I'll be sure not to use it in the bathtub." She stuck it back in the box.

Penny waited at the front door. "Oh well, Penny. Boys will be boys!" Ellen leashed her. "Call me old-fashioned, girl, but I think it's weird."

* * * *

"What, or who, put that smile on your face?"

"I can't stop grinning, Elizabeth. I'm in love. Or deep lust. Maybe both."

"What's going on? I thought you went to New Jersey to work and see friends."

Split Ends

"I did. I called an old boyfriend. *The* boyfriend. You know how there's one you never forget?"

Elizabeth sighed. "Oh yes."

"We had dinner, talked about old times. Really connected. I never felt so comfortable with another person. I spent the weekend with him. I didn't want to leave. Yesterday we had lunch in Baltimore. That's why I changed my appointment to today."

"Tell me about him."

"He's wonderful—warm, funny, bright, attentive. He gets me, Elizabeth. We're in sync. I can't believe I was depressed a week ago. I'm leading a double life: the agony—that's Ron—and the ecstasy. Did I mention that he's very attractive?"

"What is his name?"

"Drew. Drew Cushing. We hadn't seen each other since high school. He's a dream, Elizabeth. And he likes Penny."

"Is he single?"

"Of course."

"Has he been married?"

"Yes."

"What happened?"

"She left him. Met someone else, he said."

"Did he give you any details?"

"No."

"You may want to ask. There's usually a reason. Something or things missing in the marriage. He may have been unable to fulfill his wife's needs in one or more ways."

"What's the difference? That was then and this is now."

"It's a good predictor, Ellen. People tend to repeat the same patterns."

"I know what I see and feel. He's kind and he cares for me. And I'm crazy about him."

"You knew him when you were adolescents, Ellen. You hardly know him as an adult. If he's as wonderful as you say, why is he alone?"

"You're making too much of this. He was married once and it didn't work out. Big deal. He's alone because he hasn't met the right person." *But I'm working on it.*

"Be careful, Ellen. You're vulnerable."

CHAPTER 14

Sea grape leaves skittered along the sand in front of Sandy's Siesta Key condo. Ellen rolled double ones and moved two tiles on the Backgammon board. "Your turn." She watched pelicans dive-bomb the water as she waited for Sandy to move.

"You're a lifesaver, Sandy. I was dreading Thanksgiving."

"Holidays can be tough when you're single. I'm glad you came."

"I am too. I would've gone crazy alone. Anyone in your life, Sandy?"

"I started seeing someone last month. His name is Jonathan."

"And?"

"And I think this could be it."

"Good for you. I'd like to meet him."

"You will." Sandy rolled a six and moved. She would probably win. Again. "When is Drew coming back from Colorado?"

"Tomorrow. I can't wait. I miss him so much, I hurt."

"You remind me of a teenager with her first crush."

Ellen shook the dice. "I feel like a teenager. I must be going through my second puberty. He's everything I never thought I'd have. Everything I missed with Ron. Sometimes I have to pinch myself."

"You deserve it, Ellen. You paid your dues."

"Mmm."

"Why the long face?"

"I don't know what I'd do if he bailed."

"Bail? Why would he do that? You're a catch, Ellen. He'd be crazy."

* * * *

The next afternoon the women oohed and aahed over the orchids and bromeliads at a nearby nature preserve. They left the conservatory and strolled the elevated boardwalk through a mangrove swamp.

"God, I miss him, Sandy. I hope nothing's changed."

"It sounds like you're made for each other. I'm sure you'll pick up where you left off."

* * * *

"You'll go cross-eyed looking at your watch, Ellen." They finished Thanksgiving leftovers on Sandy's terrace.

"I miss talking to him most of all. I left your number on his answering machine this morning. Forgot to give it to him last week. Don't know where my head was."

"You need a cell phone."

"It's on my to-do list."

"What time does his plane arrive?"

"At 7:30. Wish I could be there to meet him."

Sandy laughed. "I think he'll understand why you're not traveling a thousand miles to meet him in Philadelphia."

"I'm going to the video store. I can't sit still."

"Maybe you can score some tranquilizers too."

Split Ends

Ellen returned half an hour later and tried watching the movie. Her eyes darted from her watch to the wall clock to the phone. *Ring, damn it!*

Unable to stand the suspense any longer, at 9:00 P.M. she dialed Drew.

Hearing his voice pushed her heart rate to dangerous.

"Welcome home, sweet thing. I missed you. How was your trip?"

"Nice."

He sounded odd. Distant. Ellen felt as though someone had kicked her in the stomach.

"I'm on the other line. Can I call you back?" he asked.

"Sure," she said, and gave him Sandy's number.

"He's home, Sandy. He's calling back."

"Good. I'll be reading in my room. See you in the morning. I expect you to act normal by then."

Ellen watched the rest of "Annie Hall." Or was it "Halls of Montezuma?" *He's probably going through mail and unpacking.* She went to bed and tossed and turned.

At dawn, she headed for the beach. *If I'm gone, he'll call. If I sit by the phone, he won't.* She crunched the sand with leathery retirees. *He'll call. I know he'll call. It's going to be all right.*

The sun pinked her nose as she passed beachcombers collecting their booty in plastic bags. Snippets of conversation floated by. She had been daydreaming about Drew when she tripped on a dead fish.

Iridescent scales covered a ravaged corpus. The eye sockets were empty and the mouth sneered at her.

Examining the corpse for clues to its demise, she thought, *I am that fish; shiny outside, rotting inside.*

She found Sandy watering the plants on the terrace. "Any messages?"

"No."

"I can't believe it. There must be a reason."

But her gut told her otherwise. She didn't want to know what it was.

Sandy reached out her hand. "I'm sorry, Ellen."

"I don't get it. Everything was fine a week ago. Why wouldn't he call?"

"I don't know. But I don't like the sound of it."

"What do you mean?"

"The same thing happened to me a few years ago."

"What same thing?"

"I was head over heels with a guy. He could have been Denzel Washington's twin. I phoned him at work. He said, 'Don't call me anymore.' I never heard from him again."

"How awful. You're not suggesting ... Drew wouldn't do that."

"You know, he might have gone to Colorado for more than skiing. Maybe there's someone else."

"Nah. He was visiting a buddy. I'm sure of it."

"That's what he told you. Maybe he lied."

"Lie? He wouldn't lie to me."

"Take it from me, Ellen, men lie."

"I know Drew. He wouldn't do that."

"You think you know him. Maybe you don't."

"I've never trusted anyone so much."

"You may be too trusting, Ellen. You've hardly been on your own. There are lots of snakes out there. You should get to know a man well before you ..."

Split Ends

"You sound like a maiden aunt."

"I'm just sharing what I've learned. Did you use condoms?"

"Of course." *Oh my God. Except for the last time.*

* * * *

They had an early supper that evening on the Gulf. Ellen picked at her yellowfin and watched the charter boats heading in.

"You haven't said a word, Ellen."

"The stuffing's been knocked out of me. I have to know what happened."

"I hope you find out, but you might not."

"Oh, I will. I can't bear being in limbo."

Sandy pasted on a smile that Ellen couldn't reciprocate.

"I think you could use a drink, Ellen. And some PIFing."

"What's that?"

"PIFing? Prolific indiscriminate fucking. I recommend it, especially in situations like these."

"Maybe in 10 years. Right now, Mel Gibson couldn't charm my panties off."

"Ellen, are you sure you want to hear Michael Feinstein tonight? He's heavy into love songs."

"I'll be fine. I'm tough." *Isn't that what Drew said?*

* * * *

Ellen felt herself sinking as the vocalist delivered songs of romance and unrequited love. The lyrics touched off images of Ron and Drew, flashing like enemy fire. She would have sacrificed Penny to stop the onslaught.

When Feinstein began to sing "Isn't it Romantic?" the words cut to her core.

She dug her nails into her flesh and began to sob.

Sandy leaned closer to whisper, "There's no need to suffer. Let's go."

"No," Ellen cried. "Let's stay. I'm having a good time." The women dissolved in laughter and tears. They ignored the clucking of the biddies behind them.

Later they sat on the terrace sipping Kahlua and searching for Orion. "I don't think the death of a loved one would hurt this bad, Sandy."

"This is worse. There's still a living body."

* * * *

"Thanks for putting me up and putting up with me."

"I would have preferred Will Smith, but you were pretty good company, Ellen."

"I enjoyed the break—until last night."

"You'll feel better when you get home and talk to Drew."

"What if he's dumped me? I couldn't handle it."

"You'll handle it. You're handling the divorce. That's far more difficult."

"I'm not so sure. This is a double-whammy. Maybe I made two disastrous choices back-to-back—one long-term, one short-term. It reminds me of 'Let's Make A Deal.' I'd like to trade them both for what's behind the curtain. With my luck, I'd end up with another schmuck."

"Don't jump to conclusions. He may have a perfectly good explanation."

"Spoken like a true friend." Ellen spied a sundries shop. "Be right back. I need a pack of ciggies." She hated herself for it. She had started smoking when the ca-ca hit the fan with Ron, and promised herself daily that she'd quit.

She paid the clerk, pocketed the pack and turned to go, then stopped. The line snaked into the corridor. They're going to kill me, she thought, eyeing the customers. She pushed the pack toward the clerk. "Time to get rid of *all* the carcinogens in my life. I'll take four bags of M&Ms instead."

The customers cheered.

"Here's something for the plane." Sandy handed Ellen a copy of *Playgirl.* "This should take your mind off your troubles, for a while at least."

Ellen stuck it in her carry-on. "I love to sink my teeth into a good man, er, mag."

Sandy walked Ellen to the gate. "Take care of yourself. I hope things work out."

"They always do. Thanks for everything. I'll call you tomorrow."

Ellen bumped her way up the aisle of the 757, scattering "sorries" like rose petals. She made eye contact with a mustached man in wire-rimmed glasses.

"Can I help you with that big bag?"

"Really? Would you? Thanks."

She slid the strap from her sunburned shoulder. Dirty laundry and shells filled the bag to bursting. The man's cheeks puffed as he hoisted it into the overhead bin.

I hope he doesn't sue me for a double hernia.

A pair of undies fell out, landing on his head like a yarmulke. "I'm sorry." She stuffed them in her purse.

He looked excited.

She shoehorned herself into the seat next to the Samaritan. *Must be designed by and for Munchkins. What do fat people do?* Her skin, gritty from a last dip in the Gulf, snagged her clothing. She looked around the cabin for signs that the odor of shells and her damp bathing suit offended other passengers.

She flipped through *Playgirl*. But her thoughts hop-scotched between Ron and Drew, not air-brushed schlongs and ads for ben wa balls.

The flight attendant pushed the cart down the aisle. The little man snored. "Wiped out from hoisting my bag. Bottled water, please." Ellen remembered that bottled water might be worse than tap water because of bacteria in the plastic. *Christ, something else to worry about.*

She ripped open a bag of pretzels and heard Elizabeth's mantra: "Nurture yourself."

As she finished the last pretzel—no calories, no fat and no taste—she wondered if self-nurturing included eating a seven-ounce Hershey bar for dinner and crying in the shower.

Somewhere over Georgia, she picked up the air phone and dialed Drew. *How could he dump me without so much as a, "So long, it's been good to know you?" Maybe he's ill. Some affliction that rendered him speechless. Maybe he's pushing up a*

Meadowlands goalpost with Hoffa. Maybe his tongue fell out.

His answering machine clicked on and his voice sent chills through her sun-warmed body. "Hello Drew. This is Ellen. E-l-l-e-n. We have some unfinished business. If you didn't break your neck skiing, call me tomorrow."

Her seatmate woke up. "My stock broker," she said. "He sold when he should have bought."

She thought of Ron doing Casey. And Drew—incommunicado. "Men. Who needs 'em?" Between her sunburn and itch to demystify The Odd Disappearance of Drew, or The Disappearance of Odd Drew, Ellen began to squirm.

Nectar dripped from the PA system as the plane began its descent over Richmond. "Those of you using portable electronic devices, please turn them OFF and stow them for landing."

Ellen thought of the sex toy buried in her bag. "For when we can't be together," Drew had said. "Think of me when you use it." She still hadn't tried it. What a strange gift, she had thought at the time. Now the gesture was pregnant with meaning. *He's gone and I'm left with a vibrating tongue.*

Ellen was sure that anyone watching their romantic comedy (PG-13), would think they had wandered onto Stephen King's latest by mistake. One second he had been there, then he was gone.

The pilot warned of turbulence. Ellen brought her seat to the upright position and tightened her belt. She heard the voice of Bette Davis in "All About Eve."

"Fasten your seatbelts. It's going to be a bumpy night."

Beth Rubin

The plane cleared the clouds near Annapolis and Ellen spied the State House and Academy. She couldn't wait to pick up Penny at the kennel and get home. As the 757 lurched toward Baltimore, she imagined a huge question mark hanging in the cabin, along with a dank smell from her bag.

CHAPTER 15

Twenty minutes early and breathless, Ellen hoped the patient before her had finished *kvetching* ahead of schedule.

When Drew reentered Ellen's life, thickening the plot faster than cornstarch, the sessions were never long enough. Every time Ellen was poised to uncover something meaningful, Elizabeth would say, "We'll have to stop now."

Ellen was sure Elizabeth had aced the graduate course in Keeping the Patient Hanging.

Elizabeth greeted her. "Come on back. You look well. Nice sunburn."

"I'm burned, all right. And burning. I'm glad to see you. I almost camped out in the hall last night."

"What's going on?"

"I called Drew from Florida and the plane and he never returned the call."

"He didn't?"

"And I called when I got home. He didn't pick up. It's obvious he wants nothing to do with me. But *why*, I keep asking myself. I'm not sleeping. And my appetite has taken a powder. You know, I had been gaining weight. What do you think?"

"That is perplexing." Ellen declined Elizabeth's offer of M&Ms.

"I don't know what to do."

"You could write him a short note, say you're concerned about him."

"I'll try it. I'll try anything."

"He may find it less threatening than a call."

"I can't believe he did this. Why?"

"I don't have an answer for you."

"I was feeling so good. I'm devastated. I cry all the time. I cry at red lights. When I hear a love song I go to pieces."

"Feel the sadness. Don't fight it," Elizabeth said, *sotto voce.*

"I can't deal with this. Maybe I need medication. Something fast-acting like arsenic."

Elizabeth gave her an enigmatic smile. "Under the circumstances, I think you're making remarkable progress without drugs."

"I trusted him. Loved him. He betrayed me."

"Slow down. Who are you talking about?"

"No. 2."

"No. 2?"

"Yes, No. 2. Ron is No. 1. Drew is No. 2."

The talk ricocheted, a bullet gone berserk, between No. 1 and No. 2. As her anger bubbled, Ellen labeled them Asshole No. 1 and Asshole No. 2. "I'm in free fall, Elizabeth."

"You're in mourning."

"Maybe I should ditch decorating and become a professional mourner."

Elizabeth looked at her watch. "We have to stop now."

She walked Ellen to the door. "Call me if you need to. You're too hard on yourself. This will take time."

* * * *

"Walkies," Ellen called. On a putty-colored day that mirrored her mood, she leashed Penny. She had been stuck in neutral since returning from Florida a

Split Ends

month before. She petted the dog, dreading the day when Penny would abandon her for the great fire hydrant in the sky. *Nothing like a dog's unconditional love and loyalty. Unlike the men in my life. Or out of my life.*

The phone rang as they reached the door. Taking the stairs two at a time, Ellen tripped and twisted her ankle. *Any explanation would be better than none. He could tell me my feet are too big, that he's engaged to Julia Roberts or insane—which I already know.*

On the third ring Ellen grabbed the receiver, nearly pulling the cord from the wall. Her heart sank.

Mady's twice-a-day calls grated. No matter how Ellen reassured her, Mady called to make sure her daughter hadn't taken a nosedive into the frigid Severn. Ellen had enough trouble keeping her own oars in the water without having to stroke for her mother.

She drew a deep breath. "So, how are things in Joisey?"

"Fine. How are you?" Ellen would have told a friend the truth. Pretending everything was hunky-dory exhausted her. She counted to 10.

"I'm doing fine, Mom. No closer than yesterday to sticking my head in the oven. Too bad it's electric."

"I'm worried about you. I don't know how you're coping."

"Faith in the goodness of men."

"You're so strong. If it was me, I'd chase some pills with a fifth of scotch. Oy gevalt! I shouldn't have said that, Ellen. No matter how bad you feel, life is precious. You're young and attractive ... and ..."

"Chill, Mom. I'm not going to commit 'sewer pipes,' as Daddy used to say. I'm hurting and I'm pissed off, but I'll get over it. Try not to worry."

"Aren't you lonely?"

"No, Mom. I haven't been lonely since Ron moved out. Lonely was living in the same house with someone who was not home. That was lonely. Alone and lonely are mutually exclusive."

"Have you heard from that prick, No. 2?"

"A month ago you thought he was a prince."

"That was then. He relinquished his title. If I could get away with it, I'd hire Dominic Matuso."

"Who?"

"Dominic Matuso, my neighbor. They don't call him the Ice Man for nothing."

"Save Dominic for someone important."

"You're too calm, Ellen. You need to get angry and stay angry."

"I don't have the energy."

"I was wondering," Mady said, "maybe No. 2 had a heart attack."

Ellen pictured Drew lying in the ICU, hooked up to a snarl of tubes and monitors. As a dyke in white removed the bedpan and wiped his ass with sandpaper, Drew would whisper his dying words, "Ellen, I love you, please forgive me." Then he'd crap out.

"Nice try, Mom. I prefer to think of him pinned at the crotch beneath an 18-wheeler." The words were barely out of her mouth when tears dripped down her cheeks. Leave it to Frank, crooning, "Where Are You?" from the family room.

Where are you, indeed? She dabbed at her eyes. Penny circled, wrapping her leash around Ellen's legs.

Split Ends

Her mother's voice dragged her back to the real world, which sucked.

"Are you eating?"

I can't tell her I'm losing weight again. She'll call in UNICEF. "Yes. I had a dozen eggs, rasher of bacon and six pieces of toast for breakfast. Remember when I blew up in college and you bugged me to lose weight? Now you bug me to eat."

"You're too thin. I'm worried about you. It's my job. I'm your mother."

"Please don't worry. This time next year I'll be on a diet of celery and watercress."

"That would be refreshing. I'll hold on to that thought."

"I think we've covered the last 12 hours of my fabulous life, Ma, and Penny is about to pee on the floor. I'll call later with the next exciting installment."

"Take care of yourself. And don't forget to eat."

"I won't."

"God bless."

"Thank her for me." Ellen hung up and stepped in a puddle of dog piss.

CHAPTER 16

"Maybe Drew disappeared until you're free. He may think he pushed you into divorcing Ron."

"That's crazy. I told him I was out of the marriage."

"He sounded like a dream."

"Well, the dream turned to a mirage."

"You had so much in common."

"I thought we did. I guess it was too good to be true."

"Maybe he couldn't handle his own feelings. Maybe he fears commitment."

"Could be, Amy. Maybe it's not about me."

Ellen sat on the rumpled spread in sweats she'd worn for 72 hours. Candy wrappers and empty tissue boxes littered Ron's former side of the bed. Scattered on the carpet were her bibles, "The Dance of Anger," "Codependent No More," "Men Are From Mars, Women Are From Venus," "Women Who Love Too Much" and "Men Who Can't Love."

"Put yourself in his shoes," Amy said. "He could have thought you and Ron would reconcile and he'd be left holding the bag. Maybe he fled to protect himself."

"I've been reading 'Men Are From Mars.' One theory holds that men retreat to their caves to solve their problems alone. They think too much intimacy robs them of their power."

"I read it. I think there's something to it."

"What I want to know is: How many sticks of dynamite would it take to blow up the cave?"

Ellen pictured Amy in her brick Tudor near Lake Erie. Amy giggled. "Could be he's in his cave, deciding his next move. Maybe he's sick or had an accident."

"He's sick all right. But I'm the one who had the accident."

"Is there anyone you could call?"

"No one. I don't think he's in touch with anyone I know. Or with reality. Amy, I feel like I've been buried under a ton of earth. If he does call, what will he say? 'I've had amnesia? Lost your number?' The schmuck."

"What bad timing. I had never heard you so elated."

"This has knocked me flat on my ass. He told me he loved me. But I guess he never gave a damn."

"I think he cared for you."

"I tell myself that normal people can't turn off their feelings like a faucet."

"Maybe he's not normal, Ellen."

Ellen used the last tissue and flung the box at the wall. "I was needy as hell. Probably scared the shit out of him with my neediness."

She poked her pinky through a cigarette burn in the spread. "Maybe I was just another notch on his bedpost." She felt weak, doubted she could walk to the bathroom unaided.

"Stop blaming yourself."

"He played me for a fool, Amy. And I let him. No, he cared. I'm sure of it." She picked at an orange M&M ground into the knee of her sweat pants.

"Maybe he backed off until your divorce is final. I'm proud of you. It took enormous courage to stand up to Ron. You have a lot of strength."

"I don't have the strength to floss."

"Remember when our kids were learning to walk? How we had to let go? Maybe Drew let go so you could take your first steps as a single woman alone."

"If that were the case, why didn't he say something about it?"

"Suppose he had. Wouldn't it have muddied the water, knowing he was waiting?"

"Who knows. He blew it. Jerk."

"You must be in pain."

"Pain it is. I feel like I'm crawling away from a wreck and I'm not sure I'll make it."

"You're spooking me."

"Don't worry. I won't OD on brownies."

"This is a huge shock, Ellen. There's a lot on your plate. Be patient."

"That's what Elizabeth says. Time is my enemy. It's moving backward. Tock-tick, tock-tick. But I'm not getting any younger." The phone went silent. Ellen thought her cousin had hung up.

"Remember when we were in high school and your parents sent you to Cleveland to get you away from him?" Amy asked.

"It was insane." Old anger sputtered inside her, corrosive as battery acid. "They thought a week in Shaker Heights would make me forget him. It didn't work. Wish it had."

"You wore his shirt all the time, even slept in it."

"I still owe your parents for the long distance calls. God, that was a long time ago. Damn, I just want an answer so I can get unstuck."

"Ellen, you have an answer. He dumped you."

Ellen heard impatience in Amy's voice. "You're right, of course."

Split Ends

"I don't mean to be cruel. What he did was horrible. Inexcusable. But you have to move on."

"I'm trying."

"Some day he may resurface. Until then, find your own answers. They're the only ones that matter."

"Thanks for the straight talk."

"What's happening with the divorce?"

"The discovery process is endless. Ron is still trying to push my buttons, trying to punish me for his sins."

"It's easier than taking responsibility."

"He says he's moving back when six months are up. Unfortunately, I agreed to that. It's soon, Amy. Too soon. If he comes back, I may have to leave."

"Why?"

"If we spend one night under the same roof it cancels the time we've lived apart. In this enlightened state it's cohabitation even if we sleep in different beds on different floors behind locked doors. You have to live apart for 365 consecutive days."

"That's medieval. My friend in Colorado divorced in three months."

"How about prehistoric?"

"Would you consider moving out?"

"I'd like to stay in the house—alone—until the divorce is final. He owes me that much."

"What can I do to help?"

"Nothing. I have to do this on my own."

"Want me to come? You want to come here for a visit?"

"Not now. I'll file your offer."

"Don't forget, you can call me anytime, even at 3 A.M."

"Thanks for sharing my garbage. You're such a good cousin ... and friend."

"That's what I'm here for. Are you sure you're all right?"

"Happy as a clam at high tide."

Ellen walked to the window and stretched. Her back was stiff from too many hours in bed. The sky and water merged in a thick gray soup. Two children lay spread-eagle making angels. They rose and ran toward a green clapboard house, snow flying off their backs. *What are they so happy about?*

Ellen petted Penny and sank into the pillows. The silence was deafening. She opened a book on astrology for clues to Drew's behavior.

"Be prepared for the unexpected ... Toss your ego into the wastebasket or his coolly impersonal approach will be sure to bruise it."

How true.

"Vague dreamy eyes ... freedom loving ... independent ... few intimates ... seldom settles down to steady relationship for more than a limited period."

Wish I had read that six months ago.

"It does little good to make an emotional appeal, but if you touch his heart, he'll come back to see what he might have missed ... don't try to interrupt his solitude ... Fights best with his hat: he puts it on and leaves."

So it seems.

She tossed the book on the floor and Penny jumped. I'll write to him, Ellen thought, and felt instantly energized.

Split Ends

It's a Hail-Mary pass, but it might provoke a response. All I want is closure. I don't want him back. If he did it once, he could do it again.

On her way to the desk she eyed her hair, hanging in lifeless strings. There was room for a family of kangaroos in the pouches under her eyes. Ellen tore herself away from the scary image before her cheek hollows devoured her.

Paper in hand, she returned to her quilted oasis.

Dear Drew:
   I have to get a few things off my chest. For the record, in many ways we're two peas in a pod. We're independent. We need lots of space. We like spontaneity. We laugh at the same things. We're sensitive. We're passionate. We revere the natural world. We enjoy books and art and music. We love to *fress* ('eat a lot,' *shegets*). I thought we were friends. Why did you dump me?

Ellen turned on the radio. Temperatures in the teens. Another six inches of snow.

Is this the winter of my discontent, or what? What else can go wrong?

* * * *

Ellen switched stations. Elizabeth's words came back.

"You're grieving over the death of the dream with Ron and you'll continue to do so. Every step toward divorce stirs up feelings of loss. It's a process. When you're feeling down, remind yourself that your husband betrayed you. And he didn't fulfill your needs."

"Okay," Ellen had said. "Do a reality check when I'm sad over Ron. What about Drew? There's no relief. I see his face on an IMAX screen. The sound track is deafening. I'm up front, pressed to that screen. All I want is a seat in the back row."

"What about the physical pain you had mentioned?"

"It's worn itself down to a dull ache."

"Good."

"Christ, you sound like a mother whose kid dumped in the potty for the first time. Big whoop."

"How does it feel, face pressed against the screen?"

"Awful. Like I'm strapped in a chair and forced to watch Wayne Newton 24-7. I can't stand the performer—or his music—but I can't leave. Drew is in my face waking and sleeping. He's with me first thing in the morning, last thing at night. Even when I'm dreaming. It's torture."

Elizabeth smiled. Elizabeth always smiled. Ellen felt like punching Elizabeth in her smiling, fuchsia mouth.

"What you're going through is normal after such an intense relationship. You're reacting to strong external stimuli."

"You're not going to believe this. I was driving on the Beltway a few days ago. I had brought a banana to eat in the car. I'm doing 70 with half a banana sticking out of my mouth, and I start to bawl. I'm talking major tears, Elizabeth. 'What's this all about?' I wondered.

Split Ends

Then I realized that it reminded me of Drew. How's that for a strong external stimulus?"

Elizabeth laughed and shook her head. "You may not think so, but you're making progress."

"Some progress. Now I'm only depressed 18 hours a day. Could you put it in language a mentally challenged mid-lifer can understand?"

"Think of it this way: Right after he dumped you, you thought about him 75 percent of the time. Then it dropped to 50 percent. Keep track of the time you spend thinking of him."

"No wonder I'm having trouble. I can't do math."

Elizabeth rubbed her forehead. "It takes time."

"Time. I wish I could propel myself into the next millennium. I feel like I'm slogging through mud trying to reach higher ground. But it's raining. And not some gentle spring shower. It's a fucking monsoon."

Elizabeth tapped the pencil to her lips. "Think of 'The Bridges of Madison County.' You read it, didn't you?"

"Read it, saw the movie twice. Cried in all the right places."

"Try to encapsulate the experience. Pretend you're Meryl Streep."

"Very funny. Can I be Mother Teresa next week?"

"It's the dream you're missing."

"There's the d-word again. I think night terror better describes it. Maybe someday he'll tell me what happened. Meanwhile, an avalanche should bury him."

Ellen read the annoyance in Elizabeth's expression.

"He's not trying to be spiteful. Some men are limited when it comes to any sense of commitment. He may feel trapped. Remember, he created the problem. You didn't do anything wrong."

"Is there an echo in here?" Ellen looked around the pastel office, soothing as a nursery.

"Ask yourself why you're drawn to difficult men. Maybe reliability and consistency are boring to you. Why? Where does it come from? Some women like a challenge."

"Yeah, I've always enjoyed a challenge. I always went for the bad boys because they had zip-a-dee-do-dah."

Ellen tuned out Elizabeth. She wedged a pillow behind her back and began reading an interview with Jack Nicholson in *GQ*.

"What accounts for all the tension between men and women these days? What would make her happy?" the interviewer asks.

"The woman needs a sense of danger in a man, whether it's fake or real," Nicholson answers.

Is that it? Do I need a sense of danger?

She turned the page to an ad for Nioxin, "for thick healthy hair." A man with a receding hairline gazes at 10 lovelies trimming, watering and fertilizing what's left of his grass. Ellen imagined a similar ad: With cautery guns, the gardeners inject an antidote to commitment phobia into the cerebral cortex.

Ellen reached over, picked up the letter and ripped it to shreds.

CHAPTER 17

Ellen sat down and opened the wrapper. "Want some?"

"Thanks. What's been going on?"

"I had the same dream three nights running. Drew shows up at my door and takes my hand. I wake up feeling euphoric. Reality kicks in and I crash and burn."

"Women often dream of white knights who will sweep them off their feet and carry them away. Especially women in unhappy relationships like your marriage. You have to recognize it for what it is—a fantasy."

"This was no fantasy." Ellen wished for his arms around her. "Maybe he's regrouping. I know what happened was real."

Elizabeth adjusted the thigh-high slit of her skirt and popped an M&M. "Most men are on remote control at the start of a relationship. In the beginning it's very romantic. Their attitude is, 'This'll be fine for now,' but they shy away from commitment. He was probably touched in a way he had not been in a long time and said, 'This is too much for me.'"

"But he was a soul mate. Until he disappeared."

"He's no soul mate. He's a schmuck. He blitzed you, changed his mind, then took the cowardly way out."

"I'm certain he was sincere."

"He was sincere in what he said and did *at the time*," Elizabeth said through clenched teeth.

"Knock, knock. Nobody home. It's so frustrating. I hang in with the marriage, my husband porks his paralegal—and maybe the Redskins' cheerleading squad. I meet someone with all the right stuff and he aborts the mission."

"You have to remember there are two kinds of men," she said between crunches. "You were married to a marathoner. Drew was a sprinter."

"I told him I enjoyed my freedom. Christ, I gave at the office."

"Rational explanations don't apply. You're giving him too much credit. You still treat him as if he was playing with a full deck."

"How come ..." Elizabeth hushed her with a raised hand, and Ellen knew that her therapist was not done spawning this pearl.

"He's not only playing with an incomplete deck, he left the game before you had a chance to discover what cards were missing."

"I was never more myself. Maybe I smothered him."

"It's not your fault. You gave him a great big gift. It's his problem. And his loss."

"Yeah, it's his problem. Meanwhile, it's worse than when I was 16. Billy Crystal makes me sad."

"What have you learned from the experience?"

"Become a lesbian."

"I've treated several gays," Elizabeth said with a straight face. "They have the same problems with relationships as heterosexuals."

"Spare me, please. I'm kidding."

"The positive thing you've learned," Elizabeth said, "is that you're capable of feeling deeply and there are people who can fulfill your needs."

Split Ends

"Great. I ate filet mignon and loved it. Now I'm sick because the meat was tainted."

"You need to balance the emotional with the cognitive in the future."

"Huh?"

"Balance your heart and head; your feeling and thinking sides."

"I did cognitive to death with Ron. I think I'll just bypass future relationships."

"I think you'll change your mind. Right now you need to get with yourself for a while."

"For how long? I'm running out of things to say to myself."

"I think you'll be ready to date in a few months."

"Yuck. Makes me think of my kids' attitude to broccoli. I don't want to share a cup of coffee with a man. A relationship? Inconceivable. As for sex, I'm a quart low. My interest is zilch."

"Don't be afraid to feel the anger."

"I've always thought anger and sadness were signs of weakness. I used to hide in the bathroom, run the water so no one would hear me crying."

"I hope you no longer do that."

Ellen nodded. "I'm learning to express it."

"What else is going on?"

"I have black cord fever at night. Keep reaching for the phone."

"You could call Drew, but you'd be stirring things up. Try to look at it as AFGE."

"What's that?"

"Another fucking growing experience."

"I love it when you talk dirty."

"When you feel the desire to call, ask yourself, What do I hope to accomplish?"

"It would accomplish nothing. There's no there there, and I won't die of him, but I still want closure."

"You'll have to be patient."

"How do you spell that?"

"You may be repeating in relationships the role you played with your parents."

"I'm beginning to connect those dots. They were loving but tough. It was their way or the highway. I was always trying to please them. Never felt I was good enough just being me."

Ellen's jaw dropped. "And I did the same in my marriage. Ron loved me as long as I was a doll. A dummy's more like it."

Her eyes met Elizabeth's.

"It sounds like you're used to receiving conditional love, with strings attached."

"Hmm. Drew offered the possibility of unconditional love. But he withdrew the offer," Ellen whispered. She slapped her thigh. "Damn, I'm not chopped liver. I deserve better."

* * * *

Ellen parked her cart in front of the onions and potatoes. She examined several heads of romaine. She put one, its glistening leaves grit-free, in a plastic bag and pitched it into the cart. It landed on a pineapple. *Just like a man. Hard and prickly on the outside. Sweet and juicy inside, but with a useless core.*

She checked her list, items sorted by aisle. Ellen couldn't get from A to B without a list. It wasn't unusual for her to make lists of lists. But she often forgot where she had put the list she needed. Especially the list of pros and cons of contacting Drew.

She lifted the cardboard lid and rolled the eggs one at a time to make sure they weren't cracked. She remembered how Drew had done the same thing.

That day, she couldn't believe that food shopping could be so much fun. She had wondered how they looked together. Did the other customers think they were siblings? Lovers? Friends?

In the produce section she had giggled.

Drew had asked, "What's so funny?"

"I feel like we're old, married geezers." Later she had realized her comment had been a mistake. Too intimate. Too threatening.

"Raisin bread, English muffins, or bagels?" he had asked.

"You choose. I like all of 'em."

He had shrugged, sexy in his leather jacket, and grabbed all three. Ron would have bought one bagel to share.

When Drew had asked the butcher to cut four strip steaks, Ellen had asked, "Why four? I don't have much of an appetite."

He had smiled, touched the tip of her nose. "That's what you said the other night."

* * * *

On her way to the dairy section, a familiar body loped by. Ellen's legs turned to rubber at the sight of the man's rear, round as Parker House rolls. Her eyes scampered up his back to the chocolate hair teasing his collar.

Ellen shifted into second gear and took off like a shot. She sideswiped an old man bent over a freezer case, nearly knocking him into a stack of pizzas. The stranger had disappeared into the canned fruits and juices.

"We might not see each other all the time, but I'll always be here for you," Drew had said. He sure picked a strange place to resurface. But strange was not out of character.

Maybe he planned to show up with a peace offering of cauliflower and laundry detergent. Maybe he'd spirit her away.

Ellen rounded Aisle 6 like a race car driver and nearly trampled a toddler. She crashed into a display stand on the hairpin turn, knocking potato chips to the floor.

She caught up with him as he examined a box of cereal. There was no mistaking Drew's beefy build. The knot in her chest tightened. He turned around. About 40, he had a pug nose and brown eyes.

He sidestepped her and rumbled down the aisle. Before he could report her weird behavior to the store manager, she wheeled toward the canned meats. Eyes brimming, she scanned the Spam and tuna.

"Paper please," Ellen said at the checkout. She envied the way the cashier's cantaloupes filled her sweater.

God, 50 and still waiting for breasts. Get real, woman.

She emptied the cart and watched the bananas riding the rubber belt. When Ellen had had diarrhea as

Split Ends

a child, Mady had always pushed bananas. "They're binding," she would say.

Whenever Ellen heard 'binding' she pictured a bottle of Lepage's glue, its flat lips drooling a mucilage stream to seal her tush forever. She wondered what Elizabeth would say about that.

Ellen searched for flaws in the cashier's complexion. It was a futile quest. A nail snapped when she tried to remove the credit card from her wallet. It hurt like hell and started to bleed. She sucked the finger. Her heart began to pound. She freed the card but couldn't slide it through the scanner.

"I'm having a panic attack," she whispered to the Cantaloupe Queen. "Please help me."

The checker patted Ellen's hand and summoned a bagger. Inhaling and exhaling until the drums moderated, Ellen glanced around to see who had watched her pathetic display. The store was quiet. Pug Nose smiled in the next aisle.

She pulled herself together in the car, then remembered what lay ahead that evening. She and Ron were to discuss living arrangements. Again.

Ellen missed Ron as much as a migraine. But dinner would be worth the discomfort if she could convince him to stay away another six months. She pulled into the driveway and began to make a mental list.

If you give me another six months in the house, you can have the remote, Phillips and plumber's helper. I want the Scrabble set, Tupperware and my grandmother's pitcher.

After unpacking the groceries she went to her closet and vacillated between her black pantsuit and beige knit dress. She wanted to look her best; to remind Ron of what he had scrapped. As if he'd notice. She reached for the black pantsuit. It was appropriate for a lady in mourning.

* * * *

"A martini straight up, hold the vermouth, and a cup of crab soup."

Ron ordered three courses and mopped his forehead with the napkin. "I'm a man of few words."

Jeez. Now he's into self-awareness?

Ellen sighed. "Yes, Ron."

"I made a mistake. I need your forgiveness."

"I forgive you."

That was easy.

"I want to come home. I want to be your husband again."

Not so easy.

"Ron. I like being on my own. I want to be on my own. Need to be on my own."

"I can't suddenly let go of our marriage."

You've been letting go for years. "For the first time in my life I'm taking care of myself, trusting myself. I have to get my act together before I can be a partner to anyone."

"I've changed, Ellen. I'll show you. I'll be more attentive. We'll go away. Anyplace you say. You can have a maid once a week. I want to come back. I want to help you."

"Help me? Help me *what*? I'm helping myself."

"You're serious about this divorce business?"

"I am."

Split Ends

His voice rose. "You're fucked up. That shrink of yours needs to talk some sense into you."

She started to titter. He got red in the face.

"I'm coming back to the house, Ellen. And you've got nowhere to go."

CHAPTER 18

On Valentine's Day—and Drew's birthday—Ellen eviscerated a chicken. Drew's face played in her mind as her fist went into the cavity. She grabbed the heart and giblets, stuffed them down the disposal and flipped the switch. "Take that, motherfucker."

Later in the morning Wilma stopped by.

"Shouldn't you be packing?"

"I'm packed, Ellen. What do I smell?"

"Jewish penicillin."

"I wish I wasn't leaving. I love your chicken soup."

"I'll freeze some for you."

"How's Penny?"

"Still in the hospital. They're running more tests. I'll pick her up at 1:00. I thought she had an upset stomach. I'm really worried." *If something happens to Penny now, I'm cashing in my chips.*

"I'm praying she'll be all right."

"Pray hard, Wilma."

"I see you got flowers." Wilma winked. "From someone special?"

"No. They're from Ron. I stuffed them into a chipped vase without adding preservative. He used to bring me half-dead mums wrapped in newspaper once in a while. Now it's roses."

"Why is he sending flowers?"

"He's pulling out all the stops. Trying to get back in my good graces. Too little, too late."

"Steven's very thoughtful that way. He brings me flowers all the time."

"That's nice."

Split Ends

"I hope someone comes along who appreciates you."

"Thanks, Wilma."

They moved to the family room and warmed themselves with spiced tea while cursing the barren winter landscape.

"Have you lost weight again?"

"A few pounds."

"Ellen, you must eat."

"Yes, mother. But there's a boulder in my throat. I wish I could bottle the appetite suppressant that comes with depression. Is it possible to be thin and happy at the same time?"

Wilma laughed. "I'd like to think so."

"You're the exception who proves the rule."

"Drink milkshakes and add a raw egg."

Ellen grimaced. "I don't think so."

"You don't seem depressed. Not like you were. In fact, you seem pretty much your old self."

"Oh, how was that?"

"Crazy."

Ellen snickered, spilling tea on herself. She dabbed at the stain. "I feel good most of the time. I'm stressed over the divorce business. The attorneys are dragging it out. And Ron's still telling everyone he hopes we'll get back together. Where is his head?"

"Where the sun don't shine. He told Steven the same thing. Denial is a powerful emotion."

"So I've heard." They walked to the kitchen and Wilma set her mug in the sink. "I'd better leave. Do you want our number?"

"No. I'll be fine. Have a wonderful trip."

Beth Rubin

"You're on your way, Ellen. Spring is coming. I'm thinking good thoughts about you and Penny. Happy Valentine's Day."

"Same to you. See you in a week."

* * * *

The technician brought Penny into the waiting room. The dog wobbled and appeared disoriented. Penny had always rushed to greet Ellen after any separation. Even when Ellen returned from taking out the trash.

Ellen kneeled to hug Penny. The dog collapsed. Ellen screamed. A swarthy man with a parrot on his shoulder looked on as Dr. Holmes rushed into the waiting room and checked Penny's heart. "We'll start an IV drip and keep a close watch on her. You may as well go home. I'll call you as soon as she's stabilized."

Ellen drove home in a daze, forgetting to lower the garage door. At least Ron wasn't there to chastise her. It also would have infuriated him to know that she left lights burning while he still paid the electric bill. *Tough titty.*

* * * *

As the aroma of warming French bread filled the kitchen, Ellen waited for the phone to ring. She had begun to fix a goat cheese salad for dinner. She whisked a vinaigrette and wondered how Drew was celebrating his birthday.

She scanned her latest phone bill—horrendous. Until the attorneys settled the marital assets (before her

90th birthday she hoped), she had cut back on extras. But she needed Amy and Sandy, her out-of-state support group.

"Damn, what's taking so long?"

She grabbed the ringing phone.

"Happy Valentine's Day? Who is this? No, I'm not interested in light bulbs with a lifetime guarantee. My husband might be. Want his number?"

Call waiting beeped.

"Mrs. Gold, this is Dr. Holmes. I'm afraid I have some bad news about Penny. Her belly feels full and I suspect she's bleeding internally. Will you give me permission to do a tap? If I draw blood, I'm afraid there's not much hope.

"Yes, of course. Call me the second you know." She broke into racking sobs.

"I'm sorry," Dr. Holmes said not ten minutes later. "The syringe was full of blood. I doubt she'll make it through the night."

"Oh my God. I can't believe this. Don't do anything until I get there. I want to be with her when you put her down."

"Are you sure you want to come? I don't think I would if it were my pet."

"I'm sure." *I have to see Penny a final time. Have to say good-bye. I wouldn't dream of letting Penny die alone.*

"I'll be there in 20 minutes."

"I don't think you're in any condition to drive. Is there someone who could bring you?"

"You're right. But I don't know who to call." Michael was in class and Wilma had left for Florida. Reluctantly, she called her next-door neighbors.

Eighty if they were a day, the Gibsons were darling; models of what she had hoped she and Ron would be in their twilight years. Ellen hated to impose. They were plagued with health problems and the evening was bitter. But the vet was right. She was in no shape to drive.

Coatless and clutching a box of tissues, she slid into the Gibsons' car. As they told of their experiences putting down family pets, Ellen tried to be polite and tune out the conversation. *I know you mean well, but not now, please.*

They pulled into the hospital parking lot. The light was on over the Dutch door.

They went into an examination room. Brown paper was taped over the door's glass panel. A clean white mat lay on the floor.

"I don't ever want to see this room again," Ellen told the Gibsons. They insisted on staying with her.

Expecting Penny would be carried in, Ellen was shocked when her dog bounded in under her own power, tail high. "Are you sure? Are you sure?" Ellen sobbed to the vet. "She seems normal. Are you sure?"

"I'm sure," Dr. Holmes said. "The medication has perked her up, but she's very sick. I'm so sorry. I wish we could save them all."

Penny lay down on the mat as if it were her favorite scatter rug at home. Ellen kneeled and buried her face in the dog's pale hair, streaked with gray like her own. She hugged her companion and whispered, "I love you Penny, I'll miss you. You're a good girl. Good dog. I love you."

Split Ends

Dr. Holmes picked up the syringe. While Ellen clung to Penny, it was done. Ellen felt spasms travel through the dog's body. Penny went still.

"She's gone," Dr. Holmes said and touched Ellen's shoulder. Ellen held onto Penny, soaking the dog's coat with tears. The vet offered her a tissue and tried to coax her up. Ellen could not let go.

Even though she couldn't afford it, Ellen arranged to have Penny cremated.

"We'll have the remains in a week. You have 120 days after that to pick them up," the technician said.

"Then what?"

"We dispose of them."

I don't care about the $300. I want Penny's ashes.

Ellen wondered why Ron hated Penny. Maybe he was jealous of her good nature and fidelity. The dog cowered whenever he entered a room, giving him a wide berth, as Ellen had. *They say things happen in threes.* She counted her losses: Ron, Drew and now Penny. I've shot my wad. Paid my dues for the next few years at least.

Ellen sniffled in the car.

"It's a shame people can't get the same consideration," Ruth Gibson said. The Gibsons were members of the Hemlock Society.

Ellen didn't doubt for a second what they would do when the time came. She thought of Penny and sensed the death spasms in her own body.

They insisted she come in for a drink and invited her to spend the night. She gulped some sherry, thanked them and assured them she'd be all right. Tears froze on her cheeks as she ran home. Her friend would never again be waiting to welcome her with a wet kiss and wagging tail. She crossed the threshold and a clump of Penny's hair flew up to greet her in the empty hallway.

CHAPTER 19

The Andouille sausage browned and Ellen tried to calculate how many meals she had fixed for Ron over the years. She lost count somewhere around 21,000.

She had been setting the table when Lisa and Josh arrived. They met in the hall and kissed. "Hi kids. Welcome to Bourbon Street north."

"It smells good, Mom. What's cooking?"

"Jambalaya, red beans and rice."

"Dessert?"

"Bread pudding and whiskey sauce."

"I'm glad I skipped lunch," Josh said and left the room.

Lisa sat down and began to rock in the chair—a childhood habit that told Ellen something was bothering her daughter.

"Everything all right, Lisa?"

Lisa stopped rocking. "Mom, I owe you an apology."

"You do? For what?"

"I gave you a hard time when you and Dad separated. I'm sorry." Ellen sat down across from her daughter.

"You were upset. I understand."

"It hit me real hard. I took it for granted you would always be together. It wasn't fair to blame you. I saw how you tried. I love Dad, but he can be difficult. I hope you're happy now. You seem to be, and you deserve it."

"Thanks, Pumpkin. I love you too."

Ellen touched her daughter's cheek. She got up to stir the sausage into the tomato mixture.

"Marriage takes work, Lisa. I'm hardly an expert, but I believe it takes day-to-day effort. Even then, there are no guarantees. Sometimes things happen that are out of our control."

Ellen went to her daughter, massaged her shoulders. "Lisa, always remember who you are."

"What do you mean?"

"It's easy to lose your identity when you're part of a couple. Hold onto who you were before you became a wife."

"An overworked, underpaid social worker?"

Ellen laughed. "You were, and are, a caring, intelligent, independent woman. I'm so proud of you."

"I'm proud of you too."

"Thanks, Sweetie. Respect yourself. And trust your instincts. Speak up when you have concerns. Most men believe they're the center of the universe. And we women have helped perpetuate that myth. While you're taking care of Josh, trying to meet his needs, take care of your own. Preserve your center, yourself. Capiche?"

Lisa reached up and took Ellen's hand. "I'm trying, Mom. You're right, it's a day-to-day thing."

"Sharing a life with someone can be a joy. Your father and I had good times. I hope you know that." Ellen kissed her daughter. "Listen to me, Dr. Laura Yenta. You and Josh are doing a wonderful job. If you hit a rough patch, I'm always here to listen."

"I'm here for you too. Are you going to be okay?"

"Absolutely."

"Where will you live?"

"I'll rent an apartment."

"Won't you miss the house?"

Split Ends

"I'm looking forward to paring down, getting rid of stuff I don't need." *Or want.*

"If Josh and I can help you move, let us know."

"I will. Thank you. Enough serious stuff. Do me a favor and find the Preservation Hall CD. I feel like dancing."

Ellen strutted barefoot, waving a potholder as if it was a handkerchief in a jazz funeral, while the spices permeated the entrée. The aromas perfumed the kitchen, bright with the colorful cachepots she had collected.

Michael tapped her on the shoulder. "Hi, Mom."

She jumped. "I didn't hear you come in." They hugged.

"The music's kind of loud. Looks like you're having fun."

"Your old lady is cutting loose. Someday I'm going to Mardi Gras. Meanwhile …" She waved the potholder. "Grab a beer or a soda. We're about to eat."

"Good. I'm really hungry. And I have to run after dinner. Paper due tomorrow."

"Have you started it?"

"It's almost done."

Miracle of miracles.

"I'm glad I'm not having my cholesterol checked any time soon," Ellen said as she carried food into the dining room. She set the casserole on the table next to a vase of white tulips that bespoke Spring.

"Michael, you sit at the head. I want to be close to the kitchen." Michael took the seat formerly occupied by his father. Ellen almost wished she missed Ron's presence at the family table, but she didn't.

Beth Rubin

* * * *

Sprawled on the bed at sunrise, Ellen watched a mandarin orange carpet unroll onto the river. She had been up for hours thinking about Penny and Drew. A nightmare had jolted her. In her groggy state, she had thought the lump on the floor was Penny. When she had reached down to pet the dog her hand landed on an old pillow.

She had cried again.

She listened to the radio and tasted the salt of her tears while reading "The Horse Whisperer." She knew exactly how Annie felt kissing Tom in the meadow. Goosebumps puckered her flesh as she replayed a similar scene in a storm-swept cottage by the sea.

Ice crusted the river. The water was phosphorescent around the dock pilings. In the early morning light an ice flow ferried a company of gulls. Once again she wondered why, with so much beauty in nature, people needed organized religion.

Her mind raced. She recalled that Elizabeth had said, "Your mind flies from zero to 60 in seconds. It's part of your creative nature. Channel the energy into your work."

"I'm trying," Ellen had replied. "But my emotions are out of control."

"Your emotions are very labile."

"Sounds prurient. What does it mean?"

"It means they're all over the place. Variable."

Ellen lunged for a tissue, but it was beyond her reach. She used her sleeve. Her thoughts jumbled like the makings of a Kahlua Smoothie. Before the ingredients fused, she tasted the essence of each.

Split Ends

The ice cubes were Ron, clear except for the hairline fissures. The vanilla ice cream was Penny who lapped her medication in the frozen treat. The Kahlua was Drew, sweet but lethal.

The sun paled to silvery gold and blurred with the clouds over the river. A coterie of tundra swans flew south, silhouetted against the pearly light.

Ellen reprised the previous evening. Lisa's apology and preparing a hearty meal for her children had satisfied her beyond measure. Yet, here she was, less than 12 hours later, lying in a heap, watching the Weather Channel.

She jumped when the phone rang. "How was your trip to New Orleans, Sandy? The French Quarter was seedy? What would rye bread be without caraway?" Ellen had been to New Orleans for clients, to scour Magazine Street for the unusual piece or two.

"Jonathan proposed? An engagement ring? In a Sazerac cocktail? Congratulations! September? At his club? That'll be a scene. How is your family handling it? Guess this makes you a member of the tribe, girlfriend. You bet your bippy I'll be there. Can I be your flower girl, or do you want me in the kitchen?

"I'm okay but I miss Penny something awful. No, nothing you can do. The divorce? The attorneys have two speeds—slow and stop. But I'm getting there, Sandy.

"Give Jonathan a hug for me. Tell him to treat you well or I'll break his legs. I'm thrilled for you. Talk soon."

She clicked through the channels, landing on "King Kong." In place of the ape, Drew swatted a plane from the top of the Empire State Building. *Does that make me Fay Wray?*

She loved New York, no matter who commanded the Empire State Building.

The sun burned through the window. Ellen took off her robe as Sarah McLachlan sang, "I Will Remember You." The bridge of her nose began to hurt, a Mayday that tears were imminent. *Damn, why did Drew have to bond and bolt?*

She picked up her journal, rested it against her flannel knees and began to write.

"MONDAY MORNING The kids were here for dinner last night. Ron and I did something right. The beast is back. I'm out of gas, with two flat tires in Harlem at 3 A.M. I'm 'The English Patient' with hemorrhoids. Will I slay the beast before it slays me? Elizabeth says I'm making headway. I hope so. Haven't felt this tired since I delivered Michael and Lisa. Will I finally deliver the Me lost in Us? Set aside sketches for the Goodmans' living room at 11 and settled into bed with *Gourmet* and *Architectural Digest.* Since the King of Energy Vampires left, it is freeing knowing there are so many:

<u>THINGS I DON'T HAVE TO DO ANYMORE</u>
Fix dinner
Lower toilet seat
Repeat things
Step on toenail clippings
Keep house neat
Keep me neat
Listen to snoring
Hang up clothes
Remake both sides of bed

Split Ends

Turn down music
Walk on eggs
Fight for blanket
Shave legs
Tiptoe after 10 P.M.
Ask, 'How was your day?'
Eat at set times
Watch sports
Clean stubble from sink
Feel lonely
Justify actions
Tolerate moodiness
Close bathroom door
Laugh at stale jokes
Have conversations edited
Hide new purchases
Sew on collar buttons
Tune out complaining
Wipe hair from shower
Feign interest in torts
Buy Preparation H
Explain everything
Pick plaque from mirror
Plan weekends
Comply ... or else
Swallow anger
Pack for two
Replace toilet paper
Straighten up
Fly right

"Sleep eludes me. I spend so much time staring at the ceiling I may paint a mural on it. *Michelangela Gold.* Running on fumes. Dr. Applebaum prescribed

Trazadone, a hypnotic. He won't give me sleeping pills. What's he afraid of? Took two. Flushed the rest. If I ask him to hypnotize me, maybe he'll prescribe sleeping pills.

"A good screwing might help. Always slept better afterward. Could resort to The Tongue, lapping lint in my underwear drawer. Doubt I could get it up. What a world. An unwanted pregnancy used to be a woman's greatest fear. Now, FUCK AND DIE is the bumper sticker of the day. Any second the Center for Disease Control will issue a warning: To practice *really* safe sex a vibrator must be sheathed with a condom. When the urge returns, where will I find a willing accomplice? Maybe I'll place an ISO ad:

"NQMNQS (not quite married, not quite single) WJF. 50 but look younger. Slim, clean, horny. ISO quick lay. No commitment sought. Like the beach, movies, laughter, back rubs, honesty. Dislike dirty fingernails, chamber music, meaningful looks and empty promises. Prefer 5'10"-6'2", under 200 lbs., broad shoulders, white teeth, flat stomach, good personal hygiene, lots of hair (but not on the back). Send color 5 x 7s in tux, jeans, naked and four references.

"There, that should do it. Sure hope the answering machine can handle the glut of responses.

"Breakfasted on coffee, garlic bagel (it's okay; nobody's been close enough to notice) and M&Ms. Called 800 number to register my distaste for aster blue M's. Color fine for eyes, bibelots, sweaters; not for candy.

"Wonder what Elizabeth would say if she knew I ate chocolate for breakfast. Probably remind me that

Split Ends

chocolate is a substitute for sex. What a revelation. I've been addicted to sex all my life and thought I was hooked on chocolate. Sure worth the bucks and time to discover that.

"Dedication from Ellen in Annapolis to Drew in NJ: 'Unbreak My Heart.' Maybe I'll leave The Coward a message—'I dreamed that you died. If you didn't, please call me.' Or a note: 'Dear Drew: If you can't call, please write. Just ask the nice orderly to untie your restraints and bring you a piece of paper and a pencil. Sincerely, Ellen.'

"In the news: A West Virginia woman has been on a respirator for 45 years. She can't move or talk. She's also allergic to anesthesia. Sure hope she doesn't need an emergency appendectomy.

"Can't wait to try this recipe from the paper: 'Hog Maul (Pig Stomach). The first requirement is for the stomach of a pig.' *That's easy. I'll pick one up next time I'm at the supermarket.* 'Clean the stomach and close the small hole.' *With Elmer's glue? Duct tape? Polident? The sausage-based stuffing looks good. I'll eat the stuffing and chuck the stomach. Or upchuck the stomach.*

"The editor must have dipped into the cooking sherry before adding the following postscript. 'Note: Overstuffing may cause the stomach to burst while baking. Leftover stomach may be sliced and fried.' *Can hardly wait to tackle those leftovers.* Wish my father was alive. He'd get a kick out of this delicacy.

"Outta juice, down to one bagel. First, I need Morpheus or Dr. Welby to pay a house call. If I hit the bars, I'll drive the beer-bellied locals into their pickups faster than a fart in a closet. Can't believe I emptied a bag of M&Ms before sun-up. Oh well, a girl's gotta do what a girl's gotta do.

"Dinner with Ron next week. One last shot at staying six more months in the house. So far, he's turned a deaf ear. What else is new? And Drew. Too bad I didn't know that he came with a 90-day limited warranty.

"On a cockamamie talk show the subject is, 'I Want a Man Who Is Not A Mama's Boy.' So do we all. Bill won't leave his mother's house and move to Chicago with his girlfriend. Bill doesn't like Chicago. It's too windy. His mother says, 'He's not a mama's boy.' Right. He can't separate from her lemon meringue pie and Mama doesn't want to lose her handyman. Where do they find these people?"

Ellen closed the journal. A few minutes later she dreamed that she was in the shower with Ron, Drew and Penny. Nobody brought soap.

Split Ends

CHAPTER 20

Ellen swallowed an anchovy. "I know we agreed to six months. It's a mistake for you to come back now. Please don't do this."

I never should have signed the agreement that he could return after six months. Marla insisted. She said half a loaf was better than none. What does she care? She'll rake in her $200 an hour whatever happens. Even if I have to move out to earn my diploma. Or if I end up in a rubber room.

"It's my house too. I've been inconvenienced long enough." Ron tossed back his Chianti. "I hate the apartment."

"But it's so close to your office." *And probably close to whomever you're screwing.* "It must be nice to walk to work, not to commute."

"That's irrelevant."

The governor walked in with an attractive blond who resembled Ellen—slim, with intense dark eyes and classic looks. And much younger. The woman smiled at Ellen and sat down with the governor at the next table.

Hmm, what's their connection? Must be someone from his staff. Ellen eyed the ID tag over the woman's designer scarf. *Maybe she's his administrative assistant or press secretary.*

"I'm coming home," Ron said loud enough for the sous chef to hear on his smoke break out back. "I want to sleep in my own bed."

"I'll mail you the bed. Just stay away."

"Very funny. Two weeks, Ellen." Ron speared a marinated mushroom from the antipasto and stuffed it in his mouth. Oil dripped on his sweater. Ellen decided not to tell him he'd made a mess again.

"The house will be yours eventually. I can't afford the mortgage, or the upkeep. All I'm asking is six more months."

"Too bad. You agreed to six months."

Ellen felt like shoving a sesame bread stick up his ass. "What will your coming home accomplish, Ron? We've chosen a course ..."

"No, you've chosen a course. I want to stay married."

"We've been over this. You want your tart and eat her, I mean, it, too." The governor and the blond put down their forks.

Ellen swept the cocktail napkin scraps into a neat pile and tried a different tack. "I know it's been a hardship, living in an apartment—a two-bedroom, two-bath apartment, with a heated garage. I appreciate your sacrifice. We have almost six months under our belts. Another six and we can move on with our lives. Don't you want to move on?"

"Move on?" Ron asked as he poured another glass of wine. "I don't want to move on. I want to move back."

Jesus, he's a one-note samba.

"Earth calling Ron. Wakey, wakey. I couldn't handle the stress of our living together again. Could you?"

"I thought we could work it out." He twirled some linguine and Ellen noticed his shiny scalp. *Gee, he's lost a lot of hair since we split. I never dreamed he'd go bald. And he's shorter.*

Split Ends

"Work it out? What's left to work out, except who gets custody of the hedge trimmer?"

"I want to give it another shot."

"Ron, we are shot. We've shot our wad. It would take a major miracle to turn this around. I don't believe in miracles. Do you? We're not getting any younger. Why drag it out?"

He dropped his voice. "Is there somebody else?"

"That's a funny question coming from you."

"Why? I don't have anyone else."

"You sure don't have me, Ron. I'm not your puppet any more." Ellen swung her hand back and forth over her head. "See, I cut the strings."

"You don't want to be married. That's clear."

I don't want to be married to you. Ellen nibbled a black olive and chose her words carefully. She didn't want to give him false hope. "Ron, if there is any chance of a reconciliation, we need another six months apart. Things are too raw."

Bread crumbs had stuck to his chin. "Then what? You'll probably smack me with another six months."

I'd like to smack you upside the head. "No. No more extensions. I promise. You want it in writing? We'll ask the governor to witness."

Ellen sipped some water. "I'm asking you, in return for 28 years of *faithful* service, please let me stay in the house another six months. I need this time. And I need it alone. I'm doing well in therapy, coming out of the depression. Losing Penny set me back. I'm dancing as fast as I can. Let's avoid any further rancor, Ron. Please don't force my back to the wall."

"You need another six months alone? You move."

"But I work at home. I'd have to move my office—the computer, all my files, swatches and sample books. And I need a place to meet with clients."

"Meet them at the library." The governor and the blond stopped talking. Ellen glanced at the woman and saw empathy in her expression. Or maybe it was pity.

"You're not supposed to talk in the library. Besides, it wouldn't make sense for me to move short-term. You're already set up in a place. And you have an office you can walk to. Don't you see? My entire life is in the house."

She saw a familiar expression on his face. A look of triumph. A look that said, Gotcha. "I'm coming back."

"Ron, all this moving back and forth would be disruptive to both of us. Don't you think?"

"I've been burdened long enough," he shouted. "Every time the toilet flushes next door I hear it. And the people above me party on weekends."

"Wear earplugs. Crash the party."

"Don't be sarcastic."

"I couldn't resist." Ellen wondered how the Maryland General Assembly would vote on her bill to secede from Ron.

"It's not fair," he continued. "I've been banished from my own home."

"You sound like a victim."

"I am."

Ellen took a deep breath and gripped the chair seat. "Have you forgotten why we're in this mess?"

"Jesus Christ, Ellen. Do you have to keep bringing it up? It's history. What do you want from me? Blood?"

About three gallons. "Where do you suggest I go, Ron?"

"How about your mother's?"

"My mother's? In New Jersey? I can't do my work in New Jersey. And I want to be near the kids. My mother would drive me nuts. She'd remind me 20 times a day that I'm not warm enough. Come in to check my breathing at night."

"You don't like that idea? Rent a furnished room. Look in the roommate ads in the paper. I'm sure you'll find something."

"Roommate? You want me to live in one room? Share space with a stranger? What about my work?" *I'd like to pour the wine on your balding head.*

The governor guffawed. Maybe over a joke. *I wish I was at their table. They're having a good time.*

"I'll tell you what I'll do. I'll let you come back to the house to work."

"Wow, thanks. What a generous guy. How did I get so lucky? May I kiss your ring?" *Or ass?*

His temples pulsated. "Watch your mouth, Ellen."

She pointed a bread stick at him. "Up yours, counselor. Your suggestion stinks. I'm not going to schlep from a furnished room to my house to work. You know I don't keep regular hours, that I often work nights and weekends." *Withholding bastard.*

"I'm coming home. If you don't like it, you move. It's your turn."

"I feel like I'm center court at Wimbledon. I'll stay, you move. No, I'll move, you stay. I'm getting whiplash from the volley, Ron. It's match point."

Ron pounded the table in his best Godfather imitation and Ellen felt every eye in the place on them, including the gov's.

"I'm coming back."

"It'll never work." She threw her napkin on the table. "Court's adjourned. I'm outta here," she said, and left.

CHAPTER 21

"Ron, I need to talk to you."

He opened the newspaper.

"I'd like your undivided attention." *Why do I bother?*

"I can do two things at once."

Says who? "Please put down the paper." She unclenched her teeth.

He balled the paper and threw it on the floor.

"I told you this wouldn't work. I'm moving. I looked at some places today. I have to pay two months' rent up front. A client owes me for a job. I should have it soon. Meantime, I'm short."

"Short?"

"Of cash. Greenbacks. Wampum."

"You'll get all my money eventually."

"I'll get a portion of *our* money when the divorce is final. Consider it an advance."

She thought she saw a sparkle in his eye.

"That's not my problem."

"You mean-spirited S.O.B."

"You want to be Ms. Independent? Fine. Don't come to me for a handout."

"Handout?" *Asshole.*

He shrugged and picked up the paper.

* * * *

Ellen charged into Elizabeth's office. She took off her raincoat and slumped in a chair. The carpet spotted as she shook her rain hat and placed it on the arm.

"I couldn't wait to see you."

"You sound anxious. What's been going on?"

"No change. He hasn't connected the dots. Since he moved back, I'm a prisoner in my own home."

"What do you mean?"

"I'm losing my power, turning back into a lifeless doll. Just being around him drags me down. I'm so angry and frustrated. I'm coming unglued, Elizabeth. Please don't tell me I'm in mourning. I'm ready to ditch the widow's weeds. Trade them in for something racy in fire engine red."

Elizabeth tapped the pencil against her temple. "What's been going on?"

"It's the pits. The house is cordoned off into His and Hers living areas. It reminds me of 'The War of the Roses,' except it's the war of the Golds. But I'm no Kathleen Turner. And for sure he's no Michael Douglas. Good thing we don't have a crystal chandelier. You can taste the tension."

Ellen began to hyperventilate. "Of course, when a friend comes over he oozes charm. What a phony."

"Men can be good at that."

"I've forgotten what it feels like to be at peace. Evenings are the worst. My stomach knots before he comes home. So I try to stay away."

"Where do you go?"

"I see every movie, memorize the merchandise at the mall. Sometimes I go to the library and read magazines with the homeless. My friends have been wonderful, calling, inviting me to dinner. Not that I eat much. I'm such a drag, I'll be lucky if I have any friends when this is over.

"I was so much better with him gone. I'm as bad as when you first saw me. In some ways I'm worse. I had

Split Ends

a taste of freedom, had begun to build a life for myself. I'm on the edge."

"Ellen, are you practicing your deep breathing?"

"Yes. Sometimes it's all I can do to curl up with Chopin. I've been having some very dark thoughts."

"You promised to tell me if you had self-destructive thoughts."

"Oh, the dark thoughts aren't about *moi*. Afternoons I pray he'll hit a tree on his way home. When the garage door goes up, my spirits sink. He's home every night nuking his freakin' TV dinner. I wish he'd go out once in a while. Or have a stroke."

Ellen pictured Ron, drool sliding from the corners of his mouth.

"How are you handling weekends?"

"I see the kids or visit friends. The children have been wonderful, supportive and non-judgmental. If I don't have plans I invent errands or drive around aimlessly." Ellen shrugged.

"But I have to go home eventually. I spent last weekend out of town at a friend's. For 48 hours I forgot about the crap. Soon as I crossed the Maryland line, my heart began to race. The contrast between how I am with others and how I am at home is startling."

"What about the negotiations?"

"It's a stalemate. Sadat and Begin had an easier time. One day he agrees to something, the next day he changes his mind. Before he came back, he said it was my turn to move."

"You agreed to six months, Ellen."

"I did it under duress. I gambled that he'd like his freedom and agree to another six months. He gambled that I wouldn't play my trump card and nail him for adultery. He won that hand. I'm sure he thought he had me by the short and curlies when he moved back."

"What did you tell him?"

"I told him that I'm looking for a place and I need some money to cover expenses short-term. A client owes me money. I'll have it soon. I have a couple of big jobs in the works."

"What about your checking account?"

"Down to a thou. It's a cushion for emergencies. Ron keeps reminding me I'll get *his* money when the divorce is final."

"Controlling."

"I'm a poor risk until things are settled. Last week Ron said he would co-sign a lease. Two days later he changed his mind. I'd like to tie his balls in a bow."

"You are facing formidable odds."

"Formidable. We're both in the house. Thanks to the wretched divorce laws in this state, every day we're at the same address, I'm another light-year away from freedom. It's like being on death-fucking-row."

"Have you taken any steps to find a place?"

"I've looked at a few. Right now I can afford $500 for rent. You can't get a bathroom in this town for $500. At best, I'd be living in a furnished room with kitchen privileges, or an efficiency near the projects where I'd be afraid to walk from my car to the front door." Ellen felt the pressure building in her head.

"The other night he said, 'Why don't you look in Bowie? It's less expensive.' Why would I want to live there? It's in the middle of nowhere and full of young families and retirees. The streets are alphabetized. Maybe he thinks it'll help me find my way home. It is cheaper, though. I'm pissed just thinking about it. He screws around and stays in the big house while I live in a dump with bars on the windows. No, I don't think so."

"Don't screen yourself out."

"What do you mean?"

"Don't cave. If you leave, you'll never get back in."

"That's what Marla said at first. Now she says to borrow what I need. She says to find someplace safe and take what I need to make a home for myself. Ron's so used to my folding—he acts as though I'll get all dewy-eyed, cook him a roast beef, medium rare and say, 'I've decided to stay in the house and be miserable with you.'"

"Have you seen any place you like?"

"The realtor showed me some hell holes. Then she took me to a place on Spa Creek. I like the location and lots of singles live there. Dating is the last thing on my mind, but I'd like to meet some women to do things with."

"How much is the rent?"

"A thousand. What I earned during the marriage was gravy. I spent it on things for the house, gifts for Ron, clothes."

"You paid for your own clothes?"

"Sure. Why?"

"It strikes me as odd, given your husband's wealth and the disparity in your earnings."

Ellen shrugged. "It gave me a small sense of independence. You know, he loved to remind me that I didn't contribute anything. He never acknowledged my putting my career on hold and taking care of family things so he could devote himself to his law practice."

"What about stocks?"

"Everything but the house is in his name. Too bad Maryland is not a community property state like California."

"What did Marla advise you?"

"She was shocked when I told her our financial arrangement. There's nothing she can do. It's legal. He always told me I had nothing to worry about. Sure, if he croaked first. It's further proof that he didn't view our marriage as a partnership. If I need more proof. Why did it take me so long to wake up and smell the poo-poo?"

"That's common for women of our generation. We were socialized to be caregivers and selfless and not to question authority. Men use money as a control."

"I don't want anyone taking care of me. Ever again."

"What about your work? How's that going?"

"Better. Sometimes my energy is zero and it's difficult to concentrate. When I help a client select wallpaper it can be as exhausting as redecorating the White House."

"Once you're in a stress-free environment, I think you will see a big change."

"I hope so. I'm looking forward to having my own place." Ellen smiled at the thought. "On a different note, I'm having slippage over Drew."

"How?"

"I can be thinking about Ron and the marriage and my thoughts shift to Drew, like a train switching tracks. I think I'm transferring my sadness over the marriage onto Drew. Maybe it's easier to fixate on him than focus on my future without Ron."

Split Ends

"I think you are on the mark. They are intertwined in your consciousness. You are a lot stronger than you give yourself credit for."

"I still miss Drew. It may have been too hot not to cool down, but I don't think feelings like that will come my way again."

"Remember, it's the *dream* you're missing."

"I'm tired of arguing the point. Let's change the subject. I have a juicy dream for you." She tore open a king-size bag of M&Ms—peanut for a change.

Elizabeth withdrew a pencil stuck in her French twist.

"Tell me about this dream." Elizabeth kicked off her shoes.

"I was standing in an empty lot behind a building. The asphalt was cracked. The building was white. Cushing, Inc. was painted on it in big red letters. I was there to meet Ron. I felt uneasy. I dreaded seeing him. You don't have to analyze that part. I've already figured it out."

Elizabeth nodded. "Go on."

"Ron and I were walking down a wide boulevard. A large fish was in the middle of the road. It was brightly colored, like a leaping dolphin fish. We got closer and I saw it was paper; it resembled a windsock. A car ran over the fish and it exploded. Hollow. Bits of colored paper scattered everywhere. Then Ron and I were walking in a flowered meadow. It was very romantic. I felt anything but romantic. The light was out of focus, gauzy."

"Then what?"

"The setting reminded me of the old 'Modess because' ads. Remember? A pretty woman is in a field.

She looks radiant and fulfilled—as though she's just been with her lover—even though she's passing clots the size of Lake Pontchartrain."

Elizabeth smiled. "And ..."

"I wondered why I was in such a romantic place with Ron. I was thinking, I'm only here by default. Then I woke up feeling sad and missing Drew. What else is new?"

Elizabeth stabbed her hair with the pencil. She smoothed her skirt. "Is that it?"

"That's it."

"You're meeting Ron in a place where the aura of Drew is present."

"Any significance to the red lettering?"

"I don't think so."

"The name was bold, overpowering."

"It could indicate that he's still a presence in your life."

"Duh. Why didn't I think of that?"

"The cracks in the pavement could be your feelings of fragmentation and frustration over your marriage. Or your desire to put together the cracked pieces of your life."

Ellen slid to the edge of the seat. "What else? Is there a Ford in my future? Or a prince?"

"You'll have to go to your psychic for those answers."

"I did. He said, 'New Jersey deserves a second chance.'"

Elizabeth appeared pained. "I wish you wouldn't. You'd be giving him a chance to sucker you in again."

Split Ends

"I have to know. Then I can hammer the final nail in his coffin." Ellen twirled some hair around her finger. "It's still a split end and I hate split ends."

"If you decide to confront him, I hope you'll wait another few months."

"Can we get back to the dream?"

"I think the fish represents your marriage, attractive on the outside but hollow inside."

"Hollow. I was in denial for a long, long time."

"Stay with this, Ellen. What about denial?"

"The truth was too painful. I didn't see how we interacted. That's not true. I buried it."

"Buried what?"

"My feelings. My needs. My essence. Me." Ellen paused to compose her thoughts. "I handed over little pieces of myself until there was nothing left. My spirit was squashed. His affair was merely the *coup de grâce*."

Elizabeth nodded like a teacher with a star pupil. "Go on."

"If I hadn't found out about Ron and Casey, I'd probably still be there. Unhappy. Unfulfilled. He wanted to be—had to be—the boss. And I let him. It's how I was raised. Don't question authority, don't rock the boat, put your own needs last."

"What did you mean about the affair? It's significance?"

"His infidelity was a wake-up call, the kick in the ass I needed to get unstuck. It forced me to take stock. I finally found my voice. He did me a big favor when he dropped his pants."

"And?"

Ellen thought of Drew and sighed. "If I had any doubt that things weren't rotten in the state of Denmark, Drew made me see what was out there—how good it could be and what I'd been missing. He opened my eyes to my own self-worth. Too bad he turned from a prince to a frog, but he did help me. Drew was the catalyst. He got me to jump from the nest and fly."

"You're giving him too much credit—and power. He didn't get you to do anything. You did it all yourself. He reflected back to you the good things that were already inside you."

"I'm working through that piece. What about the end of the dream, in the meadow?"

"No wonder you felt uncomfortable and out of place in a romantic setting. Your marriage had no romance. You used the word 'default.' The only way you would be with Ron would be by default; not by choice. You're longing for Drew because he was all the things Ron was not—attentive, warm and caring."

Ellen dabbed at a tear.

"Remember, Ellen, he betrayed you. He's an asshole."

"Is that a clinical term?" Ellen managed a tiny smile. "He's an asshole all right. But I miss the asshole."

"Are you losing weight again?"

Ellen held up the empty wrapper. "Yes. I'm living on water and chocolate vitamins."

"How much have you lost?"

"Six pounds since Ron moved back. Think there's a connection?"

Split Ends

Elizabeth noted Ellen's weight loss on her pad. "Let me know if you lose any more. It's a sign of your distress and we need to monitor it."

Ellen began to cry. "I'm breathing toxic fumes at home. I've got to move. But I'm afraid to do it until a final agreement is in place. I know two women who did. And they lost out. One was married to a jerk who smacked her around. He charged her with desertion because she had no proof. Too bad she didn't have a picture taken of her black eyes. I won't stoop to raising the adultery issue in court; mostly because of the kids."

"They're grown, Ellen. They can handle it."

"I won't do it. He's still their father. Besides, it's not the main reason the marriage crumbled."

"I think you need to follow through on your plan to move. Even if your financial business is unsettled. As long as you are there Ron will pull your strings, using money to manipulate you into staying."

"Oh, I know all about his string-pulling. I won't dance the dance anymore. My days as a Stepford wife are history. I'm hanging up my victim mask."

"Is there someone, a family member perhaps, who could help you out?"

"My cousin Amy has offered. I always say 'no.' Fifty years old and borrowing money for rent and groceries? I think I'd rather die than do that."

"You may die if you don't. I'm very concerned about you. Think about it."

CHAPTER 22

Ellen phoned her cousin. Whenever Ellen spent time with Amy and her husband she was struck by how they worked as a team. And they seemed to genuinely like each other. Ellen regarded them not with envy, but as role models.

"Amy, I can't stand it any longer. I'll swallow my pride and take you up on your offer."

"Nothing would please me more. How much do you need? Where shall I send the check?"

"Can you spare $5,000? That'll help cover the first month's rent and security deposit, the move and expenses until I get a check from a client. I expect one soon."

"No problem. Don't you need more? Please, Ellen, take it and don't worry about paying me back."

"This isn't a gift. I want that understood. We'll sign a note."

"Anything you say. I'm happy that I can help you get out of there. You've sounded on the verge of cracking."

"Thank you for saving my life," Ellen said.

She began to list the things she wanted to take with her. Although Marla had told her that she was entitled to half of the home's furnishings, there was no way they would fit in a two-bedroom apartment.

* * * *

Ellen asked the realtor to draw up a lease and contacted three moving companies. When the first two said they couldn't possibly move her on such short

Split Ends

notice, she went into a tailspin and threw herself on the mercy of the third. She pleaded until they caved in, agreeing to squeeze her in on April 1.

As she prepared to leave her old life, Ellen choked up recalling how much she had once loved Ron. *I would have done anything for him. And I nearly did. But I won't give him what's left of my life.*

"What if my husband makes trouble?" Ellen had asked.

The sales manager at A Moving Experience said, "We'll call the police if we have to. We've handled lots of moves like yours. Don't worry."

Ellen worried anyway.

Is this crazy or what? Ellen wondered as she circled April 1 in red on her calendar. It may be April Fool's Day, but I'm not fooling around. And I'm no fool any longer!

* * * *

She corralled him as soon as he walked in the door that evening. *Tough shit.*

"I'm moving, Ron. I found a place. Signing a lease tomorrow. It's not up for discussion."

He put his briefcase on a chair. "What do you mean, you're moving?"

He looks like he's hearing Swahili for the first time.

"I'm done explaining. And kowtowing. I'm suffocating. You don't look happy either." *Was he ever?*

"You want to leave? Go. But I'm not giving you one thin dime."

"I think our lawyers will decide otherwise."

Ron looked stricken.

"You can't do that."

"Yes I can, Ron. And I am doing it."

"You can't afford it."

"I borrowed enough to move. I'll manage."

"Who loaned you money?"

"That's none of your concern. I'm not going to let you manipulate me any more. I'm calling the shots."

He scowled. "You'll never make it on your own."

If I had a knife, I'd butcher him. A crime of passion. And a strong case for knife control.

She fled to her bedroom, locked the door and pushed the desk against it. She turned the radio to the most offensive hard rock station and raised the volume full blast.

All aquiver, she called Elizabeth.

"I can't take it. Him." Ellen turned down the radio.

"I'm locked in the bedroom. Shaking. Major anxiety attack. Okay. I'm breathing. In-hale. Ex-hale. Visualizing the ocean."

Elizabeth continued to talk her down to a manageable level of distress.

"I'm better. I borrowed from my cousin. I'm moving. Signing the lease tomorrow.

"Ron went ballistic. Told me I'll never make it. I'll show him. And me."

A few minutes later Ellen lay on the bed.

Ron's not violent. Why did I push the desk against the door? And then it hit her. *I didn't lock him out. I locked myself in, so I can't harm him.*

CHAPTER 23

The tension had eased since her decision. Ron had even been civil. Maybe he had run out of steam or, like a patient with a terminal illness, had come to accept the inevitable.

Acid rock, a CD Michael had brought with him, blared. The music, if you could call it that, fueled her anxiety. Ellen looked around the table at the sad faces. Lisa pushed food around her plate. Michael chewed his cheek. Ron wore a glazed look and tapped his fork on the rosewood. *The Gold's Last Supper.*

"Ron, would you like to say something?" *Please.*

He shook his head.

"Kids, I'm moving out in a week. I'll be renting an apartment nearby."

"Ron, would you help me out?"

Silence.

"Why are *you* moving, Mom?" *Because that's the only way I can win my freedom.*

"That's what your father and I decided, Michael." *I hope my nose doesn't grow.*

Ron got up. Ellen knew he would go to the broken-family room and turn on the TV.

Michael and Lisa helped Ellen to clear the table. The three of them hugged.

Elizabeth was right. This is like a death. A death that's repeated every step of the way.

"I'm so sorry."

"It's okay, Mom. You didn't do anything wrong. We'll be fine. So will you."

"Thank you, Michael."

Lisa whispered. "You have to take care of yourself, Mom. If you stay in the house much longer, I'm afraid you'll end up in a psych ward."

"Thanks, Lisa. I love you both very much. Thank you for being supportive, and not taking sides. We'll have good times again. I promise."

* * * *

She tossed and turned the night before her move. At 4:00 she woke in a cold sweat from a dream. Ron, dressed as Che Guevara, directed the Marines to circle the house, bayonets at the ready.

She dressed, but stayed in Michael's old room making lists. Her butterflies disappeared when Ron finally peeled out of the driveway.

No good-byes. No, "Have a nice life." No, "Maybe we'll do coffee sometime." No nothing.

The movers arrived, loaded the truck and followed her to her new place. Wilma arrived a few minutes later with champagne and plastic cups. Ellen eyed the cartons stacked shoulder-high in the living room.

"I did it, Wilma. I actually did it."

"I'm proud of you. How do you feel?"

"Like a bird free of its cage. It's all mine, Wilma. I can do it up any way I like. Drape fabric from the ceiling and turn it into a bedouin tent. Or hang an Elvis poster over the fireplace. I can do any damn thing I want without permission. Or fear of recrimination."

"I'm happy for you, Ellen. I know you'll give it your special touch. I wish I didn't have this meeting. I'd like to help you. Promise me you won't do it all today. I'll come by tomorrow and help you unpack."

Split Ends

"You're on. Thanks, Wilma. You've been a godsend through all this."

Ellen unpacked a couple of cartons, then glanced outside at the sunshine and the boats. She opened the patio door and plopped in a chair. She'd brought two and the umbrella table, leaving the umbrella and two chairs for Ron. She surveyed the sailing yachts and cruisers docked in the marina and craned her neck to see the State House dome.

It felt more like August. A week before, snow had dusted the daffodils in front of her former home.

Perspiration soaked Ellen's 'It Is Better to Divorce than to Murder' T-shirt. She looked down at the cotton clinging to her unsupported breasts.

Way to make a first impression. I won't win any wet T-shirt contests today, but maybe I'll get the booby prize. For little boobies.

She pulled the material from her damp skin and watched a man mopping the deck of a navy-hulled ketch. A Dalmatian snoozed in the cockpit.

He propped his string mop against the companionway. "You moving in?"

"Yes. Do you live here?"

"On my boat. I spend winters in Punta Gorda and summers here. I brought the boat back last week. You're going to love it here."

"I know I will." *I'd love the homeless shelter downtown after where I've been.*

Ellen pushed the hair from her face. She wondered if the skipper detected her body odor. "Cute dog. What's its name?"

"Carrie. It's a she. You like dogs?"

"I love them. I had to put my Lab down a few months ago. I miss her."

"Well, Carrie loves company. Feel free to visit anytime." Ellen made a mental note to buy doggy treats when she went grocery shopping.

She sat forward in the chair. "I work at home. If you need someone to walk her, I'd be happy to."

"I may take you up on that. What kind of work do you do?"

"I'm a decorator."

"My sister's a decorator in New York."

Except for the paunch, the man was attractive. Gray salted his wavy, dark hair and he had good legs. *I've heard of leg men. When did I become a leg woman?*

He was probably single. He had the look. She was growing more proficient at distinguishing marrieds from unmarrieds. Singles smiled more. Most couples wore pinched expressions and hardly spoke to their mates.

Whenever she went to Riordan's saloon with friends, they'd have a drink and make up stories about the solo men at the bar. It reminded her of the Drew fantasies she and Meg had dreamed up as kids. Ellen wondered if she would ever grow up. But it was harmless fun and all she could handle for the time being. She didn't know what she'd do if a man came on to her.

She stood up and stretched, showing off her goods to the yachtsman.

"I'm Bob. And you are ... ?"

"Ellen."

"Good luck in your new place, Ellen."

"Thanks, Bob. Gotta get back to work."

The smell of fresh paint transported her. She cranked open the windows, luxuriating in the moist breeze off the water and paused to admire the sunlit space. As she imagined decorating the room, the doorbell rang. "Ooh, a visitor," she sang to herself.

Michael stood at the door. "Hey, Mom."

Ellen hugged her son longer than usual.

"These are for you," Michael said, handing her a large bunch of daisies and cold six-pack. "Good luck in your new place. Lisa said to tell you she'll come by after work."

"Thanks, Michael. I love daisies. I could use a beer about now."

"How's it going?"

"I've barely started to unpack, but I'm happy to be here."

"Where'd you get that?" Michael asked, reading the message on her chest.

Ellen flushed. "I'd have changed if I'd known you were coming. Sandy gave it to me. Silly, isn't it?"

Ellen was showing Michael the small second bedroom that would serve as her office when the doorbell rang.

"Hi, I'm Rochelle," said the petite woman tethered to a terrier. "I live next door. I saw the moving van. I know you're busy, but I wanted to introduce myself. And this is Shayna." She patted the dog. "It means 'pretty' in Yiddish." Rochelle handed Ellen a bag from the Amish Market and her phone number.

Ellen peeked in the bag. "Thank you. I love sticky buns."

"If you need anything or want to get together for coffee, just call. My husband and I are retired and I'm always looking for something to do."

"Rochelle, this is my son Michael."

"Does he live with you?"

"No, he's too smart for that. But I hope he'll visit often."

I'm going to like it here. I better buy a giant-size box of dog biscuits. Maybe Rochelle will let me walk Shayna.

Ellen and Michael had beers on the patio, then went inside.

"I'd better get going. I have to set up for dinner."

Ellen walked Michael to his car. "Thanks for stopping, and for the daisies and beer. Can you come for brunch Sunday? I should be settled by then."

"Sounds good, Mom. Call you Saturday. Enjoy your new place."

She hugged him again. "I will."

I'm so lucky, so very lucky. She watched him drive off and went back into her home. She stepped around the cartons and into the kitchen. She slit open a box labeled POTS & PANS.

Ellen thought about the times she and Ron had moved. She'd always tackled the kitchen first. With the kitchen in place, she felt settled. The rest could wait. She wasn't going anywhere—for a year, at least.

CHAPTER 24

She latched the top and popped the trunk lever, then got out of the car.

Across the lot, Willie Nelson wailed from a low-slung sports car that a guy was waxing.

The waxer seemed to be watching her.

"Hey! I like your car," he said.

Now, there's a line. Almost as original as, "What was your major in college?"

"Hey, I like yours too." *Nice chassis.* He had shaggy black hair, an athletic build and looked about 35. *That'll work.*

He left the chamois on the roof and walked over.

She struggled to free wallpaper samples from her trunk.

"Let me help you. I'm Sean." He shook her hand.

Nice hand. Warm. Dry. Soft. Good fit.

"I'm Ellen."

"Where do you want them?"

"In my condo."

"I've seen you before. I live over there." He gestured with his chin.

She was glad she'd straightened up earlier. "Just put them on the table. Thanks, Sean."

"No problem. You need anything else, you let me know."

Anything?

He left.

A minute later he returned, as if he'd forgotten something. "How spontaneous are you?"

"Depends on what you have in mind, Sean." *Try to be a lady, Ellen.*

"I'm on my way to Quiet Waters to take pictures for photography class. Want to come along? It's a great day for a walk."

She left a basket of laundry unfolded and 10 minutes later they were at the park, in a grove of oaks and maples.

"Where are you from, Sean?"

"Wyoming. A small town near Cheyenne." He looked like a cowboy. Well-built and fit, his shirt hugged a solid chest. After a three-piece suit, plaid flannel was refreshing. She had always been a sucker for accents. The lilt of his speech enchanted her.

"Where are you from, Ellen?"

"I don't share this with everyone. New Jersey."

"You don't sound like you're from New Jersey."

"Thank you. That may be the nicest compliment I get today. But I still can't shake chalk-lit for choc-o-late."

"What do you do with those big books?"

"Practice my model's walk."

"Huh?"

"I'm a decorator. What do you do?"

"I work for the Agency."

"Motor Vehicles?"

He laughed. "No, the CIA."

"Aha! You're a spook!"

He said nothing.

"Do you wear a wire, Sean? Pack a piece?" *Is that a gun in your pocket or are you just glad to see me?*

"I think you've seen too many movies. I'm not at liberty to discuss my work."

"Are you at liberty to tell me if you travel?"

Split Ends

"Yes, I travel. Sometimes a month or two at a time. Otherwise, I'm in Langley."

"Where was your last assignment, I mean, trip?"

"Nepal."

"Nepal? How's the stewed yak? Any all-night Sherpa dance clubs? Excuse my mouth, Sean. It's not attached to my brain."

"Nepal is an interesting place. I rode a camel in the Himalayas."

"Was Hertz out of mini-vans?"

He laughed and covered his mouth in a boyish way Ellen found appealing.

They strolled the winding path along the South River and stopped to watch an osprey building a nest. Sean snapped from every conceivable angle. He changed lenses and lay on his back to shoot upward.

Ellen felt the first romantic stirrings since Drew had ditched her. She imagined Sean's body next to hers. *Nice.*

"How long have you been doing photography?"

"About five years. Took it up after my divorce. I'm planning to take a course in Rockport, Maine."

"My friend took it last summer. She said it's tough but she learned a lot. I like to take pictures, but I don't know what I'm doing."

* * * *

A fire blazed in the fireplace. They rolled around like teenagers. He unzipped her jeans and slipped his hand inside. She thought of lava spilling from a long-dormant volcano.

"Sean ..."

"Let's go to bed, Ellen. It's inevitable, you know."

"I'm not ready."

"You feel ready."

"Good line. I meant I'm not ready up here." She tapped her head and sat up. "I had a bad experience before I met you."

"What happened?"

"I fell hard for someone I thought cared about me. It was a very intense relationship. Strike that. It wasn't a relationship. I had a fling with someone I really cared about. He dropped me like a hot potato."

"He took advantage of you."

"I guess." She sighed. "I'm still healing. Super cautious. Sex complicates things. I want to get to know you—really know you—first."

"Been there. Done that."

"Really?"

"Same thing happened to me a couple of years ago. Women inflict pain too. Men don't have a monopoly on cruelty. I'm patient."

He wrapped his big arms around her and she nestled against him.

"Thanks for understanding."

* * * *

Ellen meant to stick to her guns, but she wanted to be prepared. Just in case. In sunglasses and an old kerchief she read the labels on scores of boxes, glancing over her shoulder every few seconds for a familiar face.

She couldn't believe the choices: Thin, thick, latex, sheepskin, colored, ribbed, flavored. They even had

Split Ends

extra-large. *I'd like to meet the guy who needs those. Maybe I already have.*

She looked around to see if anyone was watching her. If she ran into someone she knew, she planned to say, "It's a gift for Strom Thurmond."

She checked the unit prices as she did when shopping for groceries, and bought a box of twelve. Cheaper by the dozen. Just in case.

* * * *

Laughter and loud music filtered into the condo from the marina. Ellen set aside a pile of upholstery swatches to answer the phone.

"Hi, Meg. I'm great. Love my new place. Work's going well. Seeing someone. Not sure where it's headed. I'd love to come up for a few days. Next Friday?"

* * * *

"Meg invited me for a visit. We've known each other since we were kids and she lives not far from Drew. You know, Elizabeth, I've been biding my time."

Elizabeth screwed up her mouth. "Are you sure about this?"

"Yes. I have to do it. I need to look him in the eye and hear his explanation."

"He may not have one."

"I'll take that chance. I have to put this to rest."

"Be careful. He may try to charm you back."

Beth Rubin

"I'd rather have Strom Thurmond. I'll hang tough. I promise."

* * * *

On her way to Meg's—and Drew's—Ellen stopped at the vet hospital for Penny's ashes. The night Penny died, the technician had told Ellen to pick up the dog's remains within 120 days. Time had almost run out.

"I'm here for Penny's ashes," she choked. The receptionist, a woman with a butch haircut, handed Ellen a tissue and moved on to a man buying designer dog food. Then she went in the back.

Clutching the box, no bigger than a quart of ice cream, Ellen passed the room where Penny had died. She set the box on the backseat near the stains where Penny had thrown up rawhide treats.

Ellen balled the wet tissues, dropped them on the floor and floored the gas pedal. Pebbles pinged against the undercarriage as she skidded onto the street. Thinking of her mission three hours north, she said, "Speaking of ashes, I'm coming for you next, Drew."

* * * *

The women watched the sun dip into Barnegat Bay. As they peeled steamed shrimp, Ellen updated Meg.

"I can't believe you fell for him a second time. Still the hopeless romantic, huh?"

"Just call me Sinderella—with an 's'."

Split Ends

"After Paul died I went out with someone who was like Drew. A real looker and smooth talker. He turned out to be a heartbreaker too."

Meg licked her fingers, then wiped her hands. "You know, I think I have a recipe for the perfect relationship."

"Oh? Pray tell, what is it?"

"Feed 'em, fuck 'em and agree with everything they say."

"I think I'll needlepoint that on a pillow."

Meg gave up on the seasoning under her fingernails. "I haven't dated in over a year and it's fine by me. Be glad you're rid of him. He's always been a bad boy. Aren't you ready for a grown-up?"

"You have to be one to get one. I guess I'm young for my age."

* * * *

The next morning the clock radio went on in the middle of "I Want To Run To You." How apropos, Ellen thought.

She lay in bed, listening to the lyrics.

The element of surprise was crucial. She didn't want Drew to have time to whip up a smooth reply or reel her in like an unsuspecting flounder. He'd hooked her once. That was enough to last a lifetime.

She dragged herself to the shower.

"To make up or not to make up, that is the question," she whispered to the steamed-up mirror. A zit begged for camouflage.

She turned on the small radio on the commode then lined her eyes with white pencil. The cosmetologist at

Hecht's had guaranteed that the pencil would brighten her vitreous. She wondered if Drew would notice two of the whitest eyeballs on the entire Jersey Shore or mistake her for a walleyed pike.

The forecast was for sunshine and temperatures in the 80s with low humidity. At least her hair wouldn't frizz.

Ellen raised the volume and sang "Insensitive" with Jann Arden.

"Turn it down," Meg yelled. "I'm trying to sleep."

She'd imagined showing up at Drew's in her sleek new bathing suit, but at 7 A.M. she'd freeze. "Can't have it all, old girl," she said to the mirror.

It wasn't a bad face. The tan helped and her bangs took care of some of the wrinkles. She squeezed into white shorts, tighter than a banana peel with the weight she'd picked up since moving into her condo and tucked in her teal T-shirt.

She had thought of bringing the 'Divorce' shirt, but she didn't want to inject levity into the confrontation. The last thing she wanted was to amuse or titillate Drew, she kept telling herself.

She pulled out her white cardigan from the maple highboy and chuckled. *The purple robe would be a nice touch.* But it hung, cloaked in plastic, in her closet at home—retired like a jockey's silks.

She tiptoed downstairs for a cup of coffee. It was gritty and tasteless. Meg and Ron were the only two people she knew who still drank instant. After blotting her lips on Meg's memo pad, she wrote inside the red image: "Gone for a ride. If I'm not back by 11:00, send out the cavalry."

Split Ends

She picked up the phone and dialed Drew's number. He answered. She hung up. *Bingo!*

She put down the convertible top and cranked up the heat.

The cobalt sky had begun to lighten when Ellen joined the caravan of lights on the Garden State Parkway. "It's going to be a great day, a 10 on the tanning index all you sun lovers," the DJ proclaimed.

Flamingo pink streaked the eastern sky. She slipped a CD into the player. As Old Blue Eyes hammered, "I've Got You Under My Skin," Drew's image flashed like a video on fast forward. Drew smiling. Drew in jeans. Drew in a suit. Drew in a robe. Drew naked.

"Scumball. Prick. Coward. Schmuck," Ellen thundered, drowning out Frank. He didn't stand a ghost of a chance against her tirade.

By the time she had exhausted every pejorative in her repertoire, "Second Time Around" filled the car. It seemed a lifetime ago that the words had propelled her.

Heading east on Route 72, she passed shopping center after ugly shopping center. "I'm coming for you, asshole," she bellowed while waiting in traffic at a roundabout. A redneck in a rusted clunker leaned out his window and shouted, "Go for it, bitch."

Ellen crossed the bridge to the island and hung a left. The lighthouse came into view. She drove through the awakening town and passed Drew's house. She parked in front of a bait and tackle shop and moseyed down the street of weathered clapboards. Lights punctuated their interiors like exclamation marks.

She crossed at the blinker a block from his house and walked to the beach. She shooed a gull from a bench and sat down. *Now all I have to do is wait. And stay calm.*

A breeze chilled her and she buttoned the sweater. She watched a fisherman, his legs an inverted V, tackle box and Thermos planted in the sand.

She scanned the beach, a beacon searching for Mr. Right who done her wrong, and glanced at her watch.

When she looked up she noticed a figure striding toward the water, rod in hand. He wore faded denim shorts and the jacket she had borrowed. *No mistaking that shuffle.* If she and Drew ended up in the same nursing home she'd recognize his toddling gait in cardboard slippers; even if he'd lost his hair, teeth and bladder control.

She imagined them in a linoleum-floored rec room sharing a prune juice break between Bingo and Nerf basketball, his shriveled dick peeping through the fly of his pajamas.

Don't blow it. You've journeyed too far. In, 2, 3, 4; out, 2, 3, 4.

Deep breathing had never worked, not even when she had labored to bring Michael and Lisa into the world. And it sure hadn't helped while riding Drew.

The sun—or a hot flash—warmed her. Ellen slipped off her sweater and tied it around her waist. She regretted having left her bathing suit at Meg's. It was perfect tanning weather. Her heart returned to a tolerable clip-clop. *Chill out. You can do it.*

She squinted at Drew and sighed. *Damn, even from this distance he looks good enough to eat. Emerson was right, "Beauty is its own excuse for being."*

Split Ends

She took off her sandals and willed herself to navigate the thousand miles to the jetty. *You can do it, you can do it.*

She passed a family setting up camp near the lifeguard stand. Two red-headed kids argued over a yellow pail. *Dear God, don't let him turn around before I can surprise him.*

She climbed the jetty. The stones punished her soles.

Almost there. No turning back now. Not 10 feet from the target she tripped over a clump of kelp and stubbed her toe. "Damn it!"

She recovered to see Drew whirl like a dervish. His Day-Glo orange glasses slid toward his chin.

That's what you get for having such a gentile nose.

He gaped like a hooked bluefish and Ellen swore that, for an instant, his ruddy tan paled to alabaster. *Breathe.*

Her heart threatened to burst through her ribs. She pictured her head disengaging and drifting to Portugal.

"Hi," he said. He gathered himself and flashed his Chiclets.

Joe Cool once again.

Ellen nodded to the water. "You can jump in if you want." *I'd be happy to push you.*

She was pleased to have cornered him in a spot where he had nowhere to run, nowhere to hide.

"What a surprise. You look wonderful."

"Thank you." *No thanks to you.*

He cocked his head. "How are you?"

Ellen smiled and tucked a wisp behind her ear. "Never better." *I'm a freaking basket case. And I have to pee in the worst way.*

"How's Penny?"

"Dead." *And your rod is so limp not even the fish want to jump on.*

"Oh, I'm sorry. I know how attached you were."

"Yes, I was." *I was attached to you too. Are you sorry about that?*

"What brings you here?" Drew set his fishing rod on a rock.

"Business." *Got that right.*

"It's great to see you."

"Sure." *It's great to see you too but I'd rather walk on hot coals than admit it.*

"How about coming in for a cup of coffee?"

"I don't think so," Ellen replied. *Too many external stimuli, as Elizabeth would say. But I'd like to come in and sit on your face.*

"Aw, c'mon. My parents are visiting. I know they'd like to see you."

"Oh?" *Swell. The Maple Shade Jew haters. Wonder if his mother is still schlepping that gold cross around.*

"Please?"

If she didn't get to a bathroom she would leave a puddle on the jetty.

Ellen sighed. "No coffee. I need a john."

CHAPTER 25

The screen door slammed on Ellen's heel. The living room was dark for such a bright day. She felt disassociated from the scene, an observer dropping in for the first time.

She squeezed her thighs together. She didn't want to piss on Drew's floor. "Gotta go."

"You know where it is?" Drew asked.

"I found my way here." She heard water running behind the closed door. *Oy vey. I can't hold it much longer.*

"My mother must be in there."

Ellen's legs twisted like a pretzel. *Don't pee on the floor, don't pee on the floor.*

The door opened and a scrawny bird with a feathery white cap appeared. His mother had shrunk at least six inches. The cross had not. A bluish aura surrounded Drew's mother like the halo of the Suffering Jesus on the Cushings' mantel.

Mrs. Cushing's colorless eyes darted from Drew to Ellen. She tried to smile but her lips were frozen.

"Mom, this is Ellen Gold, er, Ellen Rosenberg. "She was my friend in high school."

"Did you marry her?"

Drew blushed through his tan. "No, Mom. We were friends in Maple Shade. Remember?"

She can't remember what day it is. Please, could we save the chitchat for later? My bladder is bursting.

Ellen pasted on a smile and extended her hand. Drew's mother strained to grasp the olive branch and wagged Ellen's fingertips.

"Hello, Mrs. Cushing. It's nice to see you," she fibbed. She felt the start of labor.

I can't believe we're having a tête-a-tête outside the john. The bitch made my life miserable because I didn't snap mackerel on Friday night. She made her son's life a living hell for lesser transgressions. Why am I being so pleasant? I'm regressing.

Ellen squirmed.

Stroking the cross as if she were coaxing it to orgasm, Mrs. Cushing chirped, "Now I remember. You were Drew's Jewish girlfriend."

"Mom ..." Drew interrupted, his mouth tight.

"Yes, Mrs. Cushing, I was the Jewish girlfriend."

Her bladder pressing into the non-conversation, the Jewish ex-girlfriend went to the bathroom. "Excuse me. We'll catch up in a minute."

Christ, are they going to stand by the door and listen?

Navy towels hung from the chrome rack. *I wonder how many snatches these towels have dried since they wiped mine.* She flushed and pulled back the shower curtain to run a finger over the tub.

Immaculate.

Not a hint of soap scum or pubic hair. *He's clean. I'll give him that much.* She recalled how they had lathered each other with lemon soap before doing it in the tub at the Four Seasons. Her back had been bruised for days. She couldn't cut into a lemon without thinking of him.

The medicine cabinet creaked when she opened it. She hoped Tina Turner's singing would cover the noise. In a pop psychology article she had read that you can learn a lot by looking in people's medicine

Split Ends

cabinets. She surveyed the neat dental/deodorant/shaving grouping on the bottom shelf. *Nothing of consequence here.*

Above it sat aspirin, antacid and pills as turquoise as the water off Virgin Gorda. Ellen rifled through the rest searching for Tampax, K-Y jelly or other signs of female life. Not even an old lipstick. And not a condom in sight. *Wonder if he still has chocolate rubbers. Maybe he's graduated to mango or tutti-frutti.*

Much relieved, Ellen washed her hands and helped herself to some of Drew's mouthwash before rejoining the Blessed Mother and Child in the living room. Drew's mother nested on the sofa. The cross rested in her gnarled fingers and she stared into space. Probably at some martyred saint.

Drew sat on the cracked leather hassock, smoking and leafing through the *Asbury Park Press.*

The ceiling fan whirred. It seemed to be seducing the morning breeze. Mini-blinds clacked. Jitters dented her composure.

She soaked up the room's details and Drew's citrus smell. On a twig table, a basket held sunscreen. A striped beach towel hung from a chair. A vase of wheat stood on the hearth where a fire had warmed their feet. A beer huggy proclaimed, "Big Boys Drive Bad Toys."

She felt as if she were visiting a Hollywood set.

The place needs a woman's touch. It's sombrous.

"Drew, I want to talk to you. Outside," Ellen said.

"Sure." He snuffed his cigarette in an ashtray and turned to his mother. "We'll be back soon. Wait for me when Dad comes back from his errands."

What else would they do? Go rollerskating?

The screen slapped shut. Ellen lifted her face to the sun.

They crossed the dune to the beach.

Don't fink out now. He's all yours.

Her anger and hurt dissipated in the velvet breeze. She feasted on the familiarity of being with Drew again. *Could I have dreamed the bad stuff? Maybe he'll prostrate himself on the beach and tell me he can't live without me. Too bad. Let him eat sand. Damn, I wish I could stop contradicting myself.*

They stopped and sat on a graffitied bench facing the ocean. They looked at each other, just smiling. "It's good to see you. I've missed you," he said. His eyes sparkled from his bronzed face.

I still want him. What's wrong with me?

Ellen spoke in a firm voice. "You owe me an explanation."

"An explanation?" His smile collapsed into a tragic mask. Pagliacci on the beach.

"Yes, an explanation. Why did you dump me?" *Damn it, I'm not letting him off the hook.*

Drew took a long moment. "I don't know what to say."

I'm the one who's suffered. Why does he look so upset? Sweat collected in the creases behind her knees. "C'mon, Drew. You're a bright, articulate guy. I'm sure you can come up with something."

"You look terrific. Things must be going well."

Don't change the subject. "Things are going well."

"I know the divorce has been a painful struggle for you."

You don't know jack shit. "I'm doing fine." She paused to blot the perspiration from her forehead. "But there's one loose screw that needs tightening." *Don't let him squirm out of this. What's his problem? Why is he taking so long? It's a simple question.* "Why did you dump me?"

He turned to face her and tears spilled from his eyes. Ellen's resolve crumbled, as though a wave had knocked her under.

She remembered the last time she'd seen him cry, when they had struggled to say good-bye. She swallowed hard.

"I handled things badly."

"You can say that again."

"I'm sorry if I hurt you," he whispered.

"*If?* You cut me off at the knees and you say if you hurt me?"

"I'm sorry." His shoulders drooped. "I cared about you," he sighed. "Still care about you. But I had to end it, for your sake more than mine."

What is he saying? Are we doing Beckett here? He dumped me for my own good?

"Remember when you called from Florida last November, after my Colorado trip?"

Remember? How could I forget. The sonofabitch never called back. "Sure," she said. "You'd been skiing with your friend."

"Well, he's more than a friend."

Oh my God.

A shiver raced up her spine clear to her scalp.

Drew took her hands in his. She didn't resist, but she felt like saying, "Hey, let's drop it and go have an ice cream cone."

"I'm bisexual."

Ellen imploded. Surf pounded in her ears—only louder.

"That's why I couldn't commit to you. Why I ran."

Ellen tried swallowing the truth. She couldn't.

"I'd made my peace with what I am. I built a life around my work and friends. I thought I had it all."

She saw her distorted reflection in his eyes. "When you visited you permeated the place. My world toppled when I realized what I'd been missing."

He loosened his grip and she wiggled her dead fingers. He offered her a cigarette.

"I don't smoke anymore." *And I'm giving up sex.*

He lit a cigarette with shaking hands. The smoke wafted toward the lighthouse. "I thought I could start over with you. I wanted to. But I couldn't handle it. I wish things were different."

Ellen wished she had remained cocooned and ignorant under Meg's quilt. She thought of the photo of the blond Twinkie in the black parka. When she had seen it in November, she couldn't put her finger on it. Now she knew why the picture had disquieted her. "What about this friend?"

"I've known him a long time. He's ill. I can't abandon him now."

"Ill? You mean ... AIDS?"

"Yes. I freaked when I found out. That's why I stopped seeing you."

Ellen's throat closed. She struggled to get the words out. "How could you sleep with me and not say something? The last time we didn't use a condom."

"You insisted. Remember?"

Split Ends

"Oh God. Yes, I remember. That's no excuse, Drew. Jesus, you outweigh me by 80 pounds. You should have pushed me away."

Drew cradled her hands to his chest. "It's all right. I've been tested since then. I'm okay. I've never tested positive, and I've always used protection. You don't have to worry. You're fine. I haven't been intimate with anyone but you in a year and a half."

Sure. Like the check is in the mail.

"Damn it, why didn't you level with me?"

He shrugged his big shoulders. "I couldn't face you with the truth. I was scared. You're strong. I knew you'd be all right."

"We have different definitions of 'all right.'"

"I knew you'd be all right."

He seemed to repeat it more for his ears than hers.

"You were in turmoil at the time. I figured I was doing you a favor. I was afraid if we continued it would cloud your judgment. You needed to gain clarity, focus on your situation. I didn't want to muddy the waters."

"Doing me a favor? Do me a favor and cut the crap, Drew. And your self-serving bullshit. You lied to me. Acted irresponsibly and put me in danger."

He gazed at the horizon. The tide was up and the waves thundered onto the beach.

"I know avoiding you was wrong. I was a coward."

As he lit another cigarette, Ellen studied his slim, nicotine-stained fingers.

"I thought of calling. I couldn't. I've been on a guilt trip ever since. I hope in time you'll understand. I don't expect or deserve forgiveness."

No you don't, asshole.

Ellen drew a deep breath and wondered if she would be all right. *Soon as I get home I'll go for a blood test. And take a vow of celibacy.*

"Isn't there a six-month window between infection and a positive test?"

"Yes."

"It's been seven months since we were together. How does that translate?"

"It would have shown up by now."

"Sure, if I'd known and gone for a test. I can't believe you did this to me."

"I'm sorry. It was only once, Ellen. Believe me, you're okay."

"Why in hell should I believe anything from your lying mouth?"

Ellen stood. She was trembling. They walked back to the house in silence. A gull munched a French fry. Drew reached for her hand. She refused him.

She left him at the door. "Say so-long to your mother for me."

"Take good care of yourself."

I hope it's not too late.

"I know you're fine. But get tested anyway."

"Thanks for the friendly advice. Don't worry, I will."

She felt as though she was swimming under water. Scratches of white blemished the sky as she walked to her car. *I guess this is the end of the line. Well, I got my answer.* "Jesus, Mary and Joseph."

She scooped her hair under a baseball cap, started the engine and lowered the top.

The light changed. She slid Judy Collins into the CD player and tried to sing, but couldn't. So she listened. "Send in the clowns. Don't bother, they're here."

CHAPTER 26

The clinic was in a frame colonial built in the '40s, decades before the neighborhood went commercial. It reminded Ellen of a fraternity house—without the keg and loud music.

The room was a stew of shapes and ages. All the chairs were taken, so Ellen leaned against the wall. The phone rang incessantly.

"The results are confidential," the receptionist said for the fifth time. "You have to make an appointment. You'll have the results in a week."

Ellen walked over and waited for a lull. "What do I do? Where do I go? Do you have a Valium?"

"Blood test?"

"And a brain transplant." Ellen felt like she was moving in slow motion.

"Have a seat at the nurse's station." The woman nodded to her left.

Ellen did as she was told. And waited.

The nurse came from somewhere in the back. She lectured Ellen about HIV.

Ellen caught every third or fourth word.

The nurse assigned her a six-digit number, wrote it on a card and handed it to her.

"For cross-referencing and to guarantee anonymity, we request an alias too."

"Alias?"

"Make up a name. Anything."

"How about 'Dumb Bitch?' If it hasn't been taken."

The nurse shrugged and picked up a pen. "You're the first. I'm writing it in the ledger along with your

Split Ends

number. Don't lose the card. Come back a week from today. We're open from 9:00 to 4:00. Are you ready?"

"No." Ellen eyed the vials, syringes and rubber tourniquets. Everything went black. She was aware of something under her nose. It smelled vile. Ammonia.

"We've got a fainter here," somebody said.

She opened her eyes. Someone had placed wet paper towels on the back of her neck.

"Breathe, ma'am. I caught you before you hit the floor. Are you okay?"

"Never worse."

The nurse pulled on rubber gloves and wrapped a tourniquet around Ellen's upper arm.

"Make a fist. You'll feel a pinch."

Ellen looked away. *Some pinch.*

"It's over." *I hope I'm not over.*

The nurse placed a cotton ball on the site and told Ellen to bend her arm.

"Sit here a few minutes. I'll get you some orange juice."

* * * *

"Sean, remember when I told you I'd been burned?"

They walked the docks of the marina.

"Hard to forget, considering my excitement at the time." He knelt to photograph two mallards on a boat transom.

"I have bad news." She sighed.

He stood up and slipped the camera strap onto his shoulder.

"What?"

"I found out the person is bisexual."

"The guy who dumped you?" She nodded. "What? He didn't tell you?"

"Nope. There's more. His boyfriend has AIDS. He claims they haven't been together in a year and a half. But who knows?"

"How could he do that? I wish you'd told me sooner. I would have been there for you."

"Thanks, Sean. You're a good friend."

"Are you okay? Were you tested?"

"I had a blood test today. It takes a week for the results. Thank heavens you and I have waited. The gods work in mysterious ways."

"Come here." He held her. "You're right about that."

She began to cry.

He stroked her hair and held her tight. "It'll be all right, Ellen. I have a feeling."

CHAPTER 27

Big Bird pecked the parched earth outside the redbrick courthouse. In Room 5 the air conditioner wheezed like a patient on a respirator, masking the traffic noise. The aroma of pine oil hung in what passed for air. Metal school lockers lined two walls of the courtroom and St. Anne's spire glistened through a window.

Behind the judge's bench the tattered flags of New Jersey and Maryland framed an altarpiece of Drew as Saint Sebastian in the style of El Greco. Instead of arrows, fishhooks pierced his sinewy flesh. Skis x-ed out his privates.

Ron's attorney, Ichabod Crane in an ill-fitting glen-plaid suit, tried to interrogate Ellen. She could tell by the way his thin lips twitched and relaxed that she was supposed to inseminate his pauses. But breast-stroking below the pool's surface, she heard only the water pulsing in her ears.

Near the entrance, her children set up a lemonade stand and argued over how much to charge. Giggling teenage girls—all Sandra Dee lookalikes—crammed the wooden pews. Ellen emerged beneath the diving board and spewed a chlorinated stream that just missed the judge's wig. She climbed out of the pool and shook like a wet retriever, then took the witness stand.

Ichabod compressed his giraffe neck like a Slinky and thrust his pinched face to within an inch of hers. "Mrs. Gold, did you at any time during your marriage have sexual intercourse with anyone other than Mr. Gold?"

Beth Rubin

Holy shit. I wonder if I have the stamina for another lap. *"No sir, your judgeship, I mean your lawyership. I did not. Would you like to subpoena my vibrator?"*

She'd been dreading the question since Marla had raised it at their pre-trial conference. Ellen had told her attorney about Drew early on. She'd seen enough courtroom scenes to know that, for a lawyer to be effective, a client had to be honest and forthcoming. Not that it hurt O.J. to tell a few white lies.

Ellen felt guiltless. And even though she and Ron had been living apart when the union with Schmuck-O took place, she hoped to avoid owning up to the brief merger in court. It was her business. And that of the 40 or so friends and relatives she'd taken into her confidence.

"Mrs. Gold, may I remind you that you're under oath. You are still legally married. Have you ever had an affair?"

Yer darn tootin'. I was fucked. I am fucked. It's over. I won't get a red cent. I'll never see my children again. And I'll probably do solitary. Maybe get the chair. *"I wouldn't call it an affair per se. It was over before it started. He was an old friend. Yeah. It was more of a reunion. It didn't mean anything. Mr. Gold and I hadn't cohabitated, um, enjoyed conjugal relations in many months. As you may recall, Mr. Gold had difficulty getting it up, er, finding himself. For me, at least. I can't speak for his paralegal or others who may have been the beneficiaries of his sexual prowess."*

Ellen scanned the cheerleading section for support. Her friends tittered in complicity. Hair lacquered into flips hugging their pert wrinkle-free faces, they wore sweater sets in a palette of pastels. She avoided eye contact with Ron.

"Would you please tell the court the circumstances surrounding your infidelity?"

"Do I have to? Can't I take the Fifth?"

"Yes to the first, no to the second," said Ron's attorney, now fully stretched to his tree-top-nibbling seven feet.

Ellen wondered if the shyster was married. He sure was ugly. She pictured him naked. Probably not a hair on his chest and a thing like a toothpick. Bet his wife weighs in at 250 or more.

"Please answer the question, Mrs. Gold."

Ellen's tongue stuck to the roof of her mouth. She took a deep breath before plunging into shark-infested waters.

"I was in New York visiting my cousin. While she was at the gym, I went to the Museum of Modern Art. I bumped into this person in front of Picasso's 'The Embrace.' That's a hot drawing of a nude couple doing the nasty. We hadn't seen each other since high school. I cannot tell a lie. He's a good-looking dude. Sort of an aging Patrick Swayze in 'Dirty Dancing.' Did I mention that he has the whitest teeth, like Chiclets? Anyway, he was my big moment when I was a teen. We chatted. He asked if I had lunch plans. I didn't. And I never pass up a free meal. We went to some little French place on Madison Avenue. Sigourney Weaver was at the next table. So I was only half-paying attention to what he was saying. I'm a groupie. Always have been."

"Mrs. Gold, please stick to the subject."

Beth Rubin

"Yessir. Sorry, sir. Well, the asshole, er, Mr. Cushing, ordered a bottle of wine, then another ... it was white, a Chardonnay I think, and we sat for two or three hours talking and drinking. I picked at a mushroom omelet. Shiitake. Sigourney left without saying goodbye, so I started paying closer attention to what the schmuck, I mean, Mr. Cushing, had to say. Mostly about his work. He's a stockbroker. Totally boring. And about being in the Air Force during Vietnam. Also boring. And about his ex-wife. A little less boring. I was getting a glow on from the wine. And he started looking like a kid. The double chin disappeared. The gray hair darkened. He dropped 20, no, 30 pounds. We were back in Latin class. And suddenly I'm feeling attractive for the first time since I can't remember when. I start loosening up. Ordered chocolate mousse even though it gives me gas. I'm licking the last of the whipped cream off the spoon and feel a stirring down below like I haven't in years. Shall I go on?"

The lawyer leered. Spittle clustered like miniature grapes in the corner of his mouth. "Yes, please."

"He paid the check with an American Express Platinum Card and called his office. As we left the restaurant, he said his three o'clock had been cancelled and he was free the rest of the afternoon. He asked if I had plans. I had nothing until that evening. My cousin and I had reservations to hear Barbara Cook at the Carlyle. The late show. Next thing I know, we're in this suite at the Four Seasons on East 57th Street. Fresh flowers everywhere. Bed the size of the Astrodome. I'm dizzy. Feel like I'm in a movie. We're holding onto each other, kind of swaying together.

Split Ends

Sinatra is singing 'Strangers in the Night.' I don't know where it's coming from. Maybe inside my head."

Ellen surveyed her support group. Minus Ron and his attorney, everyone else was on the bride's side. They were hanging over the benches, mouths agape, waiting for her to divulge the next sordid detail. Like sea lions at feeding time, they beat their flippers and arfed in preprandial anticipation of the next fish from the trainer.

"Go on."

"As I said, I'd had too much to drink. I rarely drink at lunch. Just ice tea—no sugar—or water. Well, I guess we did it. I honestly don't remember the details. I must have fallen asleep or passed out. I woke up or came to—no pun intended—and I was naked in that huge bed and there was sticky stuff running down my leg. And he was on his back snoring. Mouth hanging open. Like a cave full of bats. I could see his fillings. And he used to be so gorgeous. I can't believe I waited over 30 years for that. You want to know the truth? I don't even remember consenting. I think it was date rape. Like I said earlier, it was over before it started. He offered to pay for the taxi back to my cousin's. I walked even though it was bitter cold. Needed to clear my head. I never heard from him again."

Ellen shrugged.

"He shtupped me, then he squooshed me. That's my mother's pet phrase. After he dumped me she said, 'Ellen, he squooshed you like a bug.'"

"You may step down, Mrs. Gold."

"Thank you, your highness. I mean your lordship."

Ellen rose and curtsied to the judge. Then, as if painted by Chagall's brush, she floated to a chair next *to Marla. She glanced over at Ron, reconstituted as Pee-Wee Herman right down to the rouged cheeks, patent leather hair and a crooked smirk.* Christ, when did he change his inside-the-Beltway, button-down image?

Her dripping armpits fused with the cream polyester blouse as if the two had been glued. She detested polyester, didn't even own polyester. She had borrowed the blouse from a friend at Marla's insistence. "Don't look too affluent," her attorney had instructed. "Wear a pastel suit and no jewelry. Look a little dowdy, pathetic. You'll get more sympathy from the judge." She'd borrowed the suit also. It was pale blue, too big and in guaranteed-to-wrinkle rayon. An old stain on the skirt told of a double frozen latte that missed its target. Or the President of the United States. She couldn't wait to get home and change into a natural fiber.

"The court calls Mrs. Rosenberg to the stand."

As Mady did the so-help-me-God thing, Ellen schvitzed buckets. Could her mother stay cool? No lioness could be as fierce protecting her cubs. But if her mother screwed up on the stand, Ellen knew she'd lose points with the judge who looked like E.G. Marshall.

Mady always said she'd face water torture before wearing polyester. With fanaticism she subscribed to two fashion dictums: never wear white shoes and never wear polyester. Mady was her tasteful self in a navy St. John's knit suit over a beige silk shirt. Her helmet of teased black hair anchored tinted Gene Tierney glasses. What's with the hair? She looks like a harpy.

Split Ends

Mady's hands were locked in mortal combat, white knuckles protruding. Ellen could see she was dying for a cigarette. If Mady's lips had been pursed a skosh tighter, she would have whistled.

"Mrs. Rosenberg, I'd like to ask you a few questions about your daughter's conduct during her marriage to Mr. Gold."

"Okay, gonif. Shoot."

"Do you have any knowledge of your daughter's affair with a Mr. Drew Cushing?"

"Don't you have better things to do, young man? Mr. Cushing is hardly worth our time or the taxpayers' gelt. What's there to say? He was a good-looking goy—big shoulders, tight ass, small brain. My Ellie went for him. Twice. Look for substance, I always told her. Watch out for the handsome ones. They'll eat you alive, break your heart, rip out your spleen, eviscerate you like a Kosher chicken. She always was a pushover for a pretty face and hard body."

"Please, Mrs. Rosenberg, just answer the question."

"I'd hardly call it an affair. He besmirched my poor Ellen. She wasn't in her right mind. One thing I know for sure. I'll kill the sonofabitch if I ever get my hands on him."

"Please, Mrs. Rosenberg, just answer the question."

Ellen shifted. Sweat laminated her blouse to her boobs. She thought she'd die if she couldn't rip the synthetic layers from her fevered flesh in the next five seconds.

"I knew they had lunch in New York. Since I wasn't there and didn't see penetration, I can't swear it happened."

"Way to go, Mom."

"You know," her mother continued, *"kids never listen. I didn't trust him when they were kids. That's why Ellen's father—may his soul rest in peace—and I forced her to break up with the schmuck in high school. But did she learn anything? No! A smart person ..."*

She paused to gasp. "Got a smoke? No? Forget it, putz."

Her voice scaled up an octave and she shook an arthritic finger at Ron's attorney. "As I was saying, a smart person learns by listening to others. A stupid person has to learn the hard way—from her own dumb mistakes. She should have listened. Then this never would have happened. She could have avoided it. He shtupped her and then he squooshed her."

"You may step down, Mrs. Rosenberg."

"I'm not finished. I told her, in the words of the song, 'You're a somebody 'til a nobody loves you.'"

"Are you done, Mrs. Rosenberg?"

Ellen read relief on her mother's face. Head high, Mady returned to the peanut gallery.

"The court calls Michael and Lisa Gold to the stand."

The children—not more than six and four, respectively—raced down the aisle, screaming.

"I'm a girl, I get to sit," Lisa shrieked.

"Oh no. I'm older. And I've got a penis. I'm always first," Michael yelled as they fought for the single seat in the witness stand.

Split Ends

"*Your penis means you can stand up to pee. So you can stand up now!*"

"*I'm not going to pee here. I'm saving it for your lemonade.*"

The judge's voice squelched the fracas.

"*Simmer down, kiddies. If you're good, I'll take you for pizza and a movie after your mother gets what's coming to her.*"

As Ichabod approached the stand, the children began to giggle. "*You're funny-looking, mister,*" *Michael said. Ichabod turned scarlet.*

"*Michael and Lisa, what's your take on your old lady? I mean, what kind of wife was she to your father?*"

Michael answered first. "*I need to pee.*"

"*In a minute, kid. Cross your knees and answer the question. Then you can go pee. Waste this court's time and you can pee in your pants.*"

Michael looked contrite. He squirmed. "*Not bad I guess. But she's a bitch when she's on the rag.*"

"*Lisa, dear, what's your opinion?*"

"*It's hard to say. Daddy doesn't smile very much. Could be her fault. Can I go pee too?*"

The children were excused and stopped to stick their tongues out at their mother.

"*Comb your hair, Michael. Lisa, there's ketchup on your face,*" *Ellen called as they tore up the aisle.*

"*Andrew Cushing to the stand.*"

"*Oh, shit,*" *Ellen said, loud enough for Baltimore to hear.*

Drew materialized and took his sweet old time to shuffle through the courtroom. As he passed Ellen, the muscles of his back rippled under a white T-shirt.

Brawny shoulders exposed, a pack of Camels in the rolled right sleeve, Drew's pegged black pants left nothing to the imagination.

"I'm going to puke," Ellen whispered. Marla seemed to be assessing Drew with more than casual professional interest. Drew winked at Ellen, flashing his Chiclets, then slumped into the chair like a male stripper warming up an audience of horny spinsters.

Slouched almost to horizontal, he spread his legs. His crotch glowed, radiating heat in every direction. Ellen felt like a deer caught in the headlights—nowhere to run, nowhere to hide. Deer ticks picked at her flesh.

"Mr. Cushing," Ichabod gloated, "did you with malice of foreplay shtup and then squoosh the defendant last winter at the Four Seasons Hotel in New York City?"

"Ifuckedherifthat'swhatyouwanttoknow."

Mady jumped to her feet. "Christ, he's still mumbling. He hasn't changed. I always knew he was a bad number. He defiled my Ellie. Shtupped her and squooshed her. Like a bug."

"Mrs. Rosenberg," E.G. Marshall scolded, his wig askew, "please keep your opinions to yourself or I will cite you for contempt."

Ellen's mother, who in 71 years never hid her contempt, continued unfazed. "You want to talk contempt. I'll give you contempt. Cushing is contemptible. He's not fit to shtup the likes of my Ellen. She's a good girl. He's slime, a scumbag. He screws men. And animals for all I know."

The judge righted his wig and nodded to a pair of burly bailiffs. They lifted Mady by her scrawny elbows

Split Ends

and dragged her away kicking and screaming, "He's a shtupper, he's a squoosher, he's a schmuck. Shtup you, Drew Cushing." She flipped him the bird as the doors closed behind her.

Drew disappeared in a puff of smoke.

Elizabeth took the stand. Cleavage deeper than the Grand Canyon and gowned for a hookers' convention in a magenta and tangerine gypsy number, gold bangles up and down both arms, she told the court what she knew about Ellen's peccadillo.

Without coming up for air, Elizabeth replied in her silky, soothing, shrink's voice. "Mrs. Gold was desperate for emotional and physical bonding because her husband denied her love and affection for so long. I would have been surprised if she did not reach out for life and seek confirmation of her intrinsic femininity and in no way did her brief disastrous consensual liaison with Mr. Cushing, the aforementioned asshole, contribute to the dissolution of the marital union."

Ellen flung a thumbs-up to her therapist.

Elizabeth finished her testimony, saying: "It is unfortunate that Mrs. Gold chose such an unsuitable conjugal partner with whom to validate her self-esteem and worth as a free-thinking, independent, intelligent, attractive, sexually responsive and eminently fuckable woman. Clearly, Mr. Cushing is severely damaged emotionally. Even if he is hung like a stallion. But as I told Mrs. Gold on numerous occasions, 'Get a life. He's no soul mate, he's a schmuck.' And he wouldn't have cared if she was male, female, animal, vegetable or mineral."

Beth Rubin

As Elizabeth stepped down, bracelets jingling and ass shaking, her cheap perfume filled the air. She raised her arms overhead and turned to face the judge. Fingers snapping, she broke into Salome's dance, proving once again to Ellen that all shrinks are nuts.

The judge called the attorneys to the bench. The spectators leaned forward to hear Ellen's fate. After a brief conference, Judge E.G. Marshall said, "I think we have heard an overwhelming preponderance of evidence to determine that there occurred a shtup, followed by a squoosh, both of which were perpetrated by a schmuck. Mrs. Gold is not accountable or punishable for her actions. She's been punished enough. Although, in the opinion of this court, no woman has ever been punished enough."

The crowd erupted in cheers. Ellen's children left their lemonade stand and ran to hug their vindicated mother. Her friends rocked back and forth, beating their thighs and shouting hallelujahs. In his checkered suit and spats, Pee-Wee Ron retreated to Chick & Ruth's deli for a hot dog. Ichabod mounted Gunpowder and galloped down Main Street. Fireworks exploded over Annapolis harbor as Oprah rushed forward to interview Ellen.

A bevy of Ellen's gay decorator friends—until then models of decorum in the last two rows—formed a chorus line. In T-shirts with "FREE ELLEN" emblazoned in hot pink, they linked arms and kicked higher than the Rockettes. Stepping out in three-inch heels and swiveling their skinny hips in perfect unison, they sang, 'He shtupped her, yeah, yeah, yeah. He squooshed her yeah, yeah, yeah.' The courtroom erupted in dancing and clapping. The boys performed

Split Ends

their bump and grind down the center aisle, throwing limp wrists to the judge who, near collapse, waved his wig from a crab mallet in time to the music.

Ellen plunged into the water again, relieved to be out of the courtroom. As Marla performed a triple somersault in the tuck position, $100 bills flew from the padded bra of her bikini. The judge, metamorphosed into Tom Cruise, mixed daiquiris at the Tiki bar unfolded from his bench while Mady, a scarlet hibiscus tucked behind her ear, served drinks to Ellen's underage teen friends. Around the pool, teal lifeguard stands cupped the tight, purple-thonged butts of the gay decorators.

And then a bell rang. The frivolity stopped. Ellen groped for the phone on her bedside table, knocking over a half-eaten Hershey bar.

"Did I wake you? It's Mom."

"Oh shit. What time is it?"

"It's 8:30. Are you all right?"

"Yeah. Just groggy. What's up?"

"The divorce has been on my mind. How are the negotiations going?"

CHAPTER 28

Ellen set the throttle and started the diesel. She signaled Wilma to toss the stern lines onto the pier. One landed in the water. "Darn. Shall I get it with the boat hook?"

"Don't bother. We'll be back soon."

"I hope so." Wilma's laugh was more nervous than hearty.

"Relax. You look like you're having your tubes tied without anesthesia. We'll be fine."

The boat nosed toward open water. Wilma sat in the cockpit and leaned against a cushion. "You're a lot cooler than Ron. He was always barking orders. 'Do this. Do that.' He made Steven and me nervous."

"He made me nervous too. On and off the boat."

"I used to wonder how you handled him."

"You get used to hanging if you hang long enough."

"Well, I'm glad you cut the noose."

"Speaking of ropes, will you give me a hand with the sheets and halyards?"

"I'll try. But I'm out of my league, Ellen. I haven't sailed in a while."

"It'll come back to you. You'll do fine."

"Are you comfortable taking the boat out with just me for crew?"

"Sure. I've been sailing since I was a kid. And conditions couldn't be better. Wind out of the south, 10 to 12 knots, no chop. Piece of cake."

"Radio said there's a chance of a thunderstorm."

Split Ends

"They give the same forecast from May to October. Then they switch to '50 percent chance of snow' to cover their asses."

"Steven and I were caught in a squall years ago. We ran into a buoy off Bloody Point. I was petrified. We went home and traded the sailboat for a stink pot."

"Don't worry, Wilma. The VHF is on channel 16, just in case. We'll hear any warnings. Are you ready? I'll keep her into the wind while you raise the sails, main first.

"I think I can handle that."

Ellen's eyes followed the rising sail up the mast. "Looking good. Here." Ellen handed Wilma a winch handle.

"Read for the jib?"

"Good girl, Wilma. You remembered."

Ellen fell off the wind and silenced the diesel. Air filled the sails. "This is the best part, the first moments without the engine. No noise and no exhaust."

"I know what you mean. Power is okay, but I do miss this." *Golden Oldie* sliced through the water on a beam reach toward the shipping channel. Wilma took off her sunglasses and smoothed on sunscreen.

"Keep an eye on things for a sec." Ellen went below for diet sodas. She returned to a light chop and set the Autohelm for Tolley Point.

Wilma let go of the lifeline just long enough to take a can. "What did you want to talk about?"

"I don't know where to start."

"You're not pregnant are you?"

"I'd make a killing if I was." Ellen chewed a hangnail.

"What is it? Spill your guts."

"I saw Drew last week."

"I didn't want to pry."

Ellen spotted a puff ahead. The boat heeled. She eased the main. The wind speed gauge jumped to 18 knots. A gust forced the needle to 20. She tightened her grip on the wheel. "We're getting some heavy air. Let's reef the main. It'll be more comfortable."

Wilma clutched the stanchion, knuckles blanched. She slid toward Ellen, then took the wheel.

"Take her head-to-wind, Wilma. There's too much pressure on the main."

"Aye, aye, Skipper."

Ellen tied slip knots at the first reefing points.

"Are you okay?"

"I'm feeling more relaxed."

Ellen tied off the last reef and relieved Wilma. "Do you still volunteer at the county AIDS hotline?"

"You're changing the subject. I want to know about Drew."

"This is about Drew."

Thunderheads had begun to build in the West. "Looks like they were right for a change. Bad weather's moving in. Let's bring her about and head toward home."

"Ready about," Ellen said, and turned the wheel. "Hard-a-lee."

Wilma freed the port jib sheet and hauled in the starboard.

Wilma scuttled to the high side. "What about Drew? You're driving me crazy." The wind whistled through the rigging.

Split Ends

Ellen checked the wind speed. Up to 23 knots. She was glad Wilma was looking elsewhere. "I'm going to furl the jib and start the engine."

"Are we going to be all right?"

"Sure." *We'll be all right, but will I be all right?*

"What about Drew?"

"He's bisexual," she mumbled. The wind tore at her words.

"What?"

"Drew is bisexual."

Wilma grabbed the pedestal. "Is this a joke?"

"I wish."

"Oh, Ellen. I can't believe it, the way you described him."

"Yeah, all man."

"You must have been in shock when he told you."

Ellen nodded.

"Tell me you used condoms."

Ellen turned away.

"You did, didn't you?"

"All except once."

"Have you been checked? There's a clinic in town."

"I had a blood test. I'm going tomorrow for the results."

Thunder rumbled in the distance. Ellen saw alarm in Wilma's eyes.

"Are you afraid of the storm, Wilma?"

"I know you can handle the boat. I'm afraid for you."

"They explained everything at the clinic, but I was numb. I don't remember a thing."

"Ask away."

"If my test is negative, what then?"

"How long since you were intimate?"

"Seven months."

"If your test is negative, you don't have to be retested. Most people develop antibodies within three months after infection. The average is 25 days."

"I thought there was a six-month window between infection and a positive test, Wilma."

"In rare cases it can take up to six months. Half the people with HIV develop AIDS within 10 years. But even with an HIV-positive test, some get AIDS and some don't. There are lots of variables. I pray everything is all right."

"That makes two of us."

"Do you want me to go with you?"

"No, I don't think so. But I might need you when I get home." The sun disappeared and a charcoal cocoon enveloped them.

"Let me know if you change your mind."

Thunder boomed and Wilma jumped. "Will we make it to the creek in time?"

"I'm not even trying. Getting near shore in a storm is too risky. It's safer to ride it out. Bay squalls seldom last long. Try not to worry."

"Do you have any Not To Worry pills onboard?"

"I took them all when I learned about Drew. But I have M&Ms. Are you okay to go below? Foul weather gear is in the hanging locker. Turn up the radio and grab some crackers for seasickness. Just in case."

The women put on yellow overalls and jackets. Static crackled from the marine radio. The wind gusted to 30. Spray flew over the foredeck. The wind became a guillotine, beheading the waves.

Split Ends

"You look like Nanook of the North in that get-up, Wilma."

"So long as I stay dry."

"I can't guarantee it. Life vests are in the aft berth, if you'll feel more comfortable." Wilma struggled to get her footing on the tipsy cabin sole. Ellen saw her lower lip quiver.

"I knew we shouldn't have come out."

"It's going to be all right. Honest. I've been in dozens of squalls. Take deep breaths and focus on the horizon."

"I can't see the goddamn horizon."

"Well, pretend. I hate to ask, but I need the running lights. The control panel's to the left of the head. The switch is second from the top."

Wilma went below and returned a minute later.

"Thanks, Wilma. You're a trooper."

"I'm putting another reef in the main. Take the wheel. Please."

"I can't see the fucking wheel."

"Did my ladylike friend used the F-word?"

Ellen reached for Wilma's hand. "Sit here and play captain. Pretend you can see the fucking wheel while I reef the fucking main." *Damn. I forgot the golden rule: Reef early, reef often.*

The sky had turned to midnight. BB-size hail bombarded the deck. Ellen could no longer see the wind speed gauge, but the way the wind howled through the rigging and stung her face told her it was blowing above 30.

"Ellen, why don't you take down the mainsail?"

"It's better up. Helps with stability." The hail turned to torrential rain. Water ran down her sleeves.

The visibility fell to zero. Her biggest fear was colliding with another vessel or going aground.

"Wilma, did you hear something?"

"Just the wind. And my heart."

Ellen cut the engine. "I thought I heard a voice. It may be a distress call." She reached for the mike. "*Golden Oldie, Golden Oldie, Golden Oldie* off Greenbury Point calling boat in distress, over." She tried twice more. No response.

"Did you hear that, Wilma?"

"I don't hear anything but Mother Nature. And she sounds plenty pissed."

"Hold the spotlight, Wilma. This is no weather for a novice."

"Be careful."

"I will. I need you to put fenders out."

"Are we going to hit something?"

"I hope not. This old Girl Scout wants to be prepared." *Why didn't I think of that when I had my way with Drew?*

"Can you tie a round turn and two half-hitches?"

"Or something like it. Please don't ask me for a bowline."

"Tie the fenders to the stanchions. Two portside, two starboard."

As quickly as the deluge had begun, it slowed to intermittent spitting and the squall rolled toward the Eastern Shore. The dark curtain lifted to reveal three people, waving their arms, in what had been a small sloop. Now it was a tangle of rigging, the mast hanging over the side. Ellen put the engine in neutral and made a starboard turn 50 feet from the other boat.

"Lightning hit us," one of them shouted.

Split Ends

Ellen recognized the Naval Academy logo on their sodden sweatshirts.

"Jesus, Wilma, I'll bet they're plebes from the Academy. If these are our future naval commanders, we're in deep trouble."

"I'm going to vomit. I want to go home."

"Spoken like a true sailor, Wilma. We're in no danger. The wind is down to 15. I want to give them a tow. It'll only take a few minutes. Hang in a little longer? I'll buy you an iced cappuccino when we get back."

"Can you haul the mast on deck?"

"Maybe. We can try."

"Get it on deck, fore-and-aft. Make sure all the rigging is on deck too. Stuff the sail down below. Lash everything together as tight as you can. We'll stand by. But move fast, you're drifting.

"We're drowning," one yelled.

"Are you taking on water?" Ellen asked.

"No."

"Then you're not drowning. Get a grip. You can drown yourselves in Heineken's when I get you back to the yard. Where are your fenders?" They looked blankly at each other. "They're the plastic cushions with strings. Like big Tampax. Find them. Quickly." One went below and came back with four fenders. "Good work, admiral. Tie them on the port and starboard stanchions after you've secured the mast."

"Yes, ma'am. We were supposed to have the boat back at 1400 hours. You won't report us?"

"I don't even know you."

Ellen glanced at Wilma, retching over the side.

Beth Rubin

Ellen made a bridle, wrapped it around the cockpit winches and through the stern chocks. She threw the bitter end to one of the Mids. "Run the line through the bow eyes to what's left of your mast. Tie a good knot, a bowline if you know how to make one."

The sun peaked through the clouds. Ellen exhaled. Wilma cowered in the corner. "We're good to go, Wilma. Sip some ginger ale to settle your stomach. You've been wonderful."

"You've been pretty wonderful yourself, Admiral Ellen."

"Thelma and Louise have nothing on us, Wilma. We'll be home and dry in time for Oprah." *Men, who needs them?*

Split Ends

CHAPTER 29

Despite her fatigue after the storm, Ellen didn't sleep. It had been the longest week of her life. Her stomach had been in knots the whole time. *What will I do if the test is positive?*

With not a magazine in sight, she tried self-flagellation. *I should have suspected that Drew jumped from bed to bed faster than fleas on a dog. He wanted to make me scream? I'm ready to scream.*

Her thoughts drifted to her father. He had always said: "Do whatever you want, but be willing to live with the consequences." *Too bad I turned a deaf ear when I hopped into the sack with Drew. I miss you Daddy. I wish you were here.*

"Have a seat." The nurse spoke. A different one. "What are you here for?"

"A frontal lobotomy. When you're done, I'd like a hot fudge sundae with coffee ice cream, whipped cream and chopped nuts, but hold the cherry 'cause I'm dieting." *I'll die of embarrassment if I run into Michael here. I hope he exercises better judgement than his mother.*

"I'm here for the results of my blood test." She handed the card to the woman.

The nurse opened the ledger and looked at the card. "Let's see, you are ..."

Ellen repeated the six-digit number. "Also known as 'Dumb Bitch.' Could you pick up the pace, please? I'm afraid I'll soil the chair."

The nurse smiled. "Negative. Your test was negative."

"Thank God."

"If you're sexually active, we recommend that you come back in six months. And avoid other exposures."

"Don't worry. I'm joining the Sisters of Chastity." *Wonder if they take Jewish girls.*

"Help yourself to condoms on the way out. They're in a basket by the door."

"Better than lollipops." She got up to leave.

The woman handed Ellen a plastic patch with a smiling face that said, I AM HIV NEGATIVE. Ellen considered putting it on the rear window of her car next to the "I Love Bermuda" sticker. She helped herself to condoms and wondered if she would receive a postcard reminder.

It's time for your six-month HIV test.
If you're alive, please call for an appointment.

Her more experienced friends had bombarded her. "Use one every time. You can't count on a man to remember. They'll tell you what you want to hear, that they have been celibate for years. No matter how great the sex is, it's not worth dying over." She wondered when the next time would be. And if she'd use the condoms before they—and she—dried up.

* * * *

Across the quay the windows flamed with the setting sun's reflection. Local boats and transient yachts from Florida and the Bahamas filled the marina. New Guinea impatiens in a riot of colors flowered in the garden off the living room.

Split Ends

Ellen turned to Amy. "I'm so glad you're here. I wanted you to see my new place. And that I'm okay."

"I was scared out of my mind for you. You must be relieved."

"Relieved doesn't begin to describe it."

"You look 10 years younger than the last time I saw you with Ron. Was it only five months ago you called about moving?"

"Five months and a lifetime ago. I couldn't have done it without you, Amy. Thanks for the loan."

"My pleasure, believe me. Thanks for paying it back so quickly. You didn't have to."

"Yes I did."

"You picked a nice place to live."

"I lucked out. I'm hoping to buy it. Or another unit."

"Soon?"

"It all depends on what the court forces Ron to cough up. I fantasize about the judge chasing Ron down Duke of Gloucester Street for the money. When it comes to his assets, Ron hangs on with both hands. And his teeth."

"Do you miss your old house? That was a showplace."

"Nope. The Love Boat morphed into the Titanic. When I left, the house stank of decomposing marriage. It was just a house, Amy. I'll never again love something that can't love me back."

"It sounds like you have your act together, Ellen."

"I'm getting there."

"You're much more relaxed and you look terrific with some meat on your bones. I used to be afraid you'd break."

Ellen put down the focaccia. "I feel reborn."

"Good for you. How's your love life? Are you seeing the same man?"

"Sean and I are in a holding pattern. Friends for now."

"Tell me about him."

"He's soft-spoken, sweet and kind."

"You need someone like that."

"He's thoughtful too. He brings me flowers twice a week."

"But you're just friends?"

"Yes. I miss the romance. He kisses as well as Drew. Maybe better. But there's no man I can't live without. Besides, I'm relieved not to shave my legs every day. God forbid, I should get near a man with stubble on my legs."

"It's a girl thing."

"I liked to watch him reading the paper, his lips moving like a schizophrenic having a psychotic episode. *Nice lips, though.*

"What happened, Ellen?"

"Things heated up quickly. Then he started sending mixed signals. Green light, red light, amber light. All three at once. So I asked him, 'Why the change?'"

"Good for you, Ellen. I still shy away from confrontation."

Ellen thought about Sean and smiled. She loved running her fingers through his hair, and how he made her laugh.

"What did he say?"

Ellen swallowed some tortellini salad. "He said things were moving too fast. That I needed to finish

Split Ends

my business with Ron. I told him I could handle two things at once."

"That was wise. Don't take it personally."

"Time will tell." Ellen left half a sandwich on her plate for tomorrow's lunch and unbuttoned her jeans. "He's a wonderful friend. I want to keep the friendship. I have to be patient. Not my strong suit. I want what I want when I want it."

Ellen rose to turn on the torchiere. "I wonder if all men are babies. Dancing babies. All they seem to know is the two-step. Two steps forward, two steps back. I wish they'd learn to waltz."

"They chase you until they catch you and then they run."

"That's the dance."

"I'm sure it's hard to trust after Ron and Drew, but don't prejudge Sean."

"I'm working on it."

"Is there more?"

"Sean said I should go out with others. I told him I do. Of course, he planned to do the same. He said if he dated it wouldn't mean anything because he wasn't emotionally involved. That it was something to fill time. An activity. Like jerking off, I thought."

"Don't write him off. He sounds sincere."

"I hope so. I want to trust him. Fear keeps raising its ugly head."

"I'm an old married lady and I still don't understand men. They're little boys in suits."

Ellen put down her fork. "What I know about men would fit on a refrigerator magnet. I've lowered my expectations of anyone who stands up to pee."

"Take it one day at a time. Where did you meet him?"

"Here. Not like I was doing the meat-market scene, searching for Mr. Goodbar."

"Where do you stand?"

"He wanted to cool it, but he calls me every day. It's like having a girlfriend with a dick. Meanwhile, I'm out having fun. So 'don't cry for me Argentina, or Annapolis.'" Ellen sang as she headed to the kitchen with the dirty dishes.

* * * *

After Amy went to bed, Ellen revisited their conversation while wrapping leftovers. When she opened the refrigerator the light came on. *Jesus H. Christ. Ron was more committed to torts and tarts than to me. Drew lied and cut me off at the knees. Sean doesn't want to be in a relationship, but he behaves as if he does. Does that make him another asshole? Or am I?*

She closed the door and recalled her grandmother's favorite bon mot: "Fool me once, shame on you. Fool me twice, shame on me." *When will I learn? Homework time.*

She grabbed a Milky Way from the freezer and settled in the hickory rocker with a new book on relationships.

* * * *

Split Ends

Ellen finished with a client in St. Michael's, then stopped for crab soup to go. She crossed the Bay Bridge and got home in record time.

She tossed the mail on the kitchen table, went to the bedroom and stripped. After throwing on a robe and wiping off the greasepaint, she pushed the blinking button.

The first message was from a widower she'd met at a party. He had warm, brown eyes and a sharp wit. They'd gone out twice and Ellen found him charming and bright. He seemed very together.

"Hi, Ellen. I'm in Phoenix on business. I'd like to have dinner with you this weekend. I'll call you tomorrow."

The second message was from Marla. As Ellen dialed her attorney's office, her stomach churned. She felt panicky every time she spoke to Marla. It was worse than going to the dentist.

"Hi, Marla. What's up? Has Ron fled the country?"

"I have good news for you. Very good news. It took some doing, but he's agreed to the settlement."

Ellen sat down before she could fall down. "The terms we've been fighting for? I can't believe it."

"Believe it. I know it's been a long road. I'm glad you were able to go the distance. I think he doubted your strength and determination."

"Does that mean no trial?"

"That's right. No trial."

"Gee, Marla, I'm almost disappointed. I had it all choreographed. What happens next?"

"You have to live apart for a year. The clock is running. In the meantime, the paperwork is rolling."

"What do you think made him undig his heels?"

"I called his attorney and suggested he have a chat with Ron about the affair. I said we'd use it in court."

"You didn't! I told you not to."

"I know. It was a bluff that paid off. I'm happy for you, Ellen. You worked hard for the money."

Ellen laughed. "So did you, Marla."

"I'm glad you didn't fold."

"I'm so relieved. We have to celebrate. Someplace nice. Are you game?"

"I'd love to."

"I don't know how to thank you. I guess I can start by paying your bill. If there's anything left, I'm having a party."

Ellen was trembling when she hung up. She pinched her arm and cried until she'd soaked her peach blouse. When she'd shed the last tear she looked like a nursing mother who'd sprung a leak.

The third message was from Lisa. Ellen dialed her daughter at work. "Hi, Sweetie. How are you? Something to tell me?" When Lisa was in college "something" was flunking philosophy or running through a month's allowance in a week.

"You're what? Oh my God, Lisa, I'm so excited. How do you feel? No morning sickness? When are you due? April? What a lovely time to have a baby. I'm so happy for you and Josh. I can't wait. Do your Dad and Michael know? I'll call you at home tonight. Take care. I love you. Don't forget your grandmother."

Ellen bounced off the news. She thought about buying the layette with Lisa. And books. And toys. Then she thought of Ron and teared up. There had been a time when she assumed they would share the joys of grandparenting.

Split Ends

She poured a glass of ice tea. She couldn't wait to share the good news with her New Jersey relatives the following week. Sandy was getting married and a big shindig was planned. Ellen had been looking forward it, but her equilibrium was upset. *Hard to believe that I still get the heebie-jeebies over a visit to Drew Territory. Must be the external stimuli at work, as Elizabeth would say. Or it's the nightmare I'm missing.*

As Drew buzzed around, unbidden, in her brain, her sixth sense told her that one day she would run into him. "Enough," she said with a wave of her hand. "Go back to the graveyard for old lovers where you belong." She swatted the pesky fly and squealed, "I'm going to be a granny!"

CHAPTER 30

Ellen pushed through something dense. She heard clapping, then singing. "For she's a jolly good fellow..." She surfaced. Air. She wiped frosting from her eyes and licked her lips. Chocolate.

Ellen wiped sleepers from her eyes and licked her dry lips. *Happy Birthday to me.*

My legs may be a relief map of Colorado, and only my hairdresser knows for sure, but I feel like 22.

* * * *

She covered the table with brown paper, laid mallets and paring knives at four places. A roll of paper towels became the centerpiece.

Michael, Lisa and Josh arrived at 6:00 with steamed crabs and beer.

"Happy Birthday, Mom."

"Thanks, kiddies. The numbers are getting scary. Maybe it's time to start counting backwards."

"You'll never be old." Michael hugged her.

Lisa kissed her and put the beer in the refrigerator. "My friends think we look like sisters."

"I always liked your friends, Lisa. How're you feeling?"

"Aside from craving artichokes, I feel fine."

"I never had morning sickness either. I ate a pint of ice cream a day."

"You should try it again."

"How about a little respect for the grandmother-to-be on her birthday?"

Split Ends

Lisa walked to the door. "I left something outside." She returned with a wicker picnic hamper. Ribbons streamed from the handle.

"Is that dessert? I picked up a chocolate cake."

"No, Mom."

"Is this a gag? I hope it's not one of those exploding snakes."

Lisa lifted the hamper lid. She pulled out a chocolate lab puppy and handed it to her mother. "Happy Birthday, Mom. We figured this was the only thing missing from your life."

"I don't believe it! You are too good." Her eyes filled. She held it in her palm and pressed it to her cheek.

The puppy wore a collar with anchors on it and licked Ellen's face. The little tail was a metronome.

"I have puppy food and a crate in the car," Michael said.

"What are you going to name it?" Josh asked.

"Let's see. How about Cocoa?"

* * * *

She didn't know where she'd found the pluck, but on a whim, she had phoned Sean at work. *God, I'm turning into a brazen hussy. What's the big deal? He's a pal. I wouldn't think twice about calling a girlfriend for a drink. Why does a pecker always stir things up?*

"How spontaneous are you?" she had asked. She swallowed some M&M's and waited.

"What'd you have in mind?"

I want to jump your bones, just as friends of course. "It's such a beautiful day, I thought I'd go downtown for a marg. Want to join me?"

"I'd like to, but I have a briefing tomorrow morning. I'm bringing a lot of work home. I can't. How about a rain check?"

She was about to hang up, when he asked, "How long will you be there? If I change my mind."

God bless men. Can't even commit to a drink after work.

"Probably till 6:30 or so. No problem."

"Will you be alone?"

"No. I'm bringing a dozen midshipmen. Yes, I'll be alone. And I'm going regardless."

"Can I get that rain check?"

"Of course. This isn't a black-tie gala."

Later that afternoon, Cocoa at her feet, Ellen sat at a sidewalk table on Dock Street. She reached down to pet the puppy.

The sourwoods on the State House lawn were already turning scarlet and a cool easterly whiffled off the water. An early Fall seemed likely. People stopped to pet the dog. Ellen ordered from a pony-tailed waiter. Blender drinks were a dollar less during Happy Hour, but they reminded her of the Slurpees her kids had guzzled: all ice and no kick.

The bells of St. Mary's tolled six. An attractive, gray-haired man walked by and gave Ellen the once-over. Tall and lean, he held the hand of a young boy. *Either he's divorced or in a second marriage.* She pictured the button on her bulletin board—"If It Has Tires Or Testicles It's Going To Be Trouble." *Let him look.*

Split Ends

Ellen nursed her drink and kibitzed with two women from Wilmington at the next table. Nearby, four teenaged boys in caps and earrings flicked a Hackey Sack to one another. Their pants bagged with what appeared to be a week's worth of excrement. *Women aren't the only ones to follow fashion blindly.* A scruffy-looking woman with a mongrel read the dinner menu at the restaurant next door. Uninspired, they moved on.

Ellen faced the harbor area known as Ego Alley. Noisy muscle boats—Cigarettes and Donzis among them—bearing bikinied Barbies filed down the narrow channel on summer weekends. Seats on the sea wall were at a premium in season when day-trippers, dripping ice cream, rubbed hips with sailors provisioning for Newport or Camden.

Maybe Sean will surprise me and show up. A portly biker cruised by on a royal blue and chartreuse hog, blocking her view. She sipped the last of her drink, content with Cocoa's company and people watching.

She went back to the "His and Her Orgasms" article in *Cosmopolitan* and didn't see Sean crossing the street toward her. Chair legs scraped the sidewalk. He sat down across from her and signaled the waiter. Cocoa jumped up to greet him. "Hey, puppy. Are you taking good care of your mama?"

"What a nice surprise. I was about to leave."

"I figured my homework could wait. You're looking good."

His eyes crinkled. He had a boyish smile. And good teeth. Teeth and hands were non-negotiables. A man could be a dead ringer for Antonio Banderas, with a sparkling personality, but if he had bad teeth or stubby fingers he was *persona non grata*. Even if he had a zillion dollars, Ph.D. and a pecker from here to Pago Pago.

Sean wore his hair long. I'm robbing the cradle, Ellen had thought when she learned he was 40. She had kept her age a secret at first. When he found out, he was unruffled. "Age is just a number," he said. "You look about 35 and act like a teenager."

"I'm in touch with my inner adolescent."

Sean never looked the same twice, but any way you sliced him he was pleasing to the eye. And sweet as pecan pie. He was dressed for work, in a blue shirt and gray gabardine slacks over the legs she mused about feeling against her own. *I'm a goner.* She had tried painting him ugly as a mud fence. But the image of a hairless acned dwarf collapsed quicker than dominos whenever he was within 15 feet.

He ordered a Mexican pizza to share and a margarita. "How's Cocoa behaving?"

"Great. She's housebroken already and wonderful company. I feared being tied down, but the woman next door walks her when I can't."

Ellen told Sean a joke that she'd picked up from Jillian at her last haircut. He laughed in the little-boy way Ellen found so appealing, covering his mouth with his hand when she delivered the punch line. It felt good being with him.

"How's work?"

"Things are humming. I put a small ad in the paper and joined an association of professional women. The networking has paid off. I have more jobs than I can

Split Ends

handle. Guess I won't have to be a greeter at Wal-Mart."

"Good for you."

"Jobs are dropping in my lap. And I'm doing a room in the show house to benefit the medical center. I'm hoping it will generate more business."

"How did you get that?"

"I submitted a resume and drawings. Ten decorators were chosen from a field of about 50."

"I'd like to see it."

"There's a cocktail reception in a couple of weeks. Would you like to go?"

"Sure. Let me know when. I'll take pictures for your portfolio."

"I'd love that."

The pizza arrived.

What is it about breaking bread with someone you care for that's almost as intimate as making love? "I'm exhilarated, Sean. Especially after months when I couldn't chew gum and walk down the street at the same time."

"You were frizzed over the divorce and your scare. Anything new with the divorce?"

"Ugh. The paperwork takes more time than writing a thesis. The emotional stuff sets me back sometimes. But the end is in sight. Unmarrying is a bitch, Sean. My lawyer's bill is for more than the national debt. I'm paying it off a little at a time until I get my settlement."

"Been there. It's a pain. A year from now, you'll hardly think about it."

"I hope so. A marriage license should cost $25,000, and a divorce $25."

"I'm glad you'll be done soon. I'd like to spend time with you."

"Oh?"

"I always have. Remember? Maybe we'll celebrate your divorce with a vacation. I'm planning a trip out West next Spring. I'd like you to go with me."

"Great." *Yippee!*

"I want to visit my family then drive to Montana. Have you been to Glacier National Park? It's awesome."

"That sounds wonderful."

"We can hike and ... do you like camping?"

"As long as there's air-conditioning and room service."

He laughed. "I'll see what I can do."

"We'll have to continue this another time. I'm driving to New Jersey tomorrow for my friend's wedding. I have to pack."

"What about Cocoa?"

"My neighbor is taking care of her."

"I could've done it."

"Thanks for the offer. Next time."

"Have fun at the wedding. Don't let anyone steal you." He kissed her on the cheek. "Buzz me when you get back."

"Will do."

"I'm glad you called. It was great seeing you."

"Great seeing you too."

Ellen and Cocoa walked up Main Street toward the garage.

"He's just a friend. Stop drooling," the Wicked Witch of the West reminded her.

Split Ends

"But friends often become lovers," countered the Good Witch Glynda.

CHAPTER 31

"I don't know if I'm going to make it to the wedding, Mom. I feel lousy."

"What's wrong, Ellie?" Mady sat on the edge of the bed and felt her daughter's cheek. "No fever."

"I feel like I'm coming down with something. I can't bear the thought of dressing up and putting on a happy face, even for Sandy."

"Ellie, maybe you're just blue. This is your first wedding since you and Ron split up."

"True."

"After your father died I had trouble going out. I had to push myself. I felt like I was the only person in the world without a partner. Even now, special occasions and holidays are difficult. They remind me of happy and sad times—and missed opportunities."

"I've been jumpy for the last week or so."

"Come on." She kissed Ellen's forehead. "Push yourself a little. I think you'll feel better if you go. Besides, I want to show off my daughter."

* * * *

Ellen spotted the white limo waiting in front of the country club and took a deep breath. She handed her keys to the valet and went to help her mother out of the car.

Mady pinched Ellen's cheek. "That's my girl. You look gorgeous."

"You look damn good yourself." She pinched Mady's cheek.

Split Ends

She linked arms with her mother and they walked into the clubhouse. "Let's knock 'em dead, Mom."

* * * *

The ceremony was short and sweet, the way Ellen liked it. Sandy and Jonathan had written their own vows. The bride and groom faced each other, holding hands, while Jonathan recited Pablo Neruda's "Sonnet XVII."

Ellen thought of Drew and an unstoppable stream eroded her makeup. Mady glanced at Ellen and touched her arm. Ellen blotted the tears, careful not to soil the lace-edged handkerchief. The Irish linen square was a loaner from Mady who thought Kleenex inappropriate for special occasions.

No couple could have ordered a more beautiful setting on which to imprint their first memories as Mr. and Mrs.

Rows of gilt chairs faced the Watchung Mountains and the setting sun. An all-white *chupa* of roses, chrysanthemums, and lily of the valley framed Sandy, Jonathan, Rabbi Prinski and the minister.

Mady had told her that Rabbi Prinski had started to recite Kaddish, the traditional mourner's prayer, at another wedding a few weeks earlier. Another rabbi would likely recite it for him soon. Ellen recalled how she had bumped into him at Saks a few years before. She had been surprised that he recognized her.

"How are you?" he had asked, and enfolded her in his fleshy arms.

"I'm wonderful. And I'm still married," she had said, thrusting her ring finger in his face.

"I wish I could say the same for most of the couples I blessed."

Sandy and Jonathan bowed their heads for the blessing. With one stomp, Jonathan crushed the napkin-wrapped glass. Ellen flashed back to a similar scene nearly 30 years before and felt nothing. Ron had crushed the glass on his first attempt too—in the same shoes, he said, that he'd worn at his bar mitzvah.

Ellen waited her turn to congratulate the newlyweds. Her shoes pinched. She sipped her Cosmo, then slipped off a shoe and spread her toes. *Why don't they make sneakers in black silk? Finally.*

Tulle scratched her cheek when she hugged her friend. "Congratulations, Sandy. You look beautiful. I'm so happy for you. You know what I wish for you and Jonathan. I don't want to hold up the line. Let's meet in the girls' room later and talk about our dates."

"You brought someone?"

"Yeah, Mady. Last time I saw her she was trying to pick up a geezer at the bar. Catch you later."

Ellen extended her hand. "Jonathan, congratulations. I'm Sandy's friend, Ellen. I feel as if I know you."

"I've wanted to meet you. Sandy talks about you all the time."

"Just remember, she exaggerates. I'm not all bad."

"You'll have to visit us."

"I'd like that. Take care of my friend. She's a helluva woman."

"I know."

Can a single-breasted, Presbyterian, black woman and a double-breasted, Jewish, white man find happiness together? Maybe fairy tales do come true.

Split Ends

Cocktails and hors d'oeuvres were served in a yellow-and-white striped tent—superfluous with the beautiful evening. Ellen caught up with Mady. They crossed the lawn where a chamber ensemble set a solemn tone. After a cocktail or two, the guests seemed oblivious to spinach in their teeth or crooked cummerbunds.

The party moved into the Tudor-inspired dining room where Ellen wolfed two buttered rolls—a tip from her Russian grandmother—to soak up the vodka. The band played standards and party favorites like the Electric Slide and Macarena.

Couples took to the dance floor.

She regretted having so few opportunities to dance. Between them Ron and Drew had four left feet. Sean was a good dancer, though, and they had worked up a sweat at a roadhouse on Route 2.

Ellen bounced in the ersatz Henry VIII chair and looked around for a partner. The photographer seemed to be her only prospect.

"Excuse me, would you like to dance?"

He hesitated. "I guess I can take a short break."

"We'll make it a quickie." He handed his camera to the wedding planner and said he'd be back shortly.

"Thanks. You're a good sport," she said a few minutes later, her calves pinging. "If I ever decide to remarry, I'll call you."

"My pleasure."

Ellen grabbed her purse from the chair and headed to the ladies room.

She didn't know why she chose to return to the reception through the men's grille. Diners, many with shrink-wrapped faces, occupied a dozen tables in the

Beth Rubin

intimate, tartan-carpeted room. Ellen spotted the Fishers, old friends of her parents at a four-top near the bar. She was walking toward them to say hello when she noticed a man sitting with them, his back to her. Focused as she was on Marilyn and Ed, she didn't realize it was Drew until she was abreast of the table. Her heart began to hammer, nearly drowning out "Turn the Beat Around" in the next room.

They rose to greet her and Marilyn took Ellen's hand. "It's so nice to see you. You look sensational. Ellen, this is Drew Cushing. Drew, this is Ellen Gold. She's the daughter of dear friends."

Ellen felt the familiar ache. Her tear ducts began shifting to active mode. She struggled to regain her composure.

"Hi," Ellen whispered. His name caught in her throat. She swallowed hard and avoided his eyes. He appeared haggard and thin, thinner than he had been in high school.

"Hi, Ellen. How are you?"

"I'm very well thank you." *Christ, I sound like the Queen Mum with a stick up her arse.*

Marilyn's forehead wrinkled. "Do you two know each other?"

Ellen couldn't have replied for the world.

"Yes." Drew's voice was weak. "We went to high school together." He cleared his throat. "We ran into each other last year."

He ran over me.

Sandy's relatives had been paying Ellen compliments all evening, telling her she never looked better. And she never felt better—until she saw Drew.

Split Ends

He never looked worse. Was he ill or just overworked? *Why should I even care?* But she did.

"Would you excuse me for a minute?" Drew asked the Fishers. He struggled to get up.

"Ellen, could we talk? In private?"

"All right."

Ellen followed him to an alcove near the coat check room. He shuffled, like one of the old men at the wedding. His jacket hung loosely on his slumping shoulders.

He's little more than a scarecrow.

He turned to her. His eyes were dull and sunken.

"You look terrible, Drew. What's going on?"

"I'm sick. I was in torment over losing you. I felt I'd thrown away everything. I was never more lonely in my entire life. So I took comfort where I could. I should've been careful. But I wasn't. Now I'm paying the price."

She reached out to touch his sallow cheek.

"I wish it could have been different for us, Ellen. I'm glad you're okay."

"Yes, I am, Drew. In every way."

"I'm glad. This is probably the last time I'll see you."

"Oh God, Drew ..."

She put her arms around him. For that instant, she felt as if she alone was holding him up.

"Be kind to yourself, Drew. I hate to think of you suffering."

He took her arm. "We'd better get back."

Drew sat down with the Fishers.

They must be wondering what we had to talk about.

"Can you join us for a drink?" Marilyn asked.

Ellen shook her head side to side. All she could think to do was leave.

"I'd better get back or the bride and groom might think I've run off with the bartender. It was nice seeing you."

In a daze, she returned to the reception and sat frozen for the rest of the evening.

CHAPTER 32

She stamped the envelopes and stuck them in her purse. Paying bills provoked the same knee-jerk response as pop quizzes in high school. She exalted in having completed the unpleasant task and picked up the phone to call Lisa. Someone was on the line.

"Mrs. Gold? Mrs. Ellen Gold?"

"Ms. Gold. I hope you're not selling something. I'm a single on a fixed income."

"No, I'm not selling anything, Ms. Gold. I'm an attorney—Sam Peters of Peters & Pasternak in Livingston. I represent Mr. Andrew Cushing."

"I think you have the wrong number, Mr. Peters."

"I don't think so. Mr. Cushing gave me your phone number."

"What? He gave you my number? Are you calling for a blind date?"

"No, Ms. Gold. I'm sorry. I guess you haven't heard."

"Heard what?"

"Mr. Cushing passed away yesterday."

Ellen slumped.

"He did? How?" *I know how.*

The lawyer hesitated. "He took his own life."

"What? How?"

"Carbon monoxide. In his car. His neighbor called the police. They said there was an empty bottle and vial of pills."

She shivered. "Oh my God. Was there a note?"

"He left a note for me to call you."

"I'm sorry, I don't understand."

"I'm Mr. Cushing's executor. I called to tell you that you are the sole beneficiary of his estate."

"Excuse me?"

"Mr. Cushing deeded his house and transferred the title of his car to you. You will also receive the balance of his estate after all expenses are paid."

"One more time, please."

"Along with his home in Barnegat Light, which is mortgage-free, and his Mercedes, you will receive the residue and remainder of his estate."

"Oh my God."

"The will goes to probate in nine days. I'll contact you as soon as I know more. If you have any further questions, please call me."

"Thank you."

"One more thing, Ms. Gold. Mr. Cushing left written instructions for you to be entrusted with his remains."

"A funeral? I'm supposed to plan his funeral?"

"No. He was very clear about not wanting a funeral. He will be cremated tomorrow. He wants you to dispose of his remains."

"You mean his ashes?"

"If you prefer."

"When did he leave these instructions?"

"A couple of months ago. In September."

Her head was spinning. "When do I have to do it? Is there a time limit?"

"When you feel up to it. You can pick up the letter at my office on South Livingston Avenue. Do you know where that is?"

"Yes."

Split Ends

"Mr. Cushing's remains are at the Barnett Funeral Home in Verona. I'll give you directions when I see you, along with a copy of the will, and the keys to his house and car."

"It doesn't matter when?"

"Mrs. Gold, I would suggest sooner rather than later, for your comfort."

Ellen was not surprised to learn that Drew had died. She had already grieved for him twice—once as a teenager, again as an adult. Now she grieved for the third and final time. A lone tear inched down her cheek.

CHAPTER 33

The renters were long gone, so Ellen had her choice of parking spaces. She took Cocoa's leash and picked up the box. It was surprisingly light. A bunch of raucous 20-somethings were drinking beer and listening to Smashing Pumpkins on a rickety porch as Ellen made her way to the beach. With the temperature in the 60s it was hard to believe that Thanksgiving was less than two weeks away.

She tied her sneakers together and slung them over her shoulder. A dragon kite snaked high overhead, its multicolored tail paralleling the sand in the strong breeze. A boy of about five, with platinum curls, held onto the string for dear life.

No longer outshouted by boom boxes and noisy youths, the gulls' cries pierced the afternoon. Ellen drew in the salty air and walked toward the water.

She traced the shoreline, trying to resurrect footprints long ago washed away by the tide. Lying side by side on an old blanket, a teenaged couple seemed joined at the head. Ellen had been staring so intently she didn't see the wave before it soaked her legs. *Were Drew and I ever that young?*

Cocoa trailing, Ellen climbed the jetty as she had several months before and opened the white cardboard box.

She withdrew the small trash bag, knotted at the top. Not even a string or wire to fasten it.

She untied the bag. The funeral director had told her that the law required the contents be disposed of three or more miles offshore. The hell with that.

Split Ends

Except for the boy, the young couple and Cocoa at her side, she was alone. She stepped to the edge of the jetty.

I suppose I should say a prayer.

She scattered the ashes into the ocean. A gust blew some onto her sweatshirt. She left them undisturbed.

She took the envelope from her pocket, opened it and unfolded the letter.

> "Dear Ellen: I should have been honest with you from the start. My ambivalence had nothing to do with you, but my fear of losing you if you found out. I have questioned my decision over and over again. Now it's too late. My happiest times were those we spent together. I'm sorry for any pain I caused you. I'm appealing to your generous and forgiving nature one last time. My parents are too old and sick to make the trip East. I know I can count on you to pick the appropriate spot. Enjoy the place. I love you. I've always loved you. Drew."

She wiped her tears and crossed the sand toward the house, drawn by the screen door swinging open, shut, open, shut, open, shut. Someone would have to fix it. An umbrella rested against folded beach chairs stacked in front.

Ellen scaled the steps. The rocker creaked on the porch. *Strange. There's no breeze.*

She cupped her eyes to the living room window. All was as she remembered—the blanket on the sofa, the CD's fanning the stereo receiver, the basket of sunscreen. On the trunk sat the terra cotta dish she had given him, returned to its place of honor.

She opened the door.

Cocoa preceded her into the house.

She looked around. She imagined her grandchild-to-be in the nicotine-framed space where the photo of Drew and his lover had hung.

She followed Cocoa into the bedroom. The dog jumped onto the bed and curled up. Ellen sniffed the pillow, lay down and closed her eyes.

She felt the stranger's weight and heat. This time the feeling stayed with her.

She leaned against the headboard. The ocean sparkled beyond the glass.

A sense of peace filled her.

She glanced at the dark walls. *Sunshine yellow! White for the dresser and bedside table. A wedding ring quilt for the bed.*

She got up, smoothed the blanket and went to the kitchen for a drink—knew where to find a glass. She poured some water into a soup bowl. Cocoa lapped it up.

Ellen slapped her thigh. "C'mon, girl. Time to go."

While walking down the steps, something pierced her foot. She picked a jagged mussel shell from her toe and wiped her blood-stained finger on the wooden railing. "Rest in peace, Drew," she whispered.

She put on her sneakers and walked to her car, wondering if Drew had been ill when they were lovers.

Had he known he was ill when I confronted him in June? Had he really been tested as he said? Were there others? How many? What does it matter? He's gone. And I'm all right.

Split Ends

She got in the Toyota and unlatched the top. The dog curled up next to her, puppy paws hanging over the seat. The sky, freckled with gold, warmed her as she pulled onto the deserted street. It was a great day for tanning. From the leather case she withdrew a random CD, slid it into the player and pumped up the volume. "I've Got The World On A String." Sinatra at his buoyant best.

"Time to hit the road, girl."

THE END, THANK GOD

About the Author

Beth Rubin is the author of Frommer's Washington, D.C. With Kids, The Complete Idiot's Travel Guide to Washington, D.C., and Washington, D.C. For Dummies. A seasoned journalist, her features appear in Washington, D.C. area newspapers and magazines. She lives in Annapolis, Maryland. *Split Ends* is her first novel.

Printed in the United States
1044500001B/143